MUSIC IN THE MIND

Gulu playing the *chang*, Dai Kundi, Hazarajat

Music in the Mind

The Concepts of Music and Musician in Afghanistan

Hiromi Lorraine Sakata

SMITHSONIAN INSTITUTION PRESS
WASHINGTON AND LONDON

Table 1 on page 40 is from Reynold A, Nicholson, *A Literary History of the Arabs,* and is reprinted with the permission of Cambridge University Press.

Editor: E. Anne Bolen

Library of Congress Cataloging-in-Publication Data
Sakata, Hiromi Lorraine
   Music in the mind: the concepts of music and musician in Afghanistan/Hiromi Lorraine Sakata.
      p. cm.
Originally published: Kent, Ohio: Kent State University Press, 1983.
With new foreword and pref.
Includes bibliographical references (p.   ) and index.
   ISBN 1-58834-090-2 (alk. paper)
   1. Music—Afghanistan—History and criticism.   I. Title.
ML345.A35 S24 2002
780'.9581—dc21   2002026923

British Library Cataloguing-in-Publication Data is available

Manufactured in the United States of America
09 08 07 06 05 04 03 02   5 4 3 2 1

♾ The paper used in this publication meets the minimum requirements of the American National Standard for Information Sciences—Permanence of Paper for Printed Library Materials ANSI Z39.48-1984.

For Tom and Cuong

Contents

Illustrations

Maps

Foreword

Hiromi Lorraine Sakata's *Music in the Mind* was one of the first fully realized ethnographies of Afghanistan's expressive culture, and it stands as one of the best. This subtle and comprehensive discussion of musical genres, types of performers, instruments, and performance contexts goes well beyond formal approaches. It applies theory and method similar to those developed in ethnomethodology to elicit and compare indigenous concepts of "music" and "nonmusical" performance forms. This analysis foregrounds Afghan concepts, values, and terminology, and in the process interrogates Western definitions, revealing their own cultural contingency. Thus, this is a comparative work in the best sense: Anyone interested in ethnomusicology, comparative cultural studies, or the fate of Afghanistan and its culture can profit by reading it.

Sakata's chosen task from the 1960s onward has been to map and analyze the diversity of an important dimension of Afghan culture: music. How important musical expression is for Afghans—and how problematical in certain ways—has been tragically illustrated by the Taliban regime's late twentieth-century attempts to ban all forms of recreational music by ordering musical instruments destroyed, displacing and impoverishing already socially marginalized professional musicians, and interrupting musical traditions that are mostly oral and thus dependent on performance in social context for their survival and development. Music cassettes found in some Taliban leaders' vehicles captured during the 2001 assault against that regime and anecdotal reports from local, clandestine music sellers about music buyers in the Taliban period suggest that the effort to suppress music was not entirely embraced or fully enforced by the regime's core membership.

The controversial nature of professional music in particular was clear in the era prior to these last decades of physical and cultural warfare in Afghanistan. In charting this country's diverse musical patterns in the pre-Marxist era, Sakata consulted and recorded not only professional musicians but also those who were determinedly nonprofessional (including some considered nonmusicians), were in various walks of life, and represented a spectrum of Afghan ethnic and status groups in different socioeconomic settings. All these features of social organization figure centrally in her analysis of who performs what kinds of "music" and "nonmusic"; when, where, and for whom; and with what perceived value to the audience.

Music in the Mind reaches a new readership with a new concern for things Afghan—a concern that is motivated both by the global processes of political confrontation and by fresh understandings of the emerging effects of strategic, economic, political, and cultural globalization on expressive life in particular settings. This book merits close reading, not only as a piece of meticulously researched cultural history but also as a model for investigation of cultural developments yet to come.

Margaret Mills
Department of Near East Languages and Cultures
Ohio State University

Preface

To say that the world has changed since I first went to Afghanistan in search of the sounds and meaning of Afghan music is an understatement. What has changed dramatically is the world's view of Afghanistan and this nation's place in it. After the Soviet invasion and the efforts of Afghan *mujāhidin* (*jihād* warriors) to repossess their country from the clutches of these foreign invaders, Afghanistan moved from a place off the cognitive map of most Westerners to the outer edges of its periphery. Then, September 11, 2001, suddenly jerked Afghanistan to its very center.

If years of fighting have changed our perception of this country, think of the drastic effects these devastating wars have had on life in Afghanistan. A generation of musicians moved out while those who remained were for the most part silenced. In the introduction to this book, I wrote forlornly in 1983, "I write here about a time and place that are gone." Yet, the very ideas from that "time and place" shaped and continue to shape the place and meaning of Afghan music in the world today. They help us understand the importance of the power of music in Afghan culture and the threat that it posed for the Taliban regime in Afghanistan.

Destroying the Bamiyan Buddhas, requiring women to wear veils, ordering men to grow beards, and banning music in Afghanistan were four symbolic influences on Afghan society that were emblematic of the Taliban regime. The Danish organization Freemuse claims that music censorship is essentially an attempt to strangle a people's culture and "violate[s] international conventions of human rights."[1]

When the Taliban were pushed out of Kabul and Mazar-i Sharif, American news coverage showed images of men sitting in barbershops getting their beards shaved and of music cassette shops opening up for business. In the thirty-six years I have been studying Afghan music, never has so much attention been paid to it as since the Taliban regime politicized music. The conflation of music and politics in Afghanistan, however, is not a new phenomenon. Music has always been used to express cultural values that revolve around issues of religion, politics, authenticity, representation, gender, and identity.

The mainstay of Islam is the Qur'an, the revelations of God as passed on to the Prophet Mohammad. (Please note that I prefer the current spellings of "Qur'an" and "Mohammad" versus those that were used in the previous printing of the *Music in the Mind*.) Two great arts of Islam, music and poetry, issue forth from these revelations in the form of recitation. In the words of Seyyed Hossein Nasr in his book, *Islamic Art and Spirituality*, "Even the Quran [*sic*] itself in its traditional prosody is at once music and poetry, although traditionally it has not been classified as either, but being the Word of God, belongs to a category above all categories of human art."[2]

Proper recitation forms the basis of musical aesthetics in Islamic cultures, yet these musical sounds are identified separately either as religious chant and recitation or secular music. Herein lies the ambiguous nature of music. The Taliban reduced this sharp theoretical distinction between religious chant and secular music into a simple difference between good and evil. Therefore, it banned all forms of music that were identified as secular, accompanied by musical instruments, or performed by professional musicians.

However, historically, music in Afghanistan has been used to represent the state in one form or another. Military music accompanied soldiers into battle, court musicians represented the splendor and power of the royal courts, and state-owned radio musicians reflected the modern tastes of government bureaucrats and urban elites.

During the times of Mohammad Zaher Shah (1933–1973), army bands consisted of Western instruments played by musicians trained in Western theory and notation by Turkish military advisors. During the Communist regime in the 1980s, musicians who had formed an association in Kabul were conscripted into the army ensemble. The ensemble, consisting of forty-two musicians of whom four were female singers, included traditional instruments plus the accordion, drum, guitar, and keyboard. The musicians were sent to places such as Jalalabad, Herat, Kandahar, and Kunduz and told to sing patriotic songs in order to boost the morale of the fighting men.[3]

Opposing the Communist rule, the *mujāhidin*, particularly in Pakistan, produced cassettes glorifying the virtues of *jihād*. Songs extolling the virtues of war are not new in Afghanistan. For example, patriotic war ballads are an important genre of traditional Pashtun folk culture. The international Durand Line separates many Pashtuns located in eastern Afghanistan from their tribes in Pakistan. This division of allegiance, always a cause for disturbance, has incited a strong movement for an independent Pashtunistan. Malang Jan, poet laureate of the region, expressed the popular sentiment that it is better to die fighting for a cause rather than to die in bed.

Rather than the military, two institutions, the royal court and the radio station, determined the music of Kabul, and indeed, that of the nation. The music of Kabul developed out of the musical tastes of the urban elite and politically influential population of the capital of the country.

Under the rule of Amir Sher Ali Khan (1863–1866 and 1868–1879), Indian classical musicians were invited to become court musicians in Kabul. They were given lands in the section of old Kabul now known as *kharābāt* or entertainment quarters. From that time on, Indian classical music, the Hindustani tradition of north India, became established as the elite art tradition of Afghanistan. These transplanted Indian musicians and their descendants kept their musical ties to India and Pakistan strong. They gained a preeminent status among Afghan musicians and were accorded the title of *ustād*.[4] During the reign of Mohammad Zahir Shah, Hindustani musicians such as Ustad Villayat Khan were regularly invited to court to give private performances and music lessons for individual members of the royal family.

A radio transmitter was first introduced to Afghanistan during the reign of Amanullah Khan (1919–1929) as a part of his efforts to modernize the country, but with very limited transmission coverage, broadcasting did not last beyond a few years. In 1941, a government radio station was established in Kabul. Known as Radio Kabul and administered by the Ministry of Information and Culture, it hired radio musicians who, like government bureaucrats, enjoyed official sanction and support. In 1964, the station moved to another location in Kabul and became known as Radio Afghanistan. From its inception in 1941 until the 1980s, a number of foreign advisors from Germany, Uzbekistan, Tajikistan, and the United States not only helped the Afghans technically, but also helped shape the content and sound of radio music that most Afghans today identify as their national music.

Based on the Soviet model of a people's ensemble, the Radio Kabul orchestra and, later, the National Orchestra of Radio Afghanistan consisted of regional folk instruments brought together to play regional songs and some new songs. The orchestra members were professional musicians who learned their repertoire by rote. The leader of the orchestra played a melodic phrase that the orchestra members followed and imitated.

Another ensemble of mainly Western instruments (such as accordions, clarinets, flutes, mandolins, pianos, saxophones, trumpets, and violins) known as the "Jazz Orchestra" or "Number Two Orchestra" was established in 1953. The Jazz Orchestra was based on the principles of the Western musical system, including harmony. Musical advisers from Tajikistan and Uzbekistan were invited to the Radio to advise and teach these orchestra members the principles of composition and conducting.

In the 1960s, the leader of the Jazz Orchestra encouraged a group of young high school boys interested in music to learn to play instruments. The government later sent individuals in this group, known simply as "amateurs," to study in Moscow. When they returned to Kabul, eager to perform after two or three years of conservatory training, they found that no one (particularly the professional musicians at Radio Afghanistan) was interested in helping them pursue their careers as instrumentalists.[5] Besides the professional musicians at Radio Afghanistan, a new breed of amateur musicians from socially established families (members of the extended royal family or children of prime ministers, generals, or other officials) were heard on the radio. Their repertoire consisted of new popular songs. Madam Parwin was one of the first female radio singers in Afghanistan. She was persuaded to sing for the radio because she had a good voice and because she was related to the royal family. Her birthright was supposed to provide a bulwark against criticism, and her decision to sing for the public was made with the hope of improving the status of women in the entertainment world.[6]

The distinction between professional and amateur musicians also played a part in the social dynamics of communities outside Kabul, and even carried over into diasporic communities, particularly in the United States and Pakistan, where a musician's status is determined not by his profession but by his birthright. The most prominent musicians were amateur, nonhereditary musicians (mainly singers) who had a higher status than the professional, hereditary musicians (mainly instrumentalists.)

During the Soviet regime, many Afghans emigrated out of Afghanistan to Pakistan, India, Iran, and parts of Europe and the United States. The emigration pattern of Afghan musicians was based on the economic status of the musicians. Those musicians who were professional, hereditary musicians simply crossed the border into Pakistan where they performed with and for mainly the Pashtun population. Those amateur, nonhereditary musicians who were more affluent found their way to Europe and the United States.

This emigration pattern determined the availability or lack of availability of musical instruments and instrumentalists in the United States. The musicians who came to the United States were mainly amateur, elite singers from Kabul. The only readily available instruments to accompany their songs were the Indian *tabla*, the harmonium, and the electronic keyboard. In the United States, the distinction between musicians was not whether they were amateurs or professionals but rather about what links they might have to Afghanistan and to what generation they belonged.

One of the main performance contexts for Afghan music in the United States is the Afghan wedding. Weddings are celebrated with Kabul-style banquets at Afghan wedding halls. The bride is accompanied by the Dari song *Ahesta Buro,* and both men and women dance to the *atan*, a traditional Pashtun men's dance that is presented as the national dance of Afghanistan in the United States. Music on these occasions is of two types: music for listening and music for dancing. Musicians who started their careers in Afghanistan sing songs that transport their audiences to their homeland. Their song texts remain the main focus of attention and people rarely dance to this kind of music. For those who want to dance, young musicians sing songs in a popular style that has a fast beat suitable for dancing. Someone explained the difference between the two as "old style" (for listening) and "new style" (for dancing). Old-style musicians are accorded a higher status than the younger musicians, and are given the title of *ustād* regardless of gender. They travel widely in the

United States and Europe and identify strongly with Afghanistan before the Taliban rule.

Rare reports and recordings of music in northern Afghanistan that Jan van Belle made in the 1990s indicate many of the melody types and song genres discussed in this book were still performed and appreciated in the north.[7] Recordings made in 2001 of Afghan ensembles in Peshawar and Geneva preserve the sounds of Radio Afghanistan's National Orchestra.[8] Journalists have reported that Afghan musicians in Pakistan are returning to Afghanistan, while those who remained in Afghanistan and were silenced for so many years are finding a resurgence in the demand for both traditional and popular music.[9] Many who lost their traditional instruments are replacing them with instruments from Pakistan, including electronic keyboards, drum machines, and guitars.

Even with the incorporation of new instruments, sounds, techniques, and ideas, the essential meaning of music in the Afghan cultures presented in this book has relevance in helping us understand the development of Afghan music from the twentieth century into the beginning of the twenty-first century. When I wrote in the introduction to this book that I was presenting a historical perspective that I thought had limited relevance for the future, I could not have been more wrong. Throughout the unimaginable pain and suffering the Afghans have endured in the last thirty years, their music helped sustain their identity and culture. Today, I am ever more hopeful that it will continue to do so as long as there is an Afghanistan or Afghan communities in this world.

NOTES

1. John Baily, "Can you stop the birds singing?," *The Censorship of Music in Afghanistan* (Copenhagen: Freemuse, 2001).

2. Seyyed Hossein Nasr, *Islamic Art and Spirituality*. (Lahore: Suhail Academy, 1987), 151.

3. Nazir Ulfat, personal communication, Hayward, Calif., 19 January 2002.

4. For an example of the type of Afghan classical music developed by these musicians, listen to *Ustad Mohammad Omar, Virtuoso from Afghanistan*. Smithsonian Folkways Recordings. SFW CD 40439. Compact disk.

5. Kabir Howaida, personal communication, Walnut Creek, Calif., 23 March 2002.

6. See page 98, this volume, about Madam Parwin in Faizabad.

7. Jan van Belle, "Northern Afghanistan," in *South Asia: The Indian Subcontinent, The Garland Encyclopedia of World Music, Vol. 5.* (New York: Garland Publishing, 2000), 825–832.

8. Recordings of musicians in Peshawar were made under the auspices of the U.S. State Department. The Geneva ensemble is known as Ensemble Kaboul and can be heard on *Nastaran: Ensemble Kaboul*, Ethnomad, Arion, ARN 64543. Compact disk.

9. Andrew Solomon, "An Awakening After the Taliban," Arts and Leisure, *New York Times*, 10 March 2002, 1, 20, 21.

Acknowledgments

The research for this book is based upon field work in Afghanistan in 1966–67 and 1971–73 sponsored respectively by a Fulbright Study Grant and the Foreign Area Fellowship Program of the American Council of Learned Societies and the Social Science Research Council.

The principal contributors to this book are the many Afghans who shared their music, knowledge, and thoughts with me. Besides those mentioned specifically in the book, the following were instrumental in assisting and furthering my research in Afghanistan: Rawan Farhadi; Abdul Ghani Niksiar; Abdul Fatah; Ghulam Haidar, my *dutār* teacher; Khairuddin, who helped us survive a very cold Herat winter; Ghulam Ali Ayin; Mirza Ghulam Haidar; Wakil Ismail; Nasir Khan; our dear friend and traveling companion, Haji Latif; Amirshah Hasanyar; and my *rabāb* teacher, the late Ustad Mohammed Omar.

To Wakil Lal Mohammed Akbari and his wife, Fauzia, who generously cared for us in their home, provided us with every assistance in gathering and translating data, and offered us their lasting friendship, I am extremely indebted. Our good friends Enayatullah Shahrani, who introduced us to Badakhshan and who tirelessly transcribed many song texts, and Nazif Shahrani, who helped translate the texts and provided many insights into being Afghan, deserve special mention. Of the many friends among the "foreign community" in Kabul, I would like to thank Dr. Austin Moede, his wife Sharon, and son William, for always providing us a home away from home.

I am fortunate in having a teacher, Robert Garfias, and colleagues, Mark Slobin, John Baily, and Daniel Neuman, who have maintained an interest in my work, read my manuscript, and offered critical evaluations, advice, and above all, encouragement.

I would like to thank Guita Monfaredi for doing the Persian calligraphy found in the Appendixes.

The importance and extent of my husband Tom's contribution to this book has been invaluable. Not only has he been a source of support and inspiration to me, but he has also been actively involved in every stage of this project. He lovingly and graciously became my assistant, photographer, and traveling companion in the field, and the photographer and illustrator for this book. He is very much a part of this book and it is to him I dedicate this work.

Note on Transcriptions and Transliteration

All Persian words are transcriptions of the spoken language of Afghanistan. The following signs have been used to denote special sounds:

a: Short *a* as in *España*.

ā: Long *a* as in *almost* to distinguish from the short *a*.

kh: A velar uvular with scrape as in *Bach*.

gh: A uvular plosive, as in the French *Paris*.

': A glottal plosive representing *hamzah* ء .

c: A glottal plosive representing the letter *ᶜain* ع .

-i, -e, or *-ye*: Persian *ezafe* denoting genitive construction, as in Faiz-e Mangal.

Sometimes the long *ā* in spoken Afghan Persian sounds like an *o* and is so indicated as in *samowar* instead of *samāwar*.

The transcriptions may differ considerably from the written Persian; thus, سرغیلان is transliterated *sarghilān*, but is pronounced and transcribed as *sarghalām*. Some words, such as Koran, have a standardized English spelling which has been retained.

CHAPTER ONE

Introduction

Culture has been defined by Stephen A. Tyler as "cognitive organizations of material phenomena."[1] Ethnomusicologists have long been concerned with the material phenomenon of music, but more recently, have realized the need and advantage of studying music within its cultural context, and have made attempts to discover what people think about music, the social functions of music, and how music is ordered in society.

This work is an effort to discover an aspect of culture through the analysis of semantic and musical features concerning the concepts "music" and "musician" in Persian-speaking areas of Afghanistan. First, these concepts manifested in speech, behavior, and music are defined; and second, a relationship between the conditions which lead to different conceptions and the material phenomena which result from these conceptions is sought. The research was undertaken in three diverse locations of Afghanistan, not only to find different conditions, concepts, and material phenomena, but also because despite the differences, similarities based upon the precepts of Islam exist, and these similarities have implications not just for a small area, but for all of Afghanistan as well as the Islamic Middle East.

In order to understand the conditions which contribute to the interpretations of the concepts of music and musician, it is necessary to present a somewhat skewed overview of the country and its people as well as of the peculiarities of the three areas of Afghanistan involved in this study: Herat, Faizabad, and Khadir. I leave it to others like Donald Wilber (*Afghanistan: Its People, Its Society, Its Culture*) and Louis Dupree (*Afghanistan*) to give the reader an objective historical and ethnographic view of the country. My presentation of the social institutions of Afghanistan will be discussed from my interpretation of the Afghan point of view, that is, the outsider's perspective of the insider's popular beliefs, concerns, and biases,

for it is in the context of these notions that the concepts of music and
musician presented here are based.

Although I constantly refer to what Jean-Paul Dumont in *The Headman and I*[2] calls the "context" without stressing the "text,"—the context
being the subject of this book and the text being the interaction, relationship, and subsequent interpretation placed upon the relationship between
subject and investigator—there is no denying the role of the investigator-
writer in filtering the information through his own biases. This acknowl-
edgment, unlike the author's customary claim to all responsibility for content, mistakes and all, is important for the reader to keep in mind, for this
work is a study of concepts, of what people think, and I can only interpret
these concepts through another mind, my own.

The research for this book is based upon field work in Afghanistan
during 1966–67 and 1971–73. Many of the conditions and situations about
which I write have radically changed or ceased to exist since that time.
Heavy fighting and casualties have occurred in all the areas where I did my
research. I have lost contact with many friends in these places and pros-
pects for further research in the near future seem bleak. I write here about a
time and place that are gone. To some extent, all works based on field
research are limited to a specific time and place, but the current events in
Afghanistan have wrought upon the country and its people such drastic
and profound changes that there is no question that there is no returning to
the era of which I write, and in this sense, readers should be aware of the
historical perspective of this work.

The Setting

Afghanistan is a landlocked country bounded by Iran, the Soviet
Union, China, and Pakistan. Its most conspicuous feature is the great
Hindu Kush system of mountains which divides the country into two distinct sections, the northern and southern regions (Map 1). For the most
part, Afghanistan may be described as semiarid, but there are many regional variations and climatic contrasts according to levels of elevation.
Annual rainfall is low, but the high mountains contain sources for many
streams and rivers which supply water for cultivation.

Although no official census has ever been taken, the Ministry of Planning in 1972 estimated a total population of seventeen million, a figure
which included almost three million nomads.[3] The majority of the population at that time lived in rural areas and were sedentary agriculturalists or
herders. The main agricultural crop was wheat, while sheep constituted the
bulk of Afghanistan's livestock.

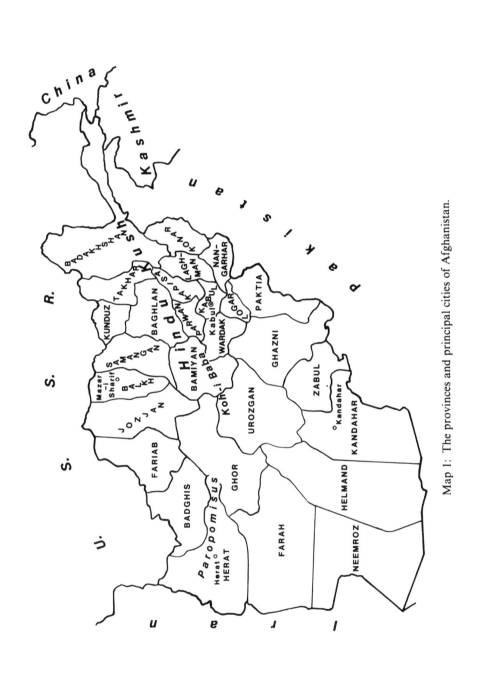

Map 1: The provinces and principal cities of Afghanistan.

PEOPLES AND LANGUAGES

Afghanistan's past history, characterized by the constant flux of populations, has contributed to today's complex ethnographic picture. Although experts do not agree on the exact number of different groups, at least fifteen major ethnic groups speaking a total of thirty-two languages live in Afghanistan. Rawan Farhadi summarizes this mosaic of languages:

> The most eastern Semitic speaking people of the world, the most southwestern Mongolian speaking, the most northern Dravidian speaking, the most southern of both western and eastern subgroups of Turkik [*sic*] speaking people of the Eurasian continent can be found in this country.[4]

An apparent effect of the existence of many different languages in close proximity is that a surprising number of people are perfectly bilingual. The official languages of Afghanistan are Pashtu and Persian (*Dari* is the official designation for the Persian spoken in the country), the two languages spoken by the overwhelming majority of the population. For purposes of this study, the complex linguistic situation can be reduced to two large language areas corresponding to the two official languages of Afghanistan, as well as the two regions demarcated by the Hindu Kush Mountains. The southern region is populated mainly by Pashtu and some Baluchi-speakers, while the northern region, which includes the central mountainous area of the Hazarajat, is inhabited mainly by Persian-speakers and some speakers of various Turkic languages.

The ethnographic complexion, however, is more complicated because a number of different ethnic groups speak Persian, and there are still basic disagreements regarding some apparent ethnic groups identified by various observers according to criteria that are by no means standardized. The problematic definition of such groups has already been noted by Louise E. Sweet: "Especially characteristic of many areas of the Middle East is the 'enclaving' of groups for whom no label is yet adequate ('tribe,' or 'confessional group,' or 'ethnic group' are among those used)."[5] Keeping in mind the problems of identification, the following recognized groups living in the three areas of Afghanistan on which this study is based—the list is obviously not inclusive of all Afghan peoples—will be discussed according to known facts or notions held about them.

Pashtuns

The Pashtuns constitute the largest single ethnic group in Afghanistan. Although a number of Pashtuns have settled in parts of northern and western Afghanistan, most of them are concentrated in the southern and southeastern regions. The Pashtun is unquestionably conceptualized as the most native of all ethnic groups living in Afghanistan. After all, the term "Afghan" is traditionally applied to Pashtuns alone; other groups still prefer to be identified by their own group affiliations such as Tajik, Hazara, and Uzbek.

The Pashtuns first gained notoriety in the West as the fierce warriors of the Northwest Frontier, the Pathans. According to Olaf Caroe, a distinction must be made between those Pashtuns who inhabit the plains and the plateaux and those who inhabit the highlands. The former are "entitled to the Afghan name."[6] The plains or plateau Pashtuns can be further considered as having two branches, the western and eastern. The western Afghans have had historical and political connections with the Persian Safavid Empire, while the eastern Afghans' main affiliations were with the Moghul Empire of Delhi. The degree of distinction between western and eastern branches was clearly perceived by Elphinstone in the nineteenth century: "The western tribes, especially those of Khorassaun, understand Persian much more generally than the eastern ones do Hindostaunee; and their dress, arms, and habitations, while they retain their national peculiarities, approach to those of Persia."[7] Approximately 150 years later, Schurmann notes the effect of long periods of association with Persian-speaking groups: "As a whole, the sedentary Afghans in the north tend to lose their language and speak Persian. Fourth-generation Herati Afghans are even no longer bi-lingual."[8] Although some groups of eastern Afghans and some hill tribes occupy eastern Afghanistan, the majority of the Pashtuns in Afghanistan are western Afghans, of whom the most important are the Durranis and the Ghilzais.

The Pashtuns—especially members of the Mohammedzai clan of the Durranis, who retained the important administrative, diplomatic, and military posts of the state—were the main ruling force in Afghanistan from the founding of the modern Afghan nation in 1747 by Ahmad Shah Durrani until the end of the Afghan monarchy in 1973.[9] In a continued campaign to keep Afghanistan dominated by the Pashtuns, most of the provincial officers were Pashtuns; many others were resettled on fertile lands in various parts of the country. Substantial subsidies were distributed to Pashtun tribes through the Department of Tribal Affairs, and rewards and pay raises were given to government employees who passed a Pashtu language examination. The practice of favoring the use of the Pashtu language was encouraged and mandated in Article 35 of the 1964 Constitution of Afghanistan: "It is the duty of the State to prepare and implement an effective programme for the development and strengthening of the national language, Pashtu."

Although there are no statistics to substantiate population counts, the government always maintained that the Pashtuns constituted a majority of Afghanistan's population. A large segment of the Pashtuns in Afghanistan seem to have had nomadic origins.[10] Although the majority of the Pashtuns today are settled agriculturalists, rural pastoralists, or urban dwellers, there are still large numbers of Pashtun nomads who traverse a seasonal route and dwell in black tents. Most of the Pashtuns are Sunni Muslims, the sect of Islam adopted by the country as the state religion.

Tajiks

The Tajiks, members of the Iranic language family, are apparently the first inhabitants of Central Asia. There is archeological evidence of fortified villages, canal systems, and irrigated agriculture of the Tajik type from the eighth and seventh centuries B.C.[11]

The name *Tajik* at first referred to the Arabs and later to the Iranians who were early converts to Islam. With the gradual Turkicization of the Central Asian Iranians, the name was applied to those Central Asians who still remained sedentary and retained their Iranian language. According to Schurmann:

> the basic medieval meaning of Tadjik: Persian-speaking, sedentary Muslim, has not changed to the present day. In recent times, the term Irânî has arisen to designate the sedentary Persian-speaking population of modern Irân. Thus, the term Tadjik today largely designates only the Persian-speaking, Muslim, sedentary populations of Afghanistan, the Central Asiatic Republics of the USSR, and Chinese Sinkiang.[12]

Schurmann's definition, although relatively clear, does not account for the different groups which fit the description, but which are not considered Tajiks by the local population. The popular notion of Tajik in Afghanistan is based on a narrower interpretation using the criterion of religion; thus, a Tajik is a sedentary, Persian-speaking, Sunni Muslim.[13] Sedentary, Persian-speaking, non-Sunnis are identified according to location, such as Herati (inhabitants of Herat), Wakhi (inhabitants of the Wakhan area of Badakhshan), and Sheghni (inhabitants of the Sheghnan area of Badakhshan). The situation is further complicated by the fact that many Persian-speaking, non-Sunni Muslims, with no visually identifiable features, will pass themselves off as Tajiks in order to escape persecution by a predominantly Sunni society. Those groups that seem to fit the Tajik description, but who have obvious ethnic identities such as settled, Persian-speaking Pashtuns, are not called Tajiks. Today's popular notion does not seem to differ greatly from that of over a century ago. In his description of the population of Herat, Elphinstone writes:

Heraut covers a great space, and contains about 100,000 inhabitants. Two-thirds of that number consist of Herautees, or ancient inhabitants of the place, who are all Sheeahs. . . . The inhabitants of the country round Heraut are, for the most part, Taujiks, and bear the character already attributed to that respectable race. They are all Soonees.[14]

Today there is a bewildering variety of groups in Afghanistan who are referred to as Tajiks, either by the local population or by historians and ethnographers. Although these divergent groups probably do not constitute a single ethnic unit, all Tajiks speak a form of Persian and are sedentary, village-dwelling cultivators, merchants, and artisans. Aside from comprising a large proportion of the urban population of Afghanistan, the Tajiks mainly inhabit the area north and west of the Hindu Kush, especially in the Herat area, north and northeastern Afghanistan, and the area just north of Kabul.

The Tajiks in the Herat area are historically and culturally related to the inhabitants of eastern Iran, and speak an eastern or Khorasan dialect of Persian called *Fārsi*. The Tajiks of northern Afghanistan are ethnically and culturally mixed with the Turkic-speaking Uzbeks of that region and are Sunni Muslims. The *lingua franca* is Persian mixed with a number of Turkic words. Although the Tajiks do not always constitute a majority in many of these northern areas, they exert a strong cultural influence on the predominantly Turkic population. The northern Tajiks are closely allied to the Tajiks of Bokhara, Samarkand, Tashkent, and other large Central Asian cities. The northern Tajiks speak a kind of Central Asian Persian called *Tājiki*. Though sometimes considered to be two separate languages, both *Fārsi* and *Tājiki* are termed *Dari* in Afghanistan.[15]

The most interesting and least known of the various groups referred to as Tajiks are the Mountain Tajiks or Pamir Tajiks, the indigenous populations living around the upper Amu Daria River, the Daria-ye Panj.[16] They speak mutually incomprehensible languages, have maintained an ancient culture, and have preserved a relatively pure race, unlike the plains Tajiks. They are Ismaili Shia Muslims and are not considered Tajiks by other inhabitants of Afghanistan.

Hazaras

The inhabitants of the mountains of central Afghanistan are known as Hazaras. They are believed to be a Mongoloid people who conquered the Tajiks of the area and adopted their culture; thus, they speak a dialect of Persian, *Hazāragi*, and are sedentary farmers.[17] Some summer transhumance is practiced.

As already shown, the question of religion, or specifically of Islamic sects, plays an extremely important part in determining identity in Afghanistan. Other historical or cultural factors seem to be of secondary importance. The Hazarajat Hazaras are predominantly Shia Muslims and form the largest single Shia group in Afghanistan.[18] Perhaps because of their religious beliefs, and perhaps partly because they have easily identifiable Mongoloid features, the Hazaras are discriminated against by Sunni Muslims. The Hazaras, in turn, feel a strong bond of unity among themselves and with other Shia groups.

Uzbeks

The Uzbeks are the principal group of Afghanistan's Turkic population. They inhabit northern Afghanistan from Maimana to Badakhshan, and in many areas overlap the Tajiks. Originally, the Uzbeks of Central Asia were predominantly nomadic, but gradually became urbanized under the influence of the sedentary Iranian element. There are still large numbers of Uzbeks in rural areas carrying out agricultural and transhumant activities. In general the Afghan Uzbeks, like the Tajiks, are Sunni Muslims and are sedentary, village-dwelling peasants, merchants, or artisans. Quite a number of Uzbek families also live in the capital city of Kabul.

Gypsies

There are a number of names for different groups who fit the gypsy description, but who may not, in fact, be real gypsies. The most commonly used names are *Jat, Chelu, Kouli, Qawāl, Ghurbati, Jogi*, and *Gharib Zāda*. A more thorough consideration of these people or peoples will be made later in reference to specific locations and to occupations, which for the gypsies is mainly that of musician.

RELIGION

Joseph Schacht states in *An Introduction to Islamic Law* that "it is impossible to understand Islam without understanding Islamic law."[19] Perhaps the axiom can be expanded to assert that it is impossible to understand Afghanistan without understanding Islam; for Afghanistan is an Islamic State and almost all of her citizens are Muslims. Islam is not just a religion; it is also a way of life.[20] Islamic law, *shariᶜat*, specifies not only religious duties regarding worship and ritual, but also establishes some political and legal rules which regulate the life of Muslims in all aspects.

In theory, the state is the political expression of the religion. In practice, however, there has never been a permanent fusion of political power and sacred law. Through this distance, Islamic law gained stability and strength. In describing the attempts of the Abbasid rulers (A.D. 750–1258) to impose state control over law, Schacht notes, "The result was that Islamic law became more and more removed from practice, but in the long run gained more in power over the mind than it lost control over the bodies of Muslims."[21] It is that spiritual ascendancy of Islamic law—or philosophy—that permeates Muslim thought and behavior and provides the main unifying element in an otherwise diverse Islamic world. It is not surprising, then, that the Afghan conceptions of music and musician are based on interpretations of Islamic law. These popular notions will be discussed in subsequent chapters dealing specifically with the concepts of music and musician. For the present, however, a brief description of Islam, as it applies to Afghanistan, is in order.

Article 2 of the 1964 Afghanistan Constitution states, "Islam is the sacred religion of Afghanistan. Religious rites performed by the State shall be according to the provisions of the Hanafi doctrine." The Hanafi doctrine is one of four orthodox systems of jurisprudence in Islam. The majority of Afghanistan's population are Sunni Muslims, while a fairly large minority of the population are Shia Muslims; the preceding section describing different ethnic groups stressed the importance of the Sunni-Shia distinction in determining Afghan social categories.

The basic disagreement between the Sunnis and Shias involves the Prophet's cousin and son-in-law, Ali, and the question of a successor to the Prophet as a temporal leader of the Muslim community. To the Sunnis, Ali was the fourth and last of the "rightly guided" Caliphs who ruled from Medina.[22] To the Shias, however, Ali and his descendants were the sole, rightful successors of the Prophet. The followers of Ali and his descendants became further divided when a faction recognized Ismail, the son of Jafar, as the seventh and last Imam and became known as the Ismaili or "Seveners." The others recognized Ismail's younger brother and his descendants down to the twelfth Imam; thus they are known as *Esnāᶜ Ashari* or the "Twelvers." The Shias are commonly referred to as *Panjtani* or followers of the "Five Holy Ones," a reference to Mohammed, Ali, Fatima (Mohammed's daughter, Ali's wife, and mother of Hasan and Husain), Hasan, and Husain. In Badakhshan province, the term more specifically applies to the Ismaili Shias of Sheghnan, Wakhan, Keran-o Munjan, Ishkashem, and Zebak (all of whom are collectively labeled as Mountain Tajiks or Pamir Tajiks). The Sunnis are colloquially called *Chāriāri* or followers of the "Four Companions," referring to the first four Caliphs—Abu Bakr, Omar, Osman, and Ali.

Originally a political faction, the Shias came to differ increasingly from Sunni doctrines.[23] The Sunni-Shia distinction leads to physical as well as social separation, and for some, accounts for all the differences in attitudes from one society to another, so that these "religious differences are the overriding criteria of social segmentations in Afghanistan."[24] Robert Canfield briefly describes the distribution of Muslim sects in Afghanistan; the country, he says,

> is also plural in a religious sense, for it is primarily made up of three muslim sects—Sunnis, Imamis [*Esnā^c Ashari*], and Ismailis—one of which, the Sunnis, predominates. Sunnis control the ruling institution and the strategic geographical regions of Afghanistan. In its southern and eastern parts, Afghan and Tajik Sunnis preponderate and in the north, Uzbek, Afghan, Tajik, and Hazara (Day Zainat) Sunnis are pre-eminent. The most numerous rural Imami groups are the Hazara-Sayyed Imamis dwelling in the inaccessible mountain massif of central Afghanistan, the Hazarajat, and the Tajik Imamis of Herat Province. The Ismaili sects follow the contours of the Hindu Kush Mountain range from its southern extremity in Besud northeastward into the Pamirs, even into Russian Central Asia and Northern Pakistan.[25]

There is no priesthood or clergy in Islam; the principles and observances are conveyed to the common people by a *mullā*, who may have charge of a mosque, give basic instruction in a *madrasa* (religious school), and give counsel.[26] In the words of Hafizullah Baghban, a folklorist from Herat, "the *mullah* was the religious leader, the charmer, the undertaker and the wise man. With other select leaders of the village, the *mullah* also had a role in solving people's disputes."[27]

In government, during the Constitutional period [1963–73], the appointees of the Ministry of Justice and the Supreme Court under the reign of Zahir Shah were respected Islamic scholars as well as civil servants, and were expected to render decisions according to the principles of Hanafi jurisprudence of *shari^cat* "whenever no provision exists in the Constitution or laws [of the State] for a case under consideration."[28]

Society

Until 1978, Afghanistan could be characterized as a traditional Middle Eastern society where families were "extended, patrilineal, patrilocal, endogamous, and occasionally polygamous";[29] where women had a lesser status than men; and where the system of purdah was observed. This statement, however, is perhaps more an ideal or a set of preferences not necessarily realized than a clear generalization. The residents of rural areas are at one and the same time more traditional and less strict than their counterparts in the cities. Their lifestyle follows the ideal as closely as possible, but for certain sociological or economic reasons, endogamy, patrilocality, purdah, and other customs cannot be strictly observed. For example, though the system of purdah is respected in the countryside, practical considerations prevent the women from being fully veiled outside their homes. The veiling of women in Afghanistan is an urban custom where many people from different families live in close quarters. The compulsory veiling of women was lifted by the government in 1959.[30] Since that time female members of the upper classes in cities and wives of government officials in the provinces have followed the examples of women of the royal family and wear only a scarf on their heads in place of the full body-covering veil called *chāderi*. In the early 1970s, the veil was more and more shunned in the cities as a symbol of backwardness, but was growing more popular in the villages where the *chāderi* had become a symbol of respectability and wealth.

Although the urban-rural dichotomy is evident elsewhere, the contrast in Afghanistan seems even greater because attributes of goodness and evil are attached to settings. Ibn Khaldun, the fourteenth-century Tunisian historian, observed that "Bedouins are closer to being good than sedentary people."[31] He notes that:

> Sedentary people are much concerned with all kinds of pleasures. They are accustomed to luxury and success in worldly occupations and to indulgence in worldly desires. Therefore, their souls are colored with all kinds of blameworthy and evil qualities. . . . Bedouins may be concerned with worldly affairs as (sedentary people are). However, such concern would touch only the necessities of life and not luxuries or anything causing, or calling for, desires and pleasures. The customs they follow in their mutual dealings are, therefore, appropriate. As compared with those of sedentary people their evil ways and blameworthy qualities are much less numerous.[32]

Although there are a number of nomads in Afghanistan called *kuchi*, Ibn Khaldun's commentary is more appropriate in assessing the urban-rural situation where nomads are included as rural inhabitants. This urban-rural dichotomy affects the activities and personalities of its inhabitants, but more important for the purpose of this study, it affects the attitudes and concepts people have of music and musicians. It is also extremely critical to remember that Muslims have had a long tradition of considering the importance of a setting in affecting its inhabitants; thus, it is in keeping with that tradition that the next chapter is devoted to the setting of the three specific locations with which this study is concerned.

CHAPTER TWO

Three Diverse Areas of Afghanistan

The three locations in Afghanistan with which this study is concerned, Herat, Faizabad, and Khadir, were chosen in part because all three are Muslim, Persian-speaking communities, and also for their diverse locality, population, ethnic composition, and way of life. I stress the differences more than the similarities in this chapter with the intention of giving a background of the conditions which may contribute to the different conceptualizations of music and musicians.

HERAT

Herat is the capital of Herat Province in northwestern Afghanistan (Map 2). It is considered one of the four great Afghan cities: Kabul, the capital, to the east; Kandahar to the south; Mazar-i Sharif to the north; and Herat to the west.[1] With an estimated population of 85,000 in the early 1970s Herat ranked as the third largest city in Afghanistan; however, Herat's importance as a great historical and cultural center even from the time of Alexander the Great to the cultural apex attained during the fifteenth-century Timurid period, is unrivaled in all of Afghanistan.

Muslim historians and geographers have referred to Herat as one of the largest and most important towns in Khorasan. J. P. Ferrier, a nineteenth-century French traveler, remarked, "The admirable position occupied by Herat must at all times have attracted the attention of the sovereigns of Persia—there is not a position of more importance in a strategical and commercial point of view, and the fertility of the soil is great."[2] Ferrier goes on to say that:

> Herat is one of the most ancient cities in Asia, and its inhabitants mention only Balkh, Maragha, and Naketchivan as of equally ancient origin. Its central situa-

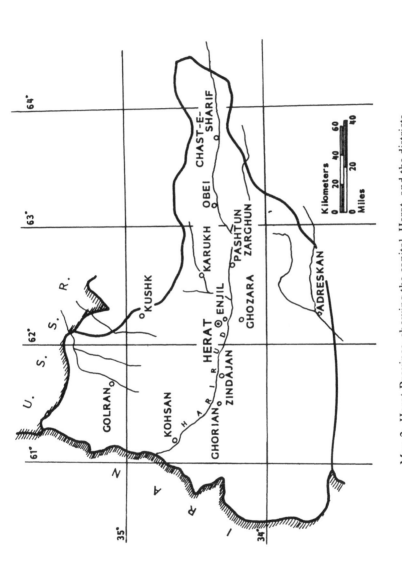

Map 2: Herat Province, showing the capital, Herat, and the districts.

tion, as I have before remarked, must ever render it a place of great importance. The merchants of Persia, Turkistan, Afghanistan, India, and the Seistan come here to exchange the various commodities of their several countries.[3]

More recently, Fraser-Tytler expressed the political significance Herat held for the British in the last century: "It guards the road to Qandahar and India and yet is itself most open to attack from the north and west."[4]

Herat's historical depth is reflected in the many great monuments of the past still visible at the time of this study. The citadel of Herat, *Qalᶜa-i Ikhtiyāruddin*, dating from 1305, apparently stands on the same site where a fortress was built at Alexander the Great's order in the fourth century B.C.[5] The old city of Herat is dominated by the Friday Mosque, *Masjid-i Jāmiᶜ*, already an important center of Islamic thought in the tenth century. The mosque was rebuilt, repaired, and enlarged through the ensuing centuries, reaching its greatest period of magnificence during the Timurid period; the present restoration was begun in 1943.[6] Six tall minarets gracefully rise out of Herat's skyline. These minarets and a mausoleum are the only remnants of an entire complex of buildings commissioned in the fifteenth century by Queen Gauhar-Shah and later by Sultan Husain-i Baiqara.[7] According to Ferrier, the mosque of the complex, still standing in 1845, was the most imposing and elegant structure in all Asia, but in 1885 the many buildings of the complex were intentionally razed for defensive purposes.[8]

Having been historically a part of Iran, Herat shares with other Iranian cities a basically Persian-Tajik tradition and population; however, the Afghans (Pashtuns) have ruled Herat for the past 250 years and now Afghans constitute a considerable part of Herat's population.[9] Many of the Afghans, originally from the area of Kandahar, have become Persianized in language and custom, but not in religion; they belong to the Sunni sect of Islam. According to Paul English, the Shias constitute only one-quarter of the city's population.[10] Hazaras, Jamshedis, Baluches, Turkmen, and Kazakhs make up the remainder of Herat's Muslim population. Ferrier notes an attempt made in 1838 by the Persians after the siege of Herat to repeople the city with several thousand nomads, including Hazaras, Jamshedis, and Taimanis.[11] A small group of Jews have lived there for centuries; many of the Jews who faced persecution in Meshed fled to and settled in Herat.[12] English notes only six Jewish families living in Herat in the 1960s, however.[13] Small groups of Russian Turkmen and Kazakhs settled in Herat following the Basmachi Revolution in the earlier part of this century.

Herat, like other Afghan cities, has expanded beyond the confines of the old city (Map 3). Government buildings are located in the new city, *Shahr-i Nau*, which sprawls east and north of the old city. The old city is

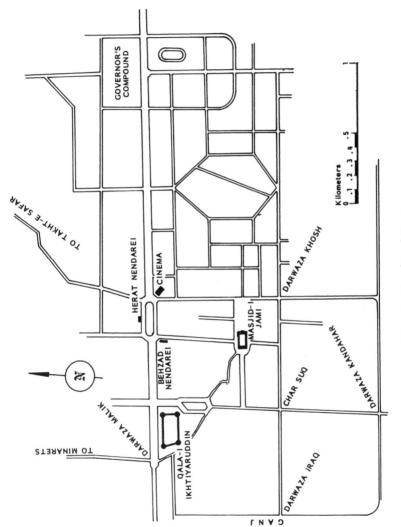

Map 3: The city of Herat.

Bazaar in old section of Herat city.

still the commercial center of Herat where specialized bazaars and quarters are maintained. The hub of these bazaars is known as *chār suq,* "four market places," where all four bazaar streets converge (Map 3).

> The bazaars of Herat have 5,542 shops and an aggregate length of approximately six miles. The city has one shop for every fifteen citizens, indicating its importance as a regional marketing center for the million or so people who live in the valley of the Hari Rud.[14]

Besides the bazaars proper, considerable commercial activity is transacted around the outer extremities of the old city in four areas known as *Darwāza Malik, Darwāza ᶜIrāq, Darwāza Kandahar,* and *Darwāza Khosh,* the four traditional "gates" surrounding old walled cities.[15] Just outside *Darwāza ᶜIrāq* is an area called *Ganj,* "mart, store, grain-market," where villagers gather to buy or sell their animals and wares on Sundays, Wednesdays, and Thursdays—the market days, *roz-e bāzār.*[16] On these market days, the street from *chār suq* to *Darwāza ᶜIrāq* is lined with peddlers from villages who squat on the pavement selling wares in front of the permanent shops. The street is generally quiet on nonmarket days and many shops, including the teahouses, are closed then. Mark Slobin has given a vivid description of *roz-e bāzār* in "local market centers" in northern Afghanistan.[17] Herat's own situation however, somewhat parallels his description of Mazar-i Sharif, a "regional market center" of the north.[18] Because of the size of the total commercial activity of the town, one is hardly aware of bazaar-day traffic in parts of town other than *Darwāza ᶜIrāq.*

Paul English contrasts the orderliness and symmetry of the general plan of the commercial area of the city with the irregularity and confusion found within its residential quarters. He relates this seeming contradiction to the observance of the difference between public and private space.

> A man's actions as a merchant or artisan, as a Muslim or an Afghan, are public actions which take place in a public space. . . . There are no shops or other facilities in the residential quarters excepting mosques, shrines, and associated baths. This is the domain of private space and private life.[19]

The distinction between public and private not only plays an important part in determining the concepts of space, but also in defining events as well as participants, which is a factor in the conceptualizations of music and musicians.

In a city the size of Herat, the demand for public entertainment in the early 1970s was constant and not dependent on the temporary influx of people on certain market days. In 1971 and 1972 a cinema and two theaters operated for a sell-out crowd every night. One theater, the Behzad Nendarei, was privately owned, while the other, Herat Nendarei, was under the sponsorship of the Ministry of Information and Culture. Both theaters had a similar format of presenting songs, dances, and a new play every week or so, but the most obvious attractions in both theaters were the female dancers, singers, and actresses who appeared in dazzling costumes after the play and sang special requests made exclusively on picture cards sold to the audiences for this purpose. The films shown at the cinema were most often Indian or Iranian movies, but sometimes old Hollywood films dubbed in Iranian Persian were offered. The audiences included a mixture of country folk attending for the first time, city regulars, and officials and their wives who attended whenever there was an especially good movie or play. Women, who comprised one percent or less of the theater audience, sat with their escorts in a special box seating ten or fewer, situated in front next to the musicians' pit. Corresponding to the rather new, nontraditional format of public entertainment, all three establishments were located on the main commercial street of the new city (see Map 3).

Other forms of public entertainment are more traditional, but more sporadic. Live music may occasionally be heard in a *samowar* (teahouse),[20] but more often than not, the musician is the owner, or a customer who has not been contracted by the teahouse. However, there are two times out of the year when traditional, live, public entertainment can be had daily: during the first days of spring and during *Ramazān*, the month of fasting.

The beginning of the new year of the Persian solar calendar corresponds with the coming of spring and is a time for celebrations, festivities, and outings. During the thirteen days following the first Wednesday of the New Year (*Chār shambe awal-e sāl*), the people of Herat and the surrounding areas like to go on picnics and outings (*mela*).[21] During this time people within the city gather in the parks to pass the day with friends, talking, eating, and listening to music. Many of the parks are assigned exclusively either to men or women. This is a busy time for vendors and musicians. Often, those with business operations in town—teahouse owners, barbers, and so on—close their shops to sell and perform at the various men's gathering grounds. Some musicians go from house to house offering a little entertainment for a small fee to those who stay at home. Besides the traditional outings, sporting events such as wrestling matches are common at this time. The spectators at these events are, of course, predominantly male.

The women's gatherings are somewhat less formal than the men's. Only women and children are allowed in those parks specially assigned to women, the vendors being the only male exceptions. A great crowd of men gathered outside these parks in 1972 and police were assigned to guard the walls of the parks to keep out male intruders or "peeping Toms." Once inside these parks, the women take off their *chāderi* or veils, and are free to relax and visit openly with each other. The favorite pastime of young girls is *chakar zadan* or "taking a stroll." Small groups of two or three girls walk slowly and proudly about the park showing off their new clothes and finery while eyeing others, occasionally stopping to talk to old friends and acquaintances and sometimes joining them to have tea or food. Many women bring their own picnic lunches. Small groups of women sing and dance to the accompaniment of tambourines called *dāira* which they bring with them or which they purchase in the park from gypsy-like women who traditionally make and sell them. Some women set up rope swings (*gāz*) in the tall trees and sell rides. Unlike the men, who eat and drink in temporary public teahouses and who are entertained by professional musicians, the women supply much of the food and entertainment for themselves. An aura of informality and abandon, lacking in the men's gatherings, prevails.

These different kinds of activity associated with men's and women's groups are not peculiar to the New Year's outings, but are applicable in general to all types of social events. The men's social events seem to be more formal, public, and professional than the women's. In any discussion of music and musicians, it becomes increasingly obvious that such features as "formal," "public," "professional," and "male" play an important role in determining the different types of music and musicians. Further, these features fall naturally into a system of binary oppositions which give insight into the relationship of the various conditions which influence the final conceptualization of music and musicians.

Fasting is one of the "Five Pillars of Islam," the others being faith, prayer, alms-giving, and pilgrimage. The Koran states, "O ye who believe! Fasting is prescribed to you as it was prescribed to those before you to ward off evil."[22] The month of fasting is *Ramazān*, the ninth month of the Islamic lunar calendar. It is the obligation of all Muslims to fast, except for the young, the sick, and the traveler. Fasting, *roza*, is observed during the daylight hours when "Muslims were commanded to eat nothing, drink nothing and abstain from sexual relations."[23] The restrictions of the day give way to a festive atmosphere at night when Muslims break the fast by feasting—if families can afford it, the meals during *Ramazān* are much more extravagant than the regular fare—and much of the night is spent socializing as Desmond Stewart's account relates:

> When the meal was over few persons slept. All night the market, streets and lanes were thronged with strollers; children rushed happily through the darkness, carrying little lanterns and begging money from grownups for more lights. In the mosques, preachers expounded to large congregations on the significance of the holy month. Outside there were various entertainments; conjurors did tricks, acrobats tumbled, and crowds surrounded poets and storytellers reciting their verses and tales.[24]

During the nights of *Ramazān* musicians perform in teahouses or in more modern "hotels" or "restaurants" located on the periphery of the old city. In these newer establishments, the entertainment takes the form of a concert where famous Kabul-oriented musicians are contracted to perform nightly for the entire month.

Most of the entertainment other than the less traditional concerts at theaters, hotels, and restaurants is private and takes place during festive, happy occasions, most typically at weddings. Although not strictly seasonal, most such special occasions are celebrated in the fall, during the mild weather and after the harvest. The most typical ensemble at these events is the *sornā* and *dohl*, the outdoor combination of oboe and drum so prevalent throughout the Middle East. These loud and penetrating instruments not only set the gay mood of the event, but also serve to announce the happy event to all those within earshot. A more intimate type of music, often voice accompanied by a string instrument and drum, is performed for male guests within the host family's compound. The musicians are most often professional. The women celebrate among themselves by participating in their own songs and dances; on rare occasions professional musicians do entertain the female guests.

An old traditional form of extravagant entertainment which has lost favor in the city but is still popular in villages is the *moqoladi* outdoor folk plays.[25] The host family hires a troupe of actors to perform for the guests. The performances usually take place at night, starting around eight o'clock and continuing into the early morning hours. A number of one-act plays are interspersed with the playing of *sornā* and *dohl*. The actors and musicians are usually a group of male residents from a single village who form an endogamous group of actors, musicians, barbers and surgeons known to outsiders as *ustā* or *jat*, but who refer to themselves as *Magad*. Until the early 1970s the city of Herat sponsored *moqoladi* performances during *Jeshen-e Isteqlāl*, national independence celebrations.

FAIZABAD

Faizabad, like Herat, is the capital of a province, but its size and character differ widely from that of Herat. Although the Ministry of Planning in 1972 quoted a population of 64,700, the most often quoted estimate during that time was 2,000 houses or approximately 20,000 people. Faizabad is the largest and most populated town in all of Badakhshan Province (Map 4).

Where Herat is well known for its favorable position in the plains of the Hari Rud River, Faizabad is equally renowned for its inaccessibility

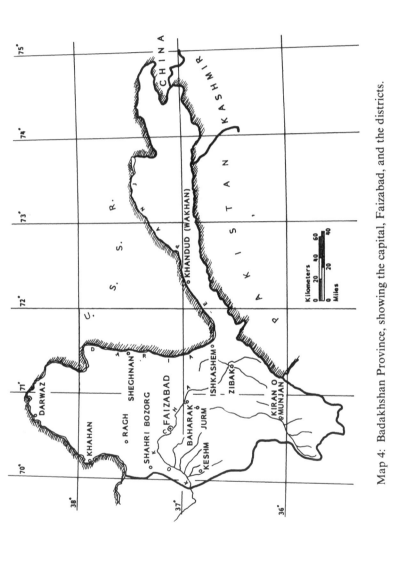

Map 4: Badakhshan Province, showing the capital, Faizabad, and the districts.

"It is a long way from here to Badakhshan": scene along the Kokcha River.

and rough, mountainous terrain. In sharp contrast to Herat, Faizabad is tucked away in a narrow valley of the Hindu Kush bordering the Kokcha River. The very task of getting to Faizabad is considerable. There is imminent danger of the roads and bridges being washed out by floods and slides, and the chance of meeting head-on traffic on the narrow road that clings perilously on the high river edge adds to the dangers. No regularly scheduled buses or trucks run between Kunduz and Faizabad; therefore, the very lack of transportation can delay the trip several days. A guidebook to Afghanistan admonishes, "This is an exciting trip through some of Afghanistan's most thrilling scenery, enjoyable only, however, if you have a strong car, spare parts, sleeping bags and an extra cache of food and petrol."[26] Bakhtar, the national Afghan airlines, served Faizabad from Kabul and Kunduz, but at the time of this study its schedule was even less dependable than the buses and trucks.

The capital of Badakhshan is equally hard to reach from within the province, as well as from without. A couplet from a popular Badakhshan quatrain aptly describes the situation, "Badakhshan" here referring to Faizabad and environs rather than the whole province, a practice begun in the nineteenth century and still common today:

Az injā tā Badakhshān khaili rāh ast
Hamagi koh ba kho sang-e siāh ast

It is a long way from here to Badakhshan
All along the way, from mountain to mountain, there are black stones

Herat has always assumed the position of the major city in the area; not so with Faizabad. The ancient capital of Badakhshan was Baharak, a lovely scenic spot in open country twenty-five miles east of Faizabad. Mountstuart Elphinstone reported that Faizabad was the capital of Badakhshan in the early nineteenth century, but by the end of that century when Captain John Wood visited Badakhshan, Jurm was the capital. "The town of Jerm, although the largest place in Badakhshan, is little more than an extensive cluster of scattered hamlets, containing at the very utmost 1500 people."[27] Even in 1972 there was talk of moving the capital back to Baharak where there was room for expansion.

Faizabad is administratively and economically the center of Badakhshan Province, but perhaps because of its size, location and its relatively newly gained status, it seems to share some of the activities of town life with three other towns on the Kokcha: Keshem, Baharak, and Jurm. The four cities form an arch (Map 4) in the general direction of southwest (Keshem), to north (Faizabad), to southeast (Baharak and Jurm). In this way Faizabad's influence seems to radiate beyond its normal sphere of influence to create a greater central area. I was first introduced to this concept of an enlarged Faizabad, or central area, when I told some Badakhshis living in Kabul about my research plans in Faizabad and asked for names of some musicians in Faizabad. I was given the names of Faiz-e Mangal from Jurm, Dur Mohammed Keshmi from Keshm, and Khan-e Baharaki from Baharak. Indeed, these musicians are extremely mobile and are often asked to perform in villages or towns throughout the central area. Thus, although this study involves Faizabad nominally as a town, it is impossible to discuss its activities without considering its interplay with other towns or regions. In this sense, the difference between a large, self-sufficient city like Herat and a small, dependent town like Faizabad becomes increasingly clear and helps determine the differing musical activities, personnel, and attitudes of the two communities.

The population of Faizabad is primarily Tajik, although there are outlying communities of Uzbeks and the Uzbek language is commonly heard in the bazaars.[28] A small percentage of Pashtuns have been encouraged by the Afghan government to settle in parts of northern Afghanistan. The Tajik element claims close ties to the Tajiks of the USSR and speaks a form of Persian known as *Tājiki* rather than *Fārsi*.

Restricted by the narrow defile where Faizabad is situated, the main street and bazaars run the length of the town, paralleling the river. The administrative center of town is an open area known as *khiābān* (Map 5). The bazaars are located in three areas: on the left bank of the Jauzun River which joins the Kokcha River just past this point; on the right bank of the Jauzun extending to the *khiābān*; and on the far side of the *khiābān* (not shown on Map 5).

Although market days are Saturdays and Thursdays, the town seems visibly unaffected by them, not because of the large size of the town as was the case in Herat, but because of the small size of the market.[29] There are perhaps three reasons for Faizabad's relatively unimportant *roz-i bāzār*. First, market functions are shared by the other towns in the central area; second, internal travel to Faizabad can be difficult, with the result that marketing is combined with other business which may take more than a market day; and third, those who raise sheep sell them locally or take their flocks all the way to Kabul where they find more demand and better prices.

Public entertainment is practically nonexistent in Badakhshan. There are no cinemas or theaters in Faizabad. Teahouses do not have musicians performing as they do in other parts of northern Afghanistan, but instead, depend on the blaring radio or old phonograph records for entertainment and atmosphere.[30] The majority of musical performances take place at private festivities—picnics, weddings, and parties.

Jeshen, the national independence celebration, is the only time of the year when there is any semblance of public entertainment in Faizabad.

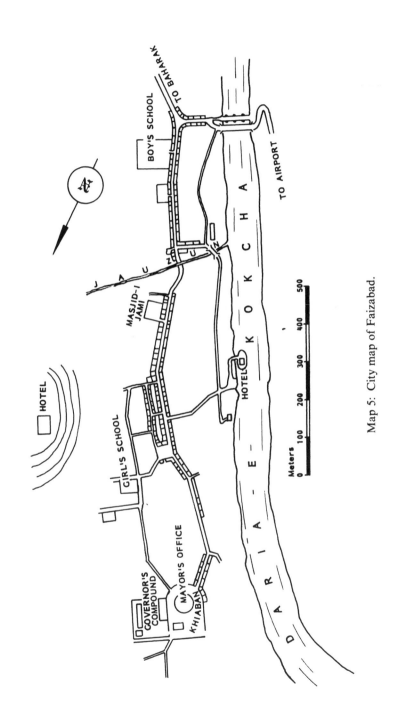

Map 5: City map of Faizabad.

A section of the Faizabad bazaar.

A teahouse in Faizabad.

Parades, musical performances, and exhibitions are held in the *khiābān* or in the schools. But even *jeshen* is handled in the same manner as private parties. The hosts are provincial and city officials; invitations are open and extended by word-of-mouth or are understood; there is no such thing as an uninvited guest. The attention accorded to individuals differs depending upon their rank and status, however. Sub-governors and local area representatives are expected to bring along the available talent from their regions.

Another semipublic event is *mela-ye chār maghz*, Walnut Festival, held in Sarghalam, a beautiful narrow green valley shaded by great walnut trees. The event is hosted yearly in the summer by a wealthy landowner of Sarghalam. Important guests from Faizabad arrive the night before and are privately entertained. The next morning, a great table is set up outside and a breakfast of trout (freshly caught in the Sarghalam River), bread, and tea is served. Other guests arrive in large numbers during the remainder of the morning and are served tea; musicians sing for the crowds. Finally, taking advantage of the number of officials and other guests present, grievances are brought up and the event turns into a political meeting.

Private events such as wedding parties and picnics take on similar forms whether they are held in the villages or in the greater Faizabad area. The amount and type of wedding music is dictated by the different events and participants associated with the marriage celebrations rather than by the locale of the wedding. Women's gatherings involve less professional and more communal or participatory music. Friends gather to help decorate the bride's hands with henna or the women of the groom's family visit the bride and her female relatives. An exchange of tea and sweets occurs and everyone (except the bride) participates in singing and dancing, usually to the accompaniment of tambourines (*daf*) played by young girls. The men's functions are more formal, involving professional musicians and dancers who entertain the guests. The outdoor, public music of weddings is performed by the *sornā* and *dohl*, the outdoor oboe and drum prevalent throughout the Middle East. It is only in this aspect that one may find a difference between the wedding music of remote villages and that of villages in the greater Faizabad area; professional *sornā* and *dohl* musicians are not readily available for hire outside the greater Faizabad area. The indoor, more private music is provided by semiprofessional musicians who accompany their songs with string instruments. In the areas of Wakhan and Sheghnan, a less formal atmosphere prevails and wedding songs are often sung by a group of men who accompany themselves on the *daf*.

Picnics are less formal occasions than weddings and the music, if any, is provided by the picnickers themselves rather than by hired musicians. An elaborate picnic may involve a two- or three-day outing to some famous shrine. Most of the days are spent in traveling, setting up camp, making pilgrimages, and preparing food, but the evenings are devoted to eating, listening to music, singing, and even dancing.

The usual setting for private music is in someone's guest house. The host hires musicians or storytellers to entertain his guests, his neighbors, and his household at night. A favorite form of entertainment during long winter nights is the traditional performance of the Central Asian epic, *Gorgholi* (also known as *Kuroghli* or *Gurogli*). The storyteller accompanies his tale with a *dambura*, a two-stringed, fretless, plucked lute, and sings in a deep, guttural voice, slowly spinning out one episode (*shākh*) of the tale which may take several nights in the telling, depending on the manipulations of the storyteller. He may stop to rest his voice and retune his instrument after every section of the story, but more calculatedly, he stops at some critical or climactic moment in order to keep his audience involved, and to demand special favors of food or money. This break is known locally in Badakhshan as *bandāna*, and can result in much time being spent in light-hearted haggling, or in long breaks while the women of the household hurriedly prepare special dishes for the teller of the tale. Many such interruptions can stretch a four- to five-hour story into a two- to three-day performance.

KHADIR

The mountainous region of central Afghanistan is known as the Hazarajat, home of the Hazaras. The Hazaras live in the high valleys of the Koh-i Baba, an extension of the Hindu Kush. The average elevation of their habitat is 9,000 feet above sea level. The mountains around them are brown and barren, yet the Hazaras carefully farm and irrigate the land, planting wheat on the mountainsides and depending upon the limited rainfall to water their fields. The winters are severe and long and most of the Hazarajat is snowbound for three or four months of the year. The one road that connects the Hazarajat to Kabul and the "outside world" is closed perhaps five months of the year while it is snowbound or washed out.

The inaccessibility of the Hazarajat perhaps equals that of Badakhshan, but here the likeness ends. Hazarajat seems inhospitable and stark when compared to the green and fertile valleys of Badakhshan. The Hazarajat appears sparsely peopled, for there are few villages of the Tajik type; only scattered, small clusters of two or three houses are apparent. At other times a few small tenant houses surround a great *qalᶜa*, a fortress which serves as the landlord's home. The Hazarajat is the most ethnically homogeneous of the three areas discussed; outsiders do not care to settle this land. There are, however, contacts with Pashtun nomads who bring their flocks to graze in the Hazarajat every summer.[31] These contacts provide for an exchange of goods and services, but more often result in quarrels and violence. Sometimes the land is even too harsh for the Hazaras, many of whom emigrate to the cities in search of a living.

Khadir is the administrative center of the district of Dai Kundi in Urozgan Province, central Afghanistan (Map 6). Dai Kundi used to be the name of a major Hazara tribe, but now designates a territory which corresponds to an administrative district known as *woleswāli*.[32] Before the reor-

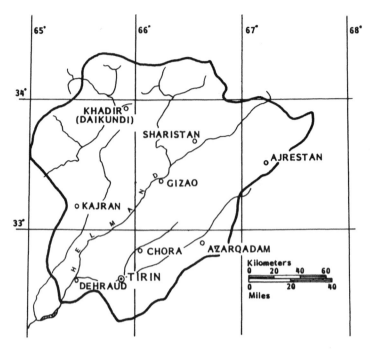

Map 6: Urozgan Province, showing the capital, Tirin, and the districts;
Khadir is at upper left.

ganization of administrative units in 1963, Dai Kundi, along with Behsud,
Lal Sarjangal, Yakaulang, and Sharistan, were subordinate divisions of
Dai Zangi, a district of Kabul Province. Therefore, Dai Zangi district included practically all of the region known as Hazarajat, with its center at
Panjao. After the reorganization, Dai Kundi became a *woleswāli* of Urozgan Province and Panjao became a *woleswāli* of Bamiyan Province. Dai
Kundi includes much of northern Urozgan and in 1973 was one of the
largest administrative districts in Afghanistan with a population of
105,000; yet only one *wakil* (congressman) represented the district in the
capital.

Just as it is difficult to isolate Faizabad and its activities from the
surrounding area, it is impossible to discuss Khadir exclusively. As the
administrative center of the district, its population and activities are atypi-
cal. The nuclear town of Khadir consists of a great *qalᶜa* which serves as the
woleswāl's (district commissioner's) home and office, two or three other
government buildings, and a little more than a dozen shops (Map 7).
Khadir is peopled mainly by civil servants, none of whom are native to the
area. The stores and the few homes in the outlying area of the town are

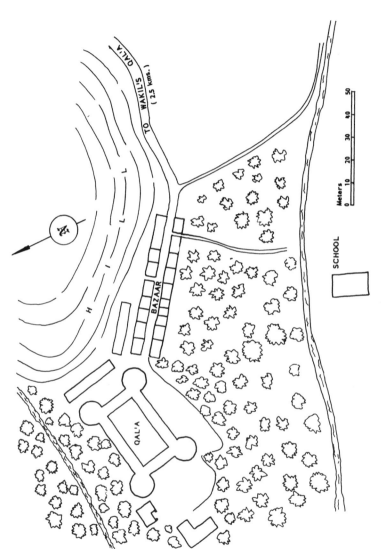

Map 7: Khadir village.

The Khadir bazaar, Hazarajat.

owned by Hazaras, but it is clear that without the function of an administrative center, the nuclear town (government buildings and bazaar) would
not exist at all. There are no figures on Khadir's population, but the
number of people who actually live in town cannot be over one hundred.
Schurmann was able to get an estimate of a total of 800 households for
Khadir and three other villages.[33] It should be noted that a village does not
necessarily designate a compact village nucleus, but may represent a
number of scattered settlements which are considered an administrative
unit. Khadir, then, consists of both a compact town and scattered settlements within Khadir Valley.

Economic and social activities center around the home of an *arbāb*,
loosely translated as "village head," or in other private homes. The *arbāb* is
most often a wealthy and respected landowner who is the head of a number
of households by consensus. His constituency does not necessarily correspond to a village unit; a village may have more than one *arbāb* or a single
arbāb can control a number of households in different villages. Generally,
the *arbāb* looks after the well-being of his tenants or those who choose an
affiliation with him, and settles local disputes; but most important, he in-
tercedes for them in official matters. In exchange for his responsibilities
and services, his constituency supplies him with whatever gifts of goods and
services they can afford. Allegiances are reaffirmed in this manner; however, alliances are not irrevocable and a person may choose to affiliate with
another *arbāb* at any time.[34]

Music as entertainment takes place almost exclusively in the context
of a private and informal setting. The musicians themselves are not professionals and most of them sing songs or poems without the accompaniment
of any instrument. Even at wedding festivities the presence of a musical
instrument is a rare luxury. The Hazara women throughout the Hazarajat
do a kind of group dance called *peshpu* which is an especially appropriate
welcome for a new bride. Shooting and riding games are also popular at
these times. The only other form of musical entertainment that I have seen
is apparently a regional form of folk pantomime about a fairy and various
jinn characters known as *Deo-Pari*, the name of two characters in the folk
play. Two jinns, *deo* and *ghol*, fight for the affections of the fairy, *pari*. Also
included in some performances is a lion, *sher*. The pantomime is accompanied by a *dambura* (two-stringed, fretless, plucked lute).

All these group activities take place outside; the solo singers usually
sing for a group within the guest house. In each type of social gathering
discussed so far, both in Herat and in Faizabad, the men and women have
been separated, either by complete exclusion to their own activities in separate quarters, or by segregation to different areas to watch the same
activity. The only exception seems to be the cinema, where the few women

who do attend have no special assigned seats. In the Hazarajat, however, men and women are quite free to mix socially, an unlikely situation else-where except in the most intimate of family gatherings. Elphinstone de-voted a great deal of his nineteenth-century description of Hazara women to what he saw as their ascendancy and their libertine characteristics.[35] It is true that many Hazara women have a strong voice in their own affairs, or even in the affairs of the community, but their libertine characteristics are not apparent today.[36] Elphinstone may have been referring to the Shia institution of legal temporary marriage.[37] Slowly, however, town or foreign mannerisms are creeping into Hazara life so that if a government official or another outsider is present as a guest, the women do not show themselves. Paradoxically, the women of high and more status-conscious families take on city airs and are more confined to their homes than less urban-oriented women.

CHAPTER THREE

Islam and Music

Music and musicians have always been regarded somewhat paradoxically in the Islamic Middle East. The paradox arises from the discrepancy between theory—the unfavorable attitude of Islam toward music—and practice—the existence of music as an almost indispensable part of Islamic social life.

ISLAMIC SOURCES

Henry G. Farmer investigates thoroughly the possible origins of Islam's authority in opposing music by citing the Koran and Hadith, but finds nothing conclusive because the Koran is interpreted by theologians according to their particular views, and because there are numerous Hadiths that indicate that Mohammed sometimes favored music and at other times condemned it.[1] Although there is not a word of direct censure against music in the Koran, exegetes on the whole treated the subject unsympathetically. It is said by some that singing is denounced in Surah 26:224-26 by virtue of its close relationship to poetry: "As for poets, the erring follow them. Hast thou not seen how they stray in every valley, And how they say that which they do not?"[2] Some point to Surah 31:19: "Be modest in thy bearing and subdue thy voice. Lo! the harshest of all voices is the voice of the ass"[3] as a dictum against singing. Others interpret "mere pastime of discourse" quoted in Surah 31:6 to include music: "And of mankind is he who payeth for mere pastime of discourse, that he may mislead from Allah's way without knowledge, and maketh it the butt of mockery. For such there is a shameful doom."[4]

Second to the authority of the Koran is Hadith. It is possible to find Hadiths that support the practice of music as well as denounce it. But on the whole, those Traditions which look upon music unfavorably are austere injunctions against music, while those that are viewed favorably are passive statements or subject to compromise. The evil of music does not seem to be balanced by its goodness. For example, many Traditions which condemn music call it the work of the devil: "Iblis (Satan) was the first who wailed and the first who sang."[5] Further, "One who sings sends for two devils. One sits on the left shoulder, the other on the right, and they kick the singer until he stops."[6] Musical instruments are "the devil's muezzin, serving to call men to his worship."[7] Those Traditions used as evidence to condone music are somewhat milder in nature: "Mohammed saw some girls playing the tambourines. Aisha, who was then nine years old, got up on his shoulder and watched, and Mohammed said nothing."[8] Mohammed also ordered, "Publish the marriage, and beat the ghirbāl [round tambourine]," and further, "His own nuptials with Khadīja were celebrated with music, and so were those of his daughter Fātima."[9]

INTERPRETATIONS

The bias against music may have been connected to Mohammed's physiological state or to his political motives, or it may have been fabricated after Mohammed's death by theologians who were jealous of the inordinate attention paid to musicians.[10] It has been said that Mohammed was hypersensitive to touch, smell, taste, and sounds; thus, any sound, including music, caused him much annoyance.[11] However, this view is not consistent with the fact that Mohammed allowed the music of the *Āzān* or call to prayer, as well as songs of war and certain festival music.

The bias in terms of Mohammed's political motives is more reasonable when it is considered that during the first years of Mohammed's Revelations, the Meccans stood aloof. More attention was paid to minstrels and poets than to the prophet. Mohammed felt a need to denounce poets, and yet he recognized the inspiration and power behind their act. Thus, the Revelations are "modelled upon the *Saj^c* or rhymed prose of the pagan soothsayers"[12] and some are charms against magic. Reynold A. Nicholson explains:

> It must, however, be borne in mind that his disavowal does not refer primarily to the poetic art, but rather to the person and character of the poets themselves. He, the divinely inspired Prophet, could have nothing to do with men who owed their inspiration to demons and gloried in the ideals of paganism which he was striving to overthrow.[13]

With or without the sanction of the theologians, music has not been viewed consistently by the caliphs who succeeded Mohammed. It has been generally acknowledged that following the death of the Prophet the energies of the orthodox caliphs were spent in battle and devoted to the ordinances of the Koran. The conquests made by Mohammed's successors brought enormous wealth and subsequently "a voluptuous and dissolute life which broke through every restriction that Islam had imposed."[14] Henry G. Farmer asks, "What has all this to do with music? A great deal. Everywhere we see culture progress dependent upon economic and political forces, and side by side with this material luxury and political grandeur we find intellectual weal and aesthetic splendour."[15]

The Umayyads, though mainly Arab in feeling, were generally indifferent to Islam; thus, they were looked upon as "Kings by right, Caliph only by courtesy."[16] Muslim purists looked upon them as usurpers not only because they were the descendants of the Meccan aristocracy who once strove to defeat Mohammed, but also because of their worldly ways. Counted among the sins of the Umayyads was their great patronage of the arts, and especially of music.

Under the Abbasids, the arts and sciences gained strength and support through adherence to a liberal Islamic theology. Although most of the learned Muslims in the religious or intellectual sciences were non-Arabs, they were recognized because "it was Islam and the sciences connected with Islam that profited thereby."[17] The "native" or Islamic sciences arising from studies of the Koran and Hadith were developed; the four great schools of Islamic law were founded; there was great intellectual and scientific activity. Under the patronage of the Abbasid caliph Mamum (A.D. 813–33) and his successors, the "foreign" or philosophical and natural sciences, which included music, flourished until Mutawakkil's reign (A.D. 847–61), which marked the return of conservatism and a stricter adherence to the text of the Koran. A reactionary spirit prevailed which was "essentially opposed to intellectual freedom and has maintained its petrifying influence almost unimpaired down to the present time."[18]

Despite such reactionary attitudes toward music, Islamic ritual often involves some sort of musical activity such as the call to prayer and the chanting of the Koran. Farmer suggests that a legal fiction was created to distinguish the cantillation of the Koran from the singing of a secular song. It was determined that anyone could grasp the modulation of the voice in cantillation, while songs were within the repertoire of professional musicians.[19]

Music and dance are also found in Sufi rituals. Many Sufis use music or dance to attain religious ecstasy or in *ziker* recitation, the use of words or syllables (to be sung, chanted, or thought) in order to remind the devotee of the presence of God.[20] This use, rather than elevating the art of music, drew suspicion to certain Sufi orders in the eyes of strict Orthodox Muslims:

This use of 'listening,' *samâ*, was the point that aroused most doubt among the 'ulamâ' scholars, who seized on such music (music being frowned upon in any case) as a singularly dubious means of spiritual discipline; sometimes they suspected that the good looks of a lad who sang might move hearers as much as words he uttered about God. Some Ṣûfîs, the more Sharīᶜah-minded, consequently avoided its use. Some, on the contrary, looked on it as peculiarly emblematic at once of the Ṣûfî's freedom and of God's beauty.[21]

Today, a general notion that music is religiously disapproved prevails. Music is looked upon with a certain degree of suspicion and people who make music their profession are relegated to a low status in society. But it must be realized that the Muslim conceptualization of music is quite different from our own; thus, it is conceivable that the paradox exists only in our minds. In Afghanistan, many Muslims find little or no paradox either within the varying Hadiths, or even between theory and practice. The differing Traditions and practices are reconciled by means of association, consequence, and definition. The Prophet probably did not censure music per se, but disapproved of its common association with debauchery, with the easy attraction of "wine, women, and song," and its intoxicating powers.[22] If music has the power to lead men astray, it also has the power to spur men to great deeds of valor; thus, it is the consequence of music which must be considered. The Sufi, Abu Sulaiman al-Darani, explains, "music and singing do not produce in the heart which is not in it."[23]

The question of paradoxy is tied closely to the problem of definition. The western notion of music emphasizes the element of sound while the Islamic sources and the interpretations of these sources speak to specific aspects, functions, consequences, or other implications of these musical sounds. It is a fallacy then, to ignore the native terms involved and their subtle nuances of meaning by simply substituting a foreign term "music" and assuming its foreign notions. It is imperative to consider the different definitions and usages of the many existing native terms that relate to music, and to recognize the varied situations which play upon the many-faceted notions of music. Only then can we begin to understand how the seeming contradiction between theory and practice is resolved, or how the contradiction does not exist in the Afghan mind.

CHAPTER FOUR

The Concept of Music

A discussion of the semantic implications of the concept of music in Afghanistan must be based on the assumption that such a domain exists and is culturally significant. Evidence supporting this assumption is found in the existence of the term *musiqi* in the Persian language. Its meaning is derived from the Greek *mousike*, from which our own term *music* is also derived. Persian-English dictionaries point out the difference between *musiqi*, the science or art of music, and *muzik*, the sounds or performances of music. Interestingly, English-Persian dictionaries include other cover terms for the concept of music, such as *āhang* and *naghma*. This is further indication that a simple one-to-one relationship does not exist between the English and Persian meanings of the term, and that cultural and philosophical disparities may exist that complicate analysis of the Afghan sense of music and musician. Still, the existence of some terminology to describe the concept of music indicates that that concept is present within the culture.

This chapter deals mainly with the meaning and usage of contemporary musical terminology in Afghanistan, but first, the traditional terminology associated with music must be reviewed briefly. Information on traditional terminology is drawn from secondary sources, while information on contemporary terminology is based on field observations in Afghanistan.

TRADITIONAL CONCEPTS

We learn from Henry G. Farmer that music in pre-Islamic times consisted of specific song types such as the caravan songs and the elegy.[1] In the seventh century a song called the *ghinā'* was introduced from al-Hira.[2] *Ghinā'* eventually came to mean "song" in particular and "music" in general. During the early Abbasid period (A.D. 750–847), a rationalist tendency developed among some Islamic thinkers which was first influenced by theological ideas of Eastern Christians and later by direct contact with Greek philosophy translated into Arabic.[3] Music became one of the courses of scientific study and the technical nomenclature *musiqi* was directly borrowed from the Greeks. "Where no Arabic equivalent was found or known the Greek term was simply transliterated with some adaptation."[4] Hence, *musiqi* came to represent the theoretical aspects of music, and *ghinā'* was reserved for the practical art.[5]

The following table from Reynold A. Nicholson shows the traditional Islamic divisions of the sciences.[6] The "native sciences" stem directly from the study of the Koran and Hadith, while the "foreign sciences" are those the Arabs learned from foreigners; *musiqi* is a division of the "foreign sciences." After A.D. 847, however, the rationalist views were rejected by the traditionalists: "The populace regarded philosophy and natural science as a species of infidelity."[7]

The categorization of *musiqi* as a "foreign science" has implications even today. *Musiqi* and things foreign are acknowledged but still suspect. As will become evident in the ensuing chapter on musicians, the distinction between native and foreign is constantly made as a measure of orthodoxy and acceptance. Further, the performance of music often involves litera-

TABLE 1

Islamic Sciences

I.   Native Sciences

1. Koranic Exegesis	*ᶜIlmu 'l-Tafsír*
2. Koranic Criticism	*ᶜIlmu 'l-Qirá'át*
3. Science of Apostolic Tradition	*ᶜIlmu 'l-Hadíth*
4. Jurisprudence	*Fiqh*
5. Scholastic Theology	*ᶜIlmu 'l-Kalám*
6. Grammar	*Nahw*
7. Lexicography	*Lugha*
8. Rhetoric	*Bayán*
9. Literature	*Adab*

II.   Foreign Sciences

1. Philosophy	*Falsafa*
2. Geometry	*Handasa*
3. Astronomy	*ᶜIlmu 'l-Nujúm*
4. Music	*Músíqí*
5. Medicine	*Tibb*
6. Magic and Alchemy	*al-Sihr wa-'l-Kímiyá*

---

ture, a "native science," as well as music. The combination of these two aspects leads to a rather specialized definition of music.

Each contemporary term associated with music will be discussed according to its meaning and usage in Afghanistan. The first term, *musiqi*, will be treated in great detail as an example of the type of data collected and the methodology used to draw conclusions. The treatment of the remainder of the words is not so lengthy. The last section will contrast the concepts of music in the three diverse areas of Herat, Faizabad, and Khadir.

Musiqi

In order to present the various ways in which the word *musiqi* is defined and used in Afghanistan, several cases of actual usage will be cited. In each case, information concerning the language, the speaker, and the setting is considered, for all these factors have a bearing on the different meanings and usages of the word *musiqi*.

Some conversations or questions were conducted in Persian, some in English. Some were cross-cultural, involving the investigator, whose native language is English, and an informant, whose native language was Persian, while other conversations overheard by the investigator were cultural, involving two native Persian speakers. Some Persian speakers are urban-oriented; many are not. The expression "urban-oriented" is loosely used here and implies a certain amount of sophistication besides formal education and literacy, and does not necessarily imply living in a city. The formality of the situation or the form of speech used is an indication of the setting. Urban-oriented informants have a choice of speaking formally or colloquially according to the situation, while others do not have that choice.

If the conversation took place in English, it is assumed that both speakers are urban-oriented. The meaning then is largely dependent upon the situation. The emphasis in such a case is not placed upon the English term "music," but upon the context in which it is used as an indication of how the Persian equivalent *musiqi* might be used. If the conversation was in Persian, the meanings are dependent both on the formality of the situation and the sophistication of the speakers.

Case 1: In cross-cultural conversations in English, this investigator always used the term "music" as a cover term, including a variety of musical settings and contexts. However, native Persian speakers using English in informal situations or off-hand remarks used "music" in the context of "instrumental music" or "musical accompaniment" as in the following examples. First, a university student commented on a recording which had been made in the provinces, "I don't like this one because there is no music in it." Second, another university student, describing the different types of activities associated with wedding celebrations in the Hazarajat said, "They sing songs, but never with music."

   Case 2: Cross-cultural conversations in Persian often resulted in the same type of definition with emphasis on instruments. The following two examples involved informants who spoke no English, but who were educated in formal institutions. In the first case, the question *chand qesm-e musiqi midānid*, "how many types of music do you know?" was put to a student at a teachers' college who was himself an amateur musician. He answered by listing various Afghan musical instruments. In the second case, a knowledgeable Shia *mullā* of the Hazarajat was asked to define *musiqi*. He answered that *musiqi* meant *sāz* (instrument), or referred to *sadāi bā naghma* (voice with instrumental accompaniment).[8]

   Case 3: The formal use of *musiqi* on the cross-cultural level in Persian is more general and similar to the Western concept of music. The same university students noted above who used "music" to mean instruments used *musiqi* in a wider sense when asked to supply a general response in Persian to the many inquiries concerning my research. The response provided was, *musiqi-ye mahalli tahqiq mekonam*, "I am doing research on folk music."

   Case 4: The usage of the expression *musiqi-ye mahalli* (folk music) in Case 3 was not concocted and tailored for my use alone, but even on a strictly cultural level, it is a common description of radio programs which include music based on folk songs or music performed by folk musicians.

   Case 5: The initial reaction of local, rural informants to inquiries about *musiqi-ye mahalli* was an almost uniform denial of the existence of any *musiqi* in the area. Only after a few examples of the type of information and music sought was there a new understanding of the term and a willingness to supply the information. The initial denial can be understood from two points of view. First, as previously discussed, there is a vague but basic notion among Muslims that music is evil; the backgrounds of its suspected associations with debauchery were noted in the preceding chapter. Thus, when a stranger inquires about musical activities in the area, it is only a natural reaction to withhold any information which may incriminate or discredit the respondent in any way. Second, the term *musiqi* was first interpreted in the narrow sense of professional music, which most often involves instrumental accompaniment and a kind of specialized knowledge attributed only to professionals. After it became clear that there was interest in unaccompanied songs, lullabies, and even children's game songs as well as professional music, a new understanding evolved in which I, as investigator, became more specific and rarely used the cover term *musiqi*; the informants then expanded this term in this particular case to include nonprofessional songs, accompanied or not, a concept which seemed more acceptable and less threatening to good Muslims.

This does not mean that basic concepts were changed, but only that those involved were capable of adaption to a unique cross-cultural situation where exceptions and compromises were made. Such compromises and changes were made because the term was just as foreign to the vocabulary of unsophisticated Persian speakers as it was to me. On the cultural level, conversations among non-urban-oriented Persian speakers rarely, if ever, included the term *musiqi*. It must be assumed, then, that the concept or concepts of *musiqi* exist mainly in the cognition of urban-oriented Afghans who are able to think of and use the term on two conceptual bases; a formal one and an informal one.

The formal basis of the term *musiqi* is similar to the Western concept of music. Its distinguishing characteristic in most situations is a common notion of musicality, organization of sound in time. At times, however, as in the case of the call to prayer (*Azān*) and the proper chanting of the Koran, the notion of musicality does not suffice, but another distinguishing feature, that of function, is used. Thus, *Azān* and the chanting of the Koran may sound like music, but by virtue of its function, is not considered music and is not called *musiqi*.[9] This switch from one distinguishing feature to another is not peculiar to this case, or even to this area. There are simply times when we cannot determine whether a talking drum is producing music or signal noise, whether *sprechstimme* is speech or song, on the basis of its sound alone.

Semantic studies of color terms indicate that man can more easily and consistently identify focal points of colors than locate the borders between colors.[10] Just as in the definition of colors, bordering regions of music are not well defined. At this point, other distinguishing features enter the decision-making process, such as the identity of the performer, the identity of the instrument of sound, and the function and association of the performance. In this way it may be determined that the talking drum is not music, but that *sprechstimme* is. In the same manner, it can be determined that songs with religious texts in Afghanistan can be considered music, but sacred chants, formulas, and so on are not. The gloss for formal *musiqi* then can be "secular music."

The colloquial definition of music is more in keeping with traditional Islamic views which emphasize theoretical aspects of music associated with professional musicians and instrumental music. Even in contemporary usage, the traditional distinction between "native sciences" and "foreign sciences" plays a great part in determining the incompatibility of sacred and secular music, of vocal and instrumental performances. The emphasis of sacred chants and strictly vocal performances is placed on the text, which is related directly to the Koran or literature. The secular and instrumental music most often at the disposal of professional musicians is considered *musiqi*. An integral aspect of the meaning of this term is a special understanding and knowledge of the art called *fahm* in Persian, which is thought to be possessed by professionals. The distinguishing feature of the colloquial term is then largely based upon the performer, as well as the sound, and may be glossed as either "instrumental music," "professional music" or "art music."

Each of the cases described above can be analyzed in another way by noting four factors of binary oppositions: urban-oriented vs. non-urban-oriented; formal vs. colloquial; cross-cultural vs. cultural; and Persian vs. English. These factors result in the permutations listed in Table 2; the first five are indicative of the cases described above, while the last four are indicative of cases not encountered.

It can be concluded that, first, the urbanized have a choice of speaking colloquially or formally, while the non-urbanized usually speak colloquially, hardly ever formally; and second, *musiqi* is not colloquially used in cultural situations, but can be brought to mind when suggested by cross-cultural environments. These two conclusions result in the two improbable combinations of Colloquial and Cultural (depicted in Cases 6 and 8) and Non-Urbanized and Formal (depicted in Cases 7 and 9). These improbable combinations which are paired in Table 2 account for all the cases not encountered.

Because *musiqi* is a cognate of "music," the convenient analytical procedure of going from the known to the unknown was utilized. This procedure, however, entailed factors which related to two languages, Persian and English. Other cover terms for different types of music find no cognates or close parallels in the English language; therefore, they can be used meaningfully only in the context of the Persian language.

As evidenced in the discussion of the term *musiqi*, the meaning of a word is conveyed not only by explicit, formal definitions, but more important, also by the implicit information derived from studying its usage, as well as the language community using it. Other words commonly used in musical contexts will also be discussed in terms of usage and language community; but further, the relationship between these words and the central concept of music embodied in the traditional, colloquial notion of music signifying the practical and theoretical aspects of professional and instrumental music vaguely disavowed by Islam will be explored in this semantic analysis of the concept of music.

For the purpose of discussion, terms commonly used in musical con-

TABLE 2
Factors Influencing the Meaning of *Musiqi*

Case	Speaker	Type of Speech	Native Language of Speakers Involved	Language Used	Meaning
1	Urbanized	Colloquial	Cross-Cultural	English	Instrumental
2	Urbanized	Colloquial	Cross-Cultural	Persian	Instrumental
3	Urbanized	Formal	Cross-Cultural	Persian	Music—General
4	Urbanized	Formal	Cultural	Persian	Music
5	Non-Urbanized	Colloquial	Cross-Cultural	Persian	Instrumental Music
6	Urbanized	Colloquial——Cultural	Persian	
7	Non-Urbanized——Formal	Cross-Cultural	Persian	
8	Non-Urbanized	Colloquial——Cultural	Persian	
9	Non-Urbanized——Formal	Cultural	Persian	

texts are grouped into three categories: first, general terms and verbs relating to music; second, more specific cover terms for different genres of music; and third, technical terminology associated with instrumental music and music theory. Unless indicated otherwise, this division and procedure of passing from the general to the specific reflects my organizational principles rather than those of the Afghans I interviewed.

General Terms Relating to Music

A perusal of common, general musical terms suggests that most terms are used in one of two contexts—vocal or instrumental.

TABLE 3
General Terms Relating to Music

Vocal		*Instrumental*	
Voice:	*Sadā* or *Āwāz*	Instrument:	*Sāz*
To Sing:	*Lalai Kardan*		*Alat-e Musiqi*
	Bait Guftan	To Play:	*Sāz Kardan*
	She^cr, Bait Khāndan		*Sāz Zadan*
Song:	*Āwāz*		*Sāz Nawākhtan*
		Instrumental	*Naghma*
		Piece:	*Sāz*

Other
Melody, Tune: *Sāz*
Musical Sound: *Āhang*

The two terms glossed as "voice" here are used in slightly different contexts. *Sadā* is a general term for voice or noise, as in a line from a famous folk quatrain:

Sadāyat meshnawom as dur o nazdik
Ma misli ghumcha-ye gul tāza mesham.

[When] I hear your voice from far or near
I become as fresh as a flower bud.

The term can even be used to refer to the sound of an instrument, as in the saying:

Sadā-ye dohl as dur khosh miyāya.

The sound of a distant drum is delightful.

The term *āwāz* is restricted more to a singing or musical voice. I asked my landlord in Faizabad, a learned scribe or *mirzā*, if a certain man were a good musician. He answered in Persian: "Khān (the musician) is not learned. He doesn't have much knowledge about poetry and he makes mistakes, but he is famous because he has a good voice (*āwāz-e khub*)."

Āwāz is often used to mean song as well as voice. During my first days in Herat, an English-speaking teacher helped me formulate sentences that could be used in recording and interviewing sessions. One such sentence was, *Lutfan, shomā yak āwāz bekhānid*, "Please sing a song." *Sadā* is never used in such a context. This negative information gives a clue to one of the features in determining the use of one term or another, the question of how musical or nonmusical an event or object is considered by the speaker. *Āwāz* is a specialized term reserved for musical, vocal sounds, while *sadā* is more general and can refer to musical or nonmusical sounds, vocal or otherwise. *Āwāz* alone can render the meaning of "song," while *sadā* alone does not. The other feature concerns the background of the speaker; just how educated or urbanized he is helps determine the vocabulary at his disposal. Thus, *sadā* can be used by all speakers, while *āwāz*, though not a particularly unusual word, is used mostly by educated or urbanized speakers who tend to use more technical or specialized terms. For example, during a recording session in Herat, the woman who was singing stopped in the middle of a song and said, *Sadā khub namera*, "The voice won't go well." It can be supposed that she used the term *sadā* because she was an unsophisticated woman who was not a musician, but also, the fact that her voice "wouldn't go well" probably meant that it was unmusical to her.

Even the usage of *sadā-ye dohl* in the saying above is an indication that the sound of a drum is not considered as musical as a stringed instrument. Although one can say *sadā-ye rabāb* (a short-necked, plucked lute), a more appropriate term would be *āhang-e rabāb*. An Afghan musician teaching at the University of Washington was preparing to give a *rabāb* concert. During rehearsal, I asked the *rabāb* player if he needed a microphone. He answered, *Uh, āhang-e rabāb aesta ast*, "Yes, the sound of the *rabāb* is soft." *Āhang* can also be used to describe a singing voice, and is even incorporated into names of professional singers such as Sarahang (Master of Harmony), but is never used to describe the sound of a drum.

The distinction between *āhang* and *āwāz* is again one of inclusiveness. *Āwāz* pertains to the voice alone, while *āhang* can be used to describe both voice and instrument, and as such is closer to the traditional concept of music than is *āwāz*. During an interview with a *mullā* in Khadir, I asked him to define some terms, among which were *musiqi* and *āwāz*. He answered:

Musiqi sāz ya sadāyi bā naghma ast. Āwāz khāndan bi naghma, misli she^cr khāni ast.

Musiqi is instrumental or vocal with instrumental accompaniment. *Āwāz khāndan* is vocal without instrumental accompaniment, like singing a poem.

At another time in Herat, during a break in a recording session, I asked professional musicians whether they thought a lullaby was *musiqi* or not. One answered, *Musiqi neist, misli āwāz ast.* "It is not *musiqi*; it is like an *āwāz*." Thus, it was made clear in both situations that *āwāz*, though considered more musical than *sadā*, was still not considered *musiqi* because it referred exclusively to the voice. *Āhang*, on the other hand, emphasizes musical sound, vocal or instrumental, and thus is closer to the concept of music.

Āhang, used alone, can mean melody. I asked my landlord in Faizabad to define the term *Āsā* and *Jog*. He answered, *Nāme āhang ast, nāme she^cr neist*, "they are names of melodies, not names of poems." In the two cases illustrating the use of *āhang*, the usage was formal and made by a literate person (landlord) or by a music specialist (*rabāb* player), but Slobin has often heard the expression *āhang-e raqs*, "dance music," used informally in northern Afghanistan.[11]

A correlation between formality of speech and specificity seems to occur in references to the concept *music*; the more formal the speech, the more technical or specific is the meaning of the term used. *Sadā* is a general term which refers to voice or to sounds. *Āwāz* refers more specifically to the vocal aspect of the meaning of *sadā* and means musical voice or song, while *āhang* refers to the sound aspect of *sadā* and means musical sound or melody (Table 4):

TABLE 4
Taxonomy of Sound: Sound (*Sadā*)

Musical: (*Āhang*)		Non-Musical
Vocal (*Āwāz*)	Instruments (*Sāz*)	

Of the two terms glossed as "instrument" in Table 3, *sāz* and *ālat-e musiqi*, the former is by far the more common and general term. *Sāz* used alone means musical instrument in general; however, in Herat the term refers specifically to the conical bored, double reed, outdoor wind instrument more commonly known as *sornā* or *sornāi*. The *sornā* is always accompanied by a large double-headed drum called the *dohl*, and the combination is referred to as *sāz-dohl* in Herat. In an article on folk plays of Herat, Baghban defines *sāz* as "the flute that is played with the drum."[12]

Sāz, like *āhang*, can also mean musical sound and melody; however, *sāz* is a colloquial term enjoying wider usage than the word *āhang*. Several

Herati drummers whistled bird calls as they played the *zirbaghali*, a single-headed, vase-shaped drum. When one drummer was asked what he was doing, he answered, *saz-e bulbul*, "sound (or song) of the nightingale." Another drummer performing at a local theater was billed as *Bulbul Herāwi*, or the "Herat Nightingale." Other parallel expressions are *sāz* combined with an instrument such as *sāz-e rabāb*, which is exactly the same but a more common way of saying *āhang-e rabāb* (the sound of a *rabāb*). *Sāz* is not restricted to instrumental referents only, but to melody in general, whether instrumental or vocal. Thus, several songs in Badakhshan were identified simply as *sāz-e watan* (native tune or melody).

With the verb *kardan* (to do) or *zadan* (to hit), *sāz* means "to play" as in the command *sāz kon* (Play!), or can be extended to mean "play a tune," as in *khub sāz mezanand* (They are playing a good tune). The former example was taught to me by my Herat translator, while the latter comment was overheard from a servant in Herat who was listening to a radio.

Sāz can sometimes refer to musicians as well as instruments and melodies. A drummer once complimented his partner by saying, *degar sāz neist*, meaning, "There's no other player like him." In gathering biographical information from a well-known Kabul musician, I asked what he learned from one of his teachers. He answered, *sāz-e āwāz khāni* (the art or form of singing). These two usages are not common; however, they serve to illustrate the wide-ranging aspects of the term. Of all the musical terms used in Afghanistan, *sāz* comes closest to being the epitome of the Afghan colloquial concept of music. Slobin considers the term *sāz* to be "the basic term for music throughout Afghanistan."[13]

Ālat-e musiqi literally translates as "instrument of music" and is never construed in any other way. I heard the term only two or three times in Herat. A village *mullā* condemned all forms of *musiqi*. I asked him to give an opinion of the *dāira* (tambourine), an instrument closely associated with women. He said the *dāira* was not bad since it was an *ālat-e chekar mezana*, an instrument of leisure as opposed to an instrument of music. Yet another informant, a student at the Herat teachers' college, referred to the *dāira*, along with other instruments, as *ālat-e musiqi*. Only my Herat translator made a distinction between *sāz* and *ālat-e musiqi*. He considered the harmonium, *sornā, tula* (flute), and *ghichak* (spiked fiddle) to be *sāz*, and all other instruments to be *ālat-e musiqi*. Although he did not express his reason for this division, one distinguishing feature seems to be tone quality; all *sāz* instruments are capable of producing long, sustained tones, while *ālat-e musiqi* instruments are either plucked strings or drums, with the exception of the *nai* (end-blown flute). However, other speakers seem to base their choice on the type of speech used, *sāz* being the colloquial term and *ālat-e musiqi* being the more formal choice.

The correlation between formality of speech and specificity is confirmed in that *ālat-e musiqi*, the formal term, refers only to musical instruments, while *sāz*, the colloquial term, relates to many aspects of music. Literally, both *sāz* and *ālat* signify any tool or instrument, yet *sāz* is always understood in a musical context, while *ālat* requires the modifer *musiqi* in order to be considered in a musical context. Because both the terms *sāz* and *ālat-e musiqi* denote musical instruments, they have a closer affinity to the Afghan concept of music than any term signifying voice.

The nouns for "song" or other references to song texts are construed with the verbs *kardan* (to do), *guftan* (to speak), and *khāndan* (to read or sing). The choice of verb seems to be affected by the user's conceptualization of the social event described in the qualifier and its relationship to the concept of music, rather than by the formality of the situation or by the social background of the speaker. An English-speaking teacher in Herat translated the sentence, "that woman is singing a lullaby" as *U zan bacha-ye khod ala mekonad*, using the verb "to do" rather than "to speak" or "to sing." The social event of lullaby includes movements as well as sounds that are not considered music. Women often find it difficult to sing lullabies for a recording unless they hold a baby in their arms or direct their song and movements to a sleeping child. The verb "to do" encompasses a wide range of actions consistent with those involved in rendering a lullaby.

The verb *guftan* is restricted to vocal action and, in conjunction with the qualifier *bait*, conveys the meaning "to sing." *Bait* is a loosely-used term corresponding to a "ditty," with the implication that it is not worthy of serious musical consideration. *Bait* literally refers to a stich or line in poetry and is considered the basic unit of poems and song texts. Most of the ditties referred to as *bait*s consist of not more than two *bait*s in a popular quatrain form consisting of four hemistichs. Women in the Hazarajat encourage other women to sing by saying, *yak bait bogo!* "Say one Verse!"

The fact that the verb *khāndan* can be glossed either as "to read" or "to sing," depending on the context, indicates that the distinction between the two actions is not so clearly defined as in English. In Persian, poetry has traditionally been sung. An excerpt from the *Cahār Maqāla* describes the famous poet Rudaki as he prepared to persuade the Amir of Samarqand to return home to Bokhara: "He picked up the *chang* (harp) and in the *ushāq* mode, he commenced this *qasida* (ode)."[14] Although deeply rooted with the concept of poetry, *khāndan* is also the closest vocal equivalent of *musiqi* or *sāz*. Professional singers are referred to as *khānenda*.

The three verbs used to denote "to play" an instrument are *sāz kardan*, *zadan*, and *nawākhtan*. Because all three verbs are associated with musical instruments, they are equally related to the traditional concept of music. Thus, the question of choice of terms no longer seems to be dependent upon the social event, as was the case with vocal verbs, but upon the formality of the situation and the social background of the speaker.

My translator in Herat gave me two versions of the command "Play!" The first, *sāz kon*, based on *sāz* and the imperative of *kardan*, is informal, while the second, *lutfan benawāz*, based on the word "please" and the imperative of *nawākhtan*, is both polite and formal. Conceivably, one can also say *bezan*, which is the most common form and falls between the two extremes as far as formality is concerned; it is the imperative of the verb *zadan*, which is the most commonly used verb for "playing an instrument." I independently asked two formally educated informants in Herat, one of whom was an amateur musician, to list all the Afghan instruments known to them. I then asked them to supply the proper verb for playing those particular instruments. *Zadan* was consistently used with every instrument; *nawākhtan* was reserved for stringed instruments only, however. The distinction between *zadan* and *nawākhtan*, where stringed instruments are concerned, seems to be a matter of formality. *Nawākhtan* translates "to fondle," "to caress," as well as "to play an instrument," and suggests a more refined technique than implied by the verb *zadan*, which translates "to hit," "to strike."

A famous Kabul *rabāb* player teaching in the United States recorded his American students for the purpose of broadcasting over Radio Afghanistan. He wanted each piece preceded by an announcement in English and Persian. When I announced in Persian, *Panj shāgerdān-e Amrikāi rāg-e Bopali mezanand,* "Five American students will play the mode Bopali," he insisted that I re-record and say, *Panj shāgerdān-e Amrikāi rāg-e Bopali menawāzand,* using the verb *nawākhtan* rather than *zadan*. Another example that shows that *nawākhtan* has a more formal connotation than *zadan* is the official title of a famous *rabāb* player, Ustad Mohammed Omar Rababnawaz (Master Mohammed Omar, Rababist). More common references would be *rabābi* with an attributive *i* or *rabābzan* from *zadan*.

Since all three verbs concern musical instruments, they are all equally related to the traditional concept of music. The choice of verb is determined by formality and referent, as shown in Table 5. The referent in the command "Play!" is nonspecific and the choice is determined by the degree of formality. When the referent is a specific stringed instrument, the choice is also determined by formality, but if the instrument is a percussion or wind instrument, there is no choice.

The two terms for musical piece or composition, *āwāz* and *sāz*, have already been discussed. Another term, *naghma,* is used by musicians and sophisticated listeners to denote purely instrumental compostions, or instrumental sections within a performance of a song.[15] In Herat *naghma* was given as a title of a *dutār* piece composed by the performer himself, *yak*

TABLE 5
Paradigm of Features for the Verb "To Play"

		FORMALITY	
R E F E R E N T		Informal	Formal
	Nonspecific	*Sāz Kardan* - - - - - - - - - - *Zadan*	*Nawākhtan*
	Specific	*Zadan*	*Nawākhtan* (stringed) - - - - - - - - - - - - - - *Zadan* (non-stringed)

naghma bud, "It was a *naghma.*" Out of five pieces he performed, three were based on songs; the remaining pieces were called *Hindi* (from Indian film music) and *naghma.* The meaning of "instrumental composition" is also evident in the classical music terminology of Kabul. The free, improvisatory introduction is called *shakal,* while the composition in fixed rhythm is called *naghma.*[16] My *dutār* teacher in Herat differentiated sections of a piece by identifying the part based on a song as *khāndan* and the interlude part not based on a song as *naghma.*

The preceding nouns and verbs have been compiled in Table 6 into three groups representing the relative distance from the traditional concept of music. The dimensions of Group A are largely functional and the terms are rarely used to refer to music. Group B stresses poetry and the voice as its

TABLE 6
General Terms in Three Categories

	Informal		Formal
A:	*Lalai Kardan* *Sadā* *Bait Guftan*	B: ←	*Āwāz* *Bait Khāndan* *Āhang*
C:	*Zadan* *Sāz*		*Nawākhtan* *Ālat-e Musiqi* *Naghma*

main dimensions which can at times be considered music, and at other times not. The main aspect of Group C is instrumental which is at all times considered music. The arrows indicate that the words *āwāz, khāndan,* and *āhang,* though quite correct and formal, are not uncommon words and are often used colloquially as well. The second arrow accompanying *āhang* indicates that it may also be used in reference to instrumental music.

Terms Relating to Genres of Music

No standard forms of identification of folk music exist in Afghanistan. The same melody may be used as a setting for different texts or the same text can be set to different melodies. Certain melodies are traditional tunes associated with certain areas; others are newly composed tunes. In only a few cases, melodies and text have been standardized by radio musicians who have popularized one version; otherwise, forms of identification are general, or refer specifically to textual content such as *Moghol Dokhtar* (Mongol Girl) or *Dandān Telāi* (Golden Tooth).

To the question, *Chand qesm-e musiqi medānid?* "How many types of music do you know?" or *Nām-e in (bait, naghma) chist?* "What's the name of this (song, piece)?" the answers are likely to refer to: (1) melody types or styles associated with certain areas or genres; (2) the subject matter of songs; or (3) the poetic forms of songs.

Melody Types or Styles. Names of melody types or styles associated with certain areas or genres are made up of two components, a place or genre name, and an attributive *i* suffix such as *Kābuli,* meaning "of Kabul" or "from Kabul;" *filmi,* meaning "of the films" or "from the films" (Indian films). The most widely known melody-type throughout Afghanistan is *shomāli,* which means "northern," and is indicative of the area north of Kabul known as Charikar. Originally a local, regional song-type, *shomāli* has been popularized by Kabul musicians to such an extent that examples of *shomāli* can be heard in Herat, Faizabad, and Khadir.

Sarhadi is the name of another melody-type whose popularity is more confined to the Herat area. *Sarhadi* means "of the border" and specifically refers to the outlying regions of Herat.[17] Two kinds of *sarhadi* are known to me: one type is simply called *sarhadi,* while the other is known as *sarhadi ghoriāni,* or *sarhadi* from Ghorian, a region west of Herat near the Iranian border. A thorough musical and poetic analysis of these forms will be made in chapter 6.

Another important regional style is known as *falak.* It is popular in northeastern Afghanistan in the areas of Badakhshan and Kataghan.[18] *Falak* translates as "sky" and metaphorically means "fortune" or "destiny." A musician in Faizabad sang six examples for me of what he called *falak.*

The first two titles were references to the subject: *falak-e zahiri* (sad *falak*) and *falak-e zarb-e zahiri* (rhythmic, sad *falak*). The following three songs were named after local areas: *falak-e Kataghani* (*falak* from Kataghan); *falak-e Farkhāri* (*falak* from Farkhar); and *falak-e Sarghalāmi* (*falak* from Sarghalam). The last of the six titles was *falak-e raqs* (dance *falak*). *Falak* is also used in a general sense meaning "verse," paralleling the term *bait* used in other parts of the country. While recording a musician in Faizabad, I tried to play back the song just recorded. I stopped the tape before reaching the beginning of the recording. The musician recognized the spot and said, *Yak falak mānda,* "One *falak* left," indicating one verse more before the beginning of the song.

Songs in the Hazarajat are generally called *bait* (stich), and are identified by local area names with an attributive suffix such as *Tamazani,* or the word *bait* is used with a modifier such as *bait-e Nili.* During an evening of musical entertainment in Khadir, eight out of nine songs were identified by such area names. Most of the names were of regions within the political boundaries of Dai Kundi of which Khadir is the center. One song was not identified at all, commonly the case when the singers are unsophisticated or are women. In this particular instance, a young boy sang two songs; one was identified as *Khadiri* by the older musicians present, and the other song was left unidentified.

All four song types mentioned above (*shomāli, sarhadi, falak, bait*) are based on popular quatrains known as *chār baiti* (four lines), *du baiti* (two lines), or *rubā^ci* (quatrain). *Chār baiti* is actually a misnomer because the Persian quatrain is composed of four *misrā^cs* (hemistichs or half lines) or two *baits* (stichs or lines), but never of four *baits.* The correct appellation for quatrain would be *char misrā^ci*; however, this term is never used. The other acceptable terms, *du baiti* and *rubā^ci,* have limited usage; the former is used mainly by those who have a formal education in Persian literature, and the latter is popularly used only in Badakhshan. Though "incorrect," *chār baiti* is still the most commonly used and understood term to designate a quatrain. *Chār baiti* not only denotes "quatrain," but the term also implies a folk form authored by illiterate peasants, shepherds, or nomads. *Chār baiti*s are, therefore, not written and the poets are unknown.[19]

Aside from the poetic form, the poetic content of these songs is uniform. The songs are most often about love, *^cishqi.* Many are about unrequited love; some are mystical love songs with hidden religious meanings. The people of Badakhshan add that *falak*s are sad (*ghamghin*). The feeling of sadness stems from a longing for a lover, friends, family, and home.[20]

Whenever a definition of one of the above forms of *shomāli, sarhadi, falak,* and *bait* is given, it contains information concerning its poetic form or its folk quality, such as *bait-e mahalli ast,* "it is a local song." The following excerpts from Shahrani's "The 'Falaks' of the Mountains," emphasizes both aspects:

> Whenever I mention the word "dobaiti" (couplets), I recall my childhood during which time the shepherds in the green valleys of Badakhshan sang in their Dari dialect what they call "falaks."
>
> . . . The Falaks or dobaitis are generally composed by four people, each contributing a line, but sometimes whole falaks are the products of one single person. However, most of these are lost because they are not recorded as their authors are usually illiterate.
>
> One thing is definite and that is that the dobaitis are a reflection of the environment where they originate.[21]

Shahrani mentions the illiterate poet, the shepherd singer, the Badakhshan locality, the Dari dialect, and the green-valley environment as characteristics of *falaks*. These characteristics emphasize the essential folk quality of these songs. Other Badakhshis described *falaks* as *naghma-ye rustāyi* (peasant tune), *ailāq* (summer pasturage), *kurdaki* (country), *kuhi ya dashti* (mountain or desert).

An examination of the terminology discussed in connection with the four song types discloses the information shown in Table 7, which indicates that the poetry and the folk or nonprofessional aspect of these songs is prominent. A look at the names of the four song types themselves also reveals information of the same nature. *Shomāli* is a local but rural region with respect to Kabul, the capital of Afghanistan. *Sarhadi* also indicates a local region outside the city of Herat. *Falak* is an expression of its poetic content, while *bait* is an indication of the poetic form of *chār baiti* which in itself implies folk origins.

Among all the terminology and definitions discussed, not one mention was made of melodic style or content, yet some songs with the same characteristics, i.e., local quatrains about love, are not identified as one of the above forms. Further, purely instrumental pieces are sometimes identified as being one of these styles. Only three informants explained the forms as being melodic types. Two were well-educated, spoke English, and worked for the Ministry of Information and Culture. One explained, "*Shomāli* has a special *naghma*." The other said, "*Tarz* [manner, style] is *sarhadi*, but they sing *chār baiti*." The third informant was a poet living in Faizabad, who explained that *falak* signified a melody type, *āhang-e makhsus ast*, and further, that there were four or five identifiable types of *falaks*.

Melody seems to be a covert concept which finds no direct equivalent term in Persian. Even the educated informants used different Persian terms to indicate melody, terms that were not exact equivalents, but which infer "melody" by their use. This, however, does not mean that melody is not an

TABLE 7
Vocabulary Associated with Four Regional Song Types

POETRY

Form	Content
Bait	*Falak*
Chār Baiti	*^{c}Ishqi*
Du Baiti	*Ghamghin*
Rubā^{c}i	

FOLK QUALITY

Regional	Rural
Shomāli	*Kurdaki*
Sarhadi	*Rustāyi*
Mahalli	*Kuhi ya dashti*
	Chopāni
	Māldāri
	Gharibi

important consideration in identifying these songs, but rather, within a particular local context, terminology implies more than what people verbalize; thus a special melodic type or style is a presupposition.

With regard to the categorization of the general terms relating to music represented in Table 6, the four song types fall into Group B for two reasons. First, the folk element present in these song types precludes any notion of professionalism so closely associated with instrumental music represented in Group C. Second, the great importance of poetry in these song types identifies them more closely with Group B, which stresses the dimensions of voice and poetry rather than with Group A, which emphasizes functionalism.

Numerous general terms describe folksongs of the *shomāli, sarhadi, falak, bait* type, but these terms do not convey any specific information concerning musical or poetic content. They only serve to stress the folk quality of these songs. All of these terms are adjectival and formed with an attributive *i* suffix. A large number of terms are generally used throughout Afghanistan to mean folksong. *Bait-e mahalli* or *musiqi-ye mahalli* in Persian and *keliwāli* in Pashtu, for example, refer to local song or music. *Bait-e māldāri* and *chopāni* both make reference to flocks. *Māldāri* refers to an owner of property or flocks. In Herat, *māldāri* refers to nomads who move from one area to another in search of grazing grounds for their flocks. *Chopān* literally means shepherd. *Gharibi, kurdaki,* and *rustāyi* are all expressions of humbleness and unsophistication associated with rural areas. *Gharib* denotes foreigners as well as poverty.[22] *Kurdaki* is an expression which indicates "country," "farmer," "unsophisticated," from *kurd*, meaning raised irrigation ditches.[23] *Rustāyi* refers to country or rural life while *kuhi ya dashti* refers to mountains and deserts. It seems that these terms, like the names of specific melody types, all suggest a product of unsophisticated rural or nomadic peoples.

Before moving to the discussion of the subject matter of these songs, two more unique styles should be considered here: first, a piece peculiar to the Herat area called *Aushāri*; and second, the epic tale of Badakhshan called *Gorgholi*. *Aushāri*, like *sarhadi*, is a melody type, but it is not based on any text. Some confusion seems to surround the meaning of the term *aushāri*. Some believe it refers to the Afshar tribe in Iran, while others think it has something to do with a waterfall (*ābshār*). Of the two contentions, the former seems more likely because a secondary mode of the Shur Dastgah named Afshari exists in Iran.[24] There is agreement, however, on the fact that *Aushāri* is a dance, but the kind or type of dance is not definite; more certain is the melody type.

Aushāri was recorded on four different occasions of this study; only one was an accompaniment to an actual dance. The instruments were, first, the *sornā* and *dohl*; second, a two-stringed *dutār* and *zirbaghali* (single-headed, vase-shaped drum); third, a multi-stringed *dutār* and *zirbaghali* accompanying a dance; and fourth, a *tula* (flute), *zirbaghali*, and *tāl* (finger cymbals). Because of its basic orientation as a purely instrumental piece, *Aushāri* can be considered a kind of *sāz* or *naghma* and can be classified as part of Group C of Table 6. The musicians involved in playing the four examples were varying degrees of professional musicians.

Gorgholi or *Kuroghli* (Son of a Blind Man), as it is sometimes known, is an epic tale known throughout Central Asia. In Badakhshan the epic is sung in Tajiki (Persian) as well as in Uzbeki and is thought to be about a hero who was born posthumously in his mother's grave (Son of the Grave).[25] The Badakhshan epic concentrates on the exploits of Awaz Khan, the son of Gorgholi, and Awaz's sons Nur Ali Khan and Sher Ali Khan, and his grandson, Jangir Khan. *Gorgholi* is considered here as an entirely separate genre of music or tradition because singers of *Gorgholi* need special training to sing these tales. Even though many *Gorgholi* singers accompany themselves with a *dambura* (two-stringed, fretless, plucked lute), its effect is mainly dramatic, not musical. The vocal quality of the singer is peculiar to this epic tradition. The singer recites in a low, guttural voice, sometimes producing audible harmonic tones. Separate from the ordinary folk music tradition as these stylistic features may be, they are still very closely associated with the *falak* folk songs of the region. These musical features will be discussed further in chapter 6.

The general makeup and division of the *Gorgholi* cycle is not clear. A number of episodes known as *dāstān* (story) or *taqsim* (division) make up major parts of the story known as *shākh*. Most people cite the number seven when referring to the number of *shākh* in a complete *Gorgholi* cycle,[26] but others refer to as many as thirty-two *shākh*. Further, there is no real consensus on the usage and meaning applied to the terms *dāstān, taqsim,* and *shākh*. The performance of a *shākh* is divided by the singing of short quatrains, *chār baiti*. These quatrains may have some relationship to the story, but more often than not, they are completely unrelated. The telling of one *shākh* may take several nights, depending on the manipulations of the storyteller.

The fact that the content or story of *Gorgholi* is its most important aspect, suggests it be categorized in Group B of Table 6. Also, the name for the singer of this epic, *Gorgholikhān*, is made up of the name of the epic and *khān* (singer), from the verb *khāndan*, which has already been classified as part of Group B. Although the unifying aspect of the story could have led me to discuss the *Gorgholi* tales under subject matter, I felt an underlying melody-type or distinct style associated with the telling of these tales justifies its treatment here.

Subject Matter. The predominant themes of Afghan folk songs are love and religion. Love songs often depict the problems lovers face in a society where Islamic tradition maintains a strict separation between the two sexes. Religious songs are often invocations to God, Mohammed, or his companions. It is common for the two themes to be combined; invocations may be made on behalf of lovers, while at other times, erotic love songs may hold hidden religious meanings.

The word *ᶜishqi* is commonly used to describe any song with the topic of love; however, the generic term *dini* for religious songs is hardly ever used. Instead, more specific titles such as *naᶜt* (song in praise of Mohammed) and *tasawwafi* (Sufi song) are used. The Persian vocabulary is particularly rich in descriptive titles such as *aklāqi* (song of moral behavior), *hamāsi* or *razmi* (patriotic songs), *fakāhi* (comic song), and so on, yet these literary terms are hardly ever applied to folk songs.[27]

Although two informants, both of whom were working for the Office of Information and Culture in Herat, gave long lists of appropriate terms for the subject matter of songs, most songs in Herat were, in fact, identified by standardized titles taken from the text, names of melody types, or poetic terminology—not subject matter. For example, a musician identified a piece he had just performed as *chār baiti* (poetic form), *Gul-e Zard* (title), and *Bairami* (melodic mode). Another song was a *chār baiti*, called *Shomāli* in the *Bairami* mode.

In Badakhshan, titles with a topical reference enjoyed greater usage and titles based on text were rare. A Badakhshi musician from Jurm played examples of seven kinds of *falak*s. Among the seven, three were said to have definite topics: *zahiri* (sad, melancholy), a song in which a poor or desperate man invokes God; *ʿishqi*, a love song; and a *tasawwafi*, a Sufi song.

Within the Hazarajat the lullaby called *lalai* or *lalu* has taken on the form of an abstract love song. The lullaby has the double function of sending a message to a lover while lulling the baby to sleep:

Bobe bacha shikār rafta
Da kohi marghozar rafta
Tanbe darga jaru ya
Pasi darga khuru ya
Tailone tanbaco biyā
Jega bale sako biyā
Lalui Lalui bobe aya, etc.

The child's father went hunting
He went to Marghozar mountain
The doorlatch is straw
The rooster stays in front of the door
Come by the path below the tobacco field
Come to the bed on the platform
Lalui Lalui mother's father [term of endearment for child].

These verses may be sung by themselves as a *bait* (song) or *lalai* (lullaby), or may be included among a number of verses on the subject of love. They are sung by men or women, accompanied by instruments or not.

Poetic Forms. As evidenced in the preceding discussion, it is impossible to speak of various terms relating to genres of music without mentioning poetic terms such as *bait, misrāʿ, chār baiti, du baiti*, and *rubāʿi*, terms which are integral in the definition of certain musical styles. It may be appropriate here to review or discuss a few technical terms associated with Afghan poetry. The basic line (verse) of a poem is called *bait*, which consists of two half lines (hemistichs) called *misrāʿ*. Saifi, in his treatise on Persian meters translated by Henry Blochmann, explains the word *misrāʿ* as "a door with two folds":

The resemblance between a verse and a folding door lies in this, that in the same manner as with a folding door you may open or shut which you please without the other; and when you shut both together, it is still one door; so also a verse you may read either of the hemistichs without the other, and when you read both together, they will form one verse.[28]

The first line of a poem is called *matlaʿ* and the last, *maqtaʿ*. The rhyme is known as *qāfia*. *Fard* is any single line or *bait* quoted from another poem.[29]

Persian poems, according to Saifi, must satisfy three conditions: they must have meaning; they must have rhyme, and they must have meter.

These three elements determine the type of the poem.[30] The general word for poem is *she^c^r*, its colloquial equivalent being *bait*. An important distinction besides formality of speech exists between the two terms, a distinction concerning the type of poem in question. If it is a classical poem, the term *she^c^r* is used. If, on the other hand, it is a folk form, such as *chār baiti*, the term *bait* is used. Classical poems are authored by a single person and the identity of the poet is usually known. The folk form, however, can be authored by more than one person, the originators are forgotten, and there is license to alter any verse according to the whims of the singer. Many folk forms are products of extemporization and are passed on orally, thus increasing the chances of change and variation.

The most common folk form in Afghanistan is the *chār baiti*, which has already been mentioned; we should briefly consider here the differing opinions regarding *chār baiti*. Blochmann simply states, "For Rubá^c^í we meet occasionally with the names Chahár baitı, Dubaití and Taránah."[31] Rawan Farhadi equates *du baiti* and *chār baiti*, pointing out that *chār baiti*, though a misnomer, is the preferred term in Afghanistan.[32] An informant in Faizabad stated that there was no distinction between *chār baiti* and *rubā^c^i*, but *du baiti* differs in that, like the *fard*, it consists of only two rhyming *misrā^c^s*. An informant in Herat made the distinction between *chār baiti* and *du baiti* on the basis of rhyme scheme: the *chār baiti* like the *rubā^c^i* consists of the rhyming scheme *aaba* while the *du baiti* scheme is *aabb*. A. J. Arberry claims that the *du baiti* is a quatrain having the same *aaba* rhyme scheme as the *rubā^c^i*, but differing in the meter.[33]

For all the differing opinions, usage indicates that all three terms— *chār baiti*, *du baiti*, and *rubā^c^i*—are used in Afghanistan to mean generally the same thing. *Chār baiti* is the most general and preferred term. It also implies a folk form, while *du baiti* is formal and is used for songs composed by a known poet whose quatrains are organized in a series. *Rubā^c^i* is the preferred term in the Badakhshan region. The subject, rhyme scheme, and meter do not seem to affect the usage of one term or another in general.

The following discussion, then, concerns the common characteristics of the folk quatrain by any name in Afghanistan. The quatrain is most often concerned with the subject of love: love of God, friends, family, home, and lover. The settings are local or pastoral and the mood is often melancholy. The following quatrain was recorded in Badakhshan by Mark Slobin:[34]

> *Az xāneie padar, ei mardom, digar raftam*
> *Bā sad ālam du didei geryān raftam.*
> *Yārān o barādarān salāmat bāshid.*
> *Shughnān be shomā, man dar badakhshān megardum.*

I left my father's house, O people.
With a hundred sorrows and two tearful eyes.
Friends and brothers, be well!
Shughnān is for you; I'm going to travel in Badakhshān.

The most common rhyme scheme of quatrains is *aaba*; that is, *misrā͑s* (half lines) one, two, and four rhyme, while *misrā͑* three does not.[35] Occasionally there are quatrains with the rhyme scheme *aabb* as in the following from Herat:

Sare kuhi baland nei mezanam man
Shitor gum kardaam pāi mezanam man
Shitor gum kardaam shitore shāhi
Daringas mekonad Lailā Kojāi.

I play the flute on a high mountain top,
I have lost a camel. I am searching.
I have lost the camel, the lead camel.
Its bell is clanging. "Lailā, where are you?"

or *aaaa* as in another example from Herat:

Sahar shod sob bedam shod jān be nālam
Delam dariā-e gham shod chun be nālam
Nāzok az dasti pādshāh kuli ālam
Khorāsan dar ba dar shod chun be nālam

It has become dawn, morning is near, I am crying;
My heart has become a river of sadness because
Delicate, in the hands of "the King of the World,"
Khorasan has been ruined, so I cry.

The rhyming *misrā͑s* and the repetition of certain words and themes contribute to the unity and completeness of the quatrain. The first part of the third *misrā͑* is often a repetition of the first part of the second *misrā͑*, a technique which renders for the third *misrā͑*, or the last two *misrā͑s*, as the case may be, a relationship to the other *misrā͑s* without the benefit of a rhyme. Such an example is the quatrain from Herat with the rhyme scheme of *aabb* quoted above. Another popular quatrain quoted in Farhadi[36] displays the same technique:

Maqorbān-e sar-i darwāza mesham
Sadāyat meshnawam estāda mesham
Sadāyat meshnawam az dur o nazdik
Ma misli ghumcha-ye gul tāza mesham.

I sacrifice myself at your doorstep
[When] I hear your voice, I stand
[When] I hear your voice from far or near,
I become as fresh as a rosebud.

The meter of these quatrains may be problematical. Theoretically, the meters, like those of the classical *rubāᶜi*, are special modifications of the *hazaj* meter which is based on the foot ∪ - - -. There are twelve varieties of *rubāᶜi* meters based on long-short syllable combinations shown in the following diagram:[37]

Misrā:

‒ ‒	‒ ‒	‒ ‒ ‒	‒ ‒	‒ ‒
	∪ ∪ ‒	‒ ∪ ∪		∪ ∪ ‒
		∪ ‒ ∪		

Browne[38] points out that most Persian dialect poetry is "not written in the usual *rubāᶜi* meters, but in the apocopated hexameter *hazaj; i.e.*, the foot (∪ - - -) six times repeated in the *bayt*, but 'docked' to (∪ - -) in the third and sixth feet."

Even this exception to the classical meters is hard to accept as a rule when one realizes that most folk musicians in Afghanistan are illiterate and hardly versed in the intricacies of Persian prosody. This, however, does not preclude any notion of poetic meter in these quatrains. Proper scansion of Persian poetry involves the counting of consonants and short and long vowels which form series of short or long syllables.[39] Although a musician may be ignorant of the fine rules of scansion, he is capable of hearing the rhythm of a poetic meter and can thus realize the poetic meter musically, or attempt to improvise verses in a particular meter. (Analyses of musical realizations of poetic meter will be made in chapter 6.) Otherwise, his song may be based on the number of syllables within a *bait*. Slobin related what a Soviet researcher found in the folk music of Tajikistan: "She found that while some folk melodies could be considered as having classical meters followed by music, other folk songs relied on a strictly syllabic basis outside of metric schemes."[40]

Of all the classical-type poems in Afghanistan, the *ghazal* enjoys the greatest popularity. The *ghazal* is originally an Arabic term denoting a love song. It was, however, the Persians who developed this classical form from the *qasida*.[41] The *qasida* is a long ode consisting of rhyming couplets. The first *bait*, or *matlaᶜ*, is special in that it consists of an internal rhyme—that is, the two *misrāᶜ*s of the *matlaᶜ* must rhyme—and thereafter only the second *misrāᶜ* carries through the rhyme. According to Edward G. Browne, "the *ghazal* differs from the *qasida* mainly in subject and length"; the *qasida*, Browne notes, is usually a panegyric or satire of great length, "often extending to more than a hundred *bayts*," preceded by an amatory prelude.[42] The *ghazal* is a lyrical poem of four to fourteen *baits* in the same rhyme scheme as the *qasida*. The same meters are used in both the *ghazal* and *qasida*: "For a *Qacídah* and a *Ghazal*, a poet may choose any meter (except the *Rubá^c í* meters)," but once chosen, the meter remains through-out.[43] It has become customary for the poet to introduce his *takhallus* (pen name) in the last *bait* or *maqta^c* of the *ghazal* as in the following *maqta^c* by a contemporary Badakhshi musician, Faiz-e Mangal:

> *Mane Mangal ke hairānam zi Jurm o az Badakhshānam*
> *Ghulāme shāh-e mardānam qalandarwār o megardam*
>
> I am Mangal from Jurm and from Badakhshān who is perplexed,
> A servant of the people's King, I wander carelessly like a *qalandar* (a dervish).

It is interesting to note here that the quatrain is related to the *ghazal* as the *ghazal* is to the *qasida* (Table 8). Arberry credits Umar ibn Abi Rabia of Mecca for detaching the amatory prelude from the *qasida* and developing the prelude into a love poem in its own right; however, "it was left to the Persians to recognize this kind of writing as belonging to a separate genre and to call it *ghazal*."[44] The quatrain, according to Browne, "is formally two *bayts* (whence called *dú baytí*) or four hemistichs (whence called *rubá^c í*) from the beginning of a *qasída* or *ghazal* written in certain varieties of a particular meter, the *hazaj*."[45] Besides the poetic meter, the structure and rhyme scheme of these poems have implications for the music which will be explored in chapter 6.

Other classical-type poems are not frequently encountered in Afghanistan; therefore, the discussion and explanation concerning them will be made only with particular examples.

Technical Terminology

Terminology associated with Afghan musical theory is borrowed from Hindustani (North Indian) or Persian classical music vocabulary. Thus, the Hindustani term *rāg* is used as a reference to musical modes with names

TABLE 8
Relationship Between *Qasida*, *Ghazal*, and *Chār Baiti*

Q a s i d a			*G h a z a l*			*Chār Baiti*	
Matla^c:	a	a	*Matla^c:*	a	a	a	a
	b	a		b	a	b	a
	c	a		c	a		
	d	a		d	a		
	e	a	*Maqta^c:*	e	a		
	f	a					
	g	a					
	etc.						

such as Bairami (Bhairavi in Hindustani), Bairo (Bhairav in Hindustani), Pelo (Pilu in Hindustani), and Pari (Pahari in Hindustani) for individual modes.[46] The Persian equivalent of *rāg* is *maqām,* sometimes used by classically oriented musicians in Herat and Kabul, but most of the time, the term is incorporated into the title of pieces such as *Maqām-e Jal* (Tune of the Lark). Baily points out that *sor,* generally meaning tone or pitch, can also be used to refer to a set of tones or scale used in a melodic mode.[47] The concept of the Indian *alap,* a free-rhythm, improvisatory introduction where the modal characteristics are expressed and developed, is recognized by the Persian word *shakal,* meaning form or shape.[48] Other less technical terms are *sar āwāz,* which means beginning of a song, or *shoruwa,* the beginning.

Many urban-oriented professional musicians use Hindustani technical terms for pitches, scales, intervals, and so forth.[49] Two Afghan terms that I did not collect have been mentioned by John Baily and Mark Slobin, but with slightly different meanings. The terms, *raft* (went) and *āmad* (came), are equated by Baily to the Hindustani derived terms, *ārui* and *amrui,* for ascending and descending scales, respectively.[50] Slobin mentions that the two terms are used in describing important sections of a piece, *āmad* being the "more stable and important of the two."[51]

Two terms borrowed directly from Iranian are *tarz* and *tasnif.* Both terms are used strictly by educated musicians or official personnel. *Tarz* means "manner" or "mode" and was used in this way by a student at Herat Teachers' College who was also an amateur musician. He indicated that he could play the *dutār* in *tarz-e mahalli,* folk style, and *tarz-e ustādi,* classical style. In a narrower sense, *tarz* is used to mean melody as distinguished from text. *Tasnif* in Iran signifies a composed song based on relatively contemporary poetry. A Herati musician working for Radio Afghanistan defined *tasnif* as text written to fit a composed melody. In most contexts, *tasnif* is used to refer to text rather than melody.

The Indian rhythmic concept of *tala* is not widely understood and only three terms that refer specifically to rhythm are generally used by Afghan musicians: *mogholi,* to designate a rhythm of seven, divided 3+2+2; *dadra,* to designate a variety of rhythms in three or six;[52] and *geda,* to designate a rhythm of four. Other terms such as *zarb* and *paron* are indications of tempo rather than meter. *Zarb* means striking or stamping and usually refers to a slow section in duple meter, or a slow rhythm of five. *Paron* literally means "flying" and refers to a fast section, usually in a rhythm of seven. These terms are combined with names of modes or pieces to identify sections such as *zarb-e āsā, paron-e āsā* or *sāz-e paron.* Informants in Faizabad explained these tempo indications in terms of dance movements. *Zarb* is a slow, regular dance; *paron* is a faster dance, while a third type called *shamār* represents a dance with very fast, turning or circling motions. Dance, in general, is called *raqs, bāzi* in the colloquial language, and *atan* in Pashtu.

Another technical term likely to have evolved from dance is *pāzarb* (*pāi* meaning foot; and *zarb*, stamping). It is most easily recognized in the context of a song in free rhythm in which the *pāzarb* functions as a recurring refrain in fixed rhythm. Although the etymology would suggest the fixed rhythm as its most obvious aspect, it can still be recognized as a *pāzarb* within the context of a song in fixed rhythm. In such cases, the *pāzarb* can be recognized as a short refrain with short, repeated phrases of varying rhyme schemes: *aaaa, aaba,* or *aabb.*

> *Shirin dokhtar māldār*
> *Be sar mezana kaldār*
> *Hami khālā negindār*
> *Khodā bāsha negahdār*

> Sweet nomad girl
> She puts coins around her head
> All her spots are like jewels
> May God keep her.

The general terms *khāndan* and *naghma* are sometimes used to designate sections of a song; the part based on the song text is called *khāndan* and the part that is purely instrumental is called *naghma*. I once asked a group of musicians in Herat about a singer's vocal ornamentation, which was like a miniature *tahrir* of Persian classical music, "a particular kind of glottal vibration."[53] They responded by using a number of expressions, including Hindustani terminology: *zonga, min, gamak,* and *tal*; and two Persian expressions: *rez dādan* (to scatter) and *gulun zadan* (to strike the throat).

Other expressions used in musical contexts are descriptive rather than technical, and are borrowed considerably from the culinary arts. A *rabāb* teacher berated his students by saying *khām ast,* a reference to their playing technique which he considered "raw," "uncooked," meaning unskilled or not developed enough. A *dutār* player in Herat explained that he first played the melody in a pure, unornamented manner; then he ornamented the melody by striking the drone strings in order to make it "boil," *jush mekona.* A song sung in a mixture of languages such as Persian and Uzbek is referred to in Badakhshan as *shir o shekar,* "milk and sugar."

Technical names for the parts of classically oriented plucked lutes, i.e., *rabāb* and multi-stringed *dutār,* are most numerous. Other plucked lutes such as the three-stringed *dutār* and the *dambura* share limited basic terminology with their more sophisticated relatives. The neck of a lute is called *gardan* (neck) or *dasta* (handle). The body is called *kāsa* (bowl) and *rutāl* (surface or lid), or, if it happens to be covered with a membrane, *post* (skin). Pegs are known as *gushak* (little ears); bridges are called *kharak* (little donkey). The small bone bridges over which the sympathetic metal strings are stretched are called *magasak* (little fly), carrying the zoomorphic phraseology further. All the strings are tied around a peg or *tārgir* (string catch). The frets on the *dutār* and *rabāb* are known as *parda* (curtain). The wire plectrum for the *dutār* is *nākhonak* (little nail, talon, claw), and the wooden plectrum for the *rabāb* is *shāhbāz* for which a meaning can only be surmised; that is, "the longest feathers in a falcon's wing."[54] The bow for the *ghichak* is called *kamān* (bow). Strings are usually referred to as *tār*, which includes *lailon* (nylon) and *roda* (gut) strings. If the strings are metal, they are called *sim* (wire). The main playing strings of a *rabāb* and multi-stringed *dutār* are further identified as *jalau*, the first or front string; *miāna*, middle string, and *kata*, the largest string. Slobin cites the use of terms *zil* and *bam* for upper and lower string of the *dambura*, whereas Baily has heard the term *bam* used in describing the lowest-sounding and largest string on both the *rabāb* and Herat multi-stringed *dutār*.[55]

The decorations found on *rabāb*s or *dutār*s are identified by material or design. *Gul* (flower) refers generally to round-shaped designs of inlaid mother-of-pearl, bone, or white plastic. Other designs are generally referred to as *sadaf kāri* (mother-of-pearl work) or *sadaf bandi* (mother-of-pearl lines or bands). *Khanjari* (sword-shaped) is a name for a specific design utilizing *sadaf* and *mosāla* (a dark bone or plastic). Other designs are *kamand* (rope ladder), *khesh* (yoke), and *zāu* (cleft). Slobin reports the term *sheraz* is used in northern Afghanistan to refer to the small concentric circle designs (not unlike the circles in the *kamand*, Figure 1) often found on *dambura*s.[56]

Aside from the two verbs, *zadan* and *nawākhtan*, meaning "to play an instrument," there are two verbs for "tuning an instrument": *kuk kardan* (to tune or wind) and *sor kardan* (to tune machinery). One can use the expression *sor neist* to mean "it is out of tune."[57]

In summary, technical musical terminology seems generally limited to words borrowed from Hindustani or Persian classical music and dance. Terminology pertaining to musical instruments is descriptive of function, design, and material. These terms relate to anatomy, animals, and familiar physical objects.

From the preceding discussion, it is apparent that the usage of musical terms is largely dependent upon the musicality of a descriptive term. Three categories representing three degrees of musicality are:

—Category A, which consists mainly of functional terms that are hardly ever used in talking about music

Khanjari:

Kamand:

Khesh:

Zāu:

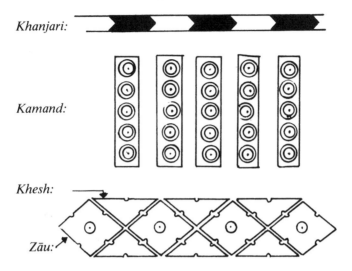

Figure 1: Examples of Some Instrument Ornamentation

—Category B, which consists mostly of vocal and poetic terms which are sometimes used in talking about music

—Category C, which includes instrumental and technical terms that are almost always used in talking about music

These three degrees of musicality are represented in Table 9. The categories are further subdivided into three parts, representing the three groups of terms used in our general discussion of all musical terms, i.e., general terms, genre terms, and technical terms. General terms pertaining to music fall into all three categories; terms relating to genres of music fall mostly into Category B, with the exception of *Aushari*, which is definitely instrumental and restricted to the professional repertoire; the majority of the technical terms fall into Category C. Those technical words that refer to the voice or text fall into Category B. The two terms that come closest to the traditional concept of music in Afghanistan referring to the practical and theoretical aspects of professional and instrumental music vaguely disavowed by Islam are the formal *musiqi* and the informal or colloquial *sāz*.

Concepts of Music in Herat, Faizabad, and Khadir

The number of terms used in each area is consistent with the size and makeup of each area; in other words, Herat, as the most urban of the three areas, used the largest number and variety of terms. Looking more closely

TABLE 9
Categories of Musical Terminology

	Category A		Category B		Category C
General Terms		——Bait Guftan——		——Āhang——	
	Lalai Kardan		Khāndan		Zadan
	Sadā		Āwāz		Sāz Kardan
					Nawākhtan
					Ālat-e musiqi
					Naghma
					Sāz
					Musiqi
Genre Terms		——Bait——			Aushāri
		——Lalai——			
			Gorgholi Shomāli		
			Māldāri Chār Baiti		
			Chopāni Rubāᶜi		
			Kurdaki Du Baiti		
			Rustāyi Qasida		
			Gharibi Ghazal		
			Zahiri Sheᶜr		
			ᶜIshqi Fard		
			Falak Keliwali		
			Sarhadi Mahalli		

Technical Terms

—zarb—
—paron—

Pāzarb	Bāzi	Tār
Rez Dādan	Atan	Nākhonak
Shir O Shekar	Raqs	Shāhbāz
Tasnif	Geda	Jush Kardan
Khāndan	Dadra	Kuk Kardan
	Mogholi	Sor Kardan
	Dasta	Sar Āwāz
	Gardan	Shakal
	Post	Raft
	Kāsa	Āmad
	Rutāl	Ārui
	Parda	Amrui
	Tārgir	Maqām
	Kharak	Rāg
	Gushak	Tarz
	Magasak	Naghma
	Sim	

Music in the Mind

at the general terms, one finds that all three areas share the informal vocabulary, such as *sāz, sadā, lalai kardan, bait, āwāz,* and so on, but such formal terms as *musiqi, ālat-e musiqi,* and *naghma* were commonly used in Herat only. Not only are these terms formal, but they are also more specific to the musical concept. Terms commonly used in the most rural area, Khadir, are nonspecific, informal terms dealing with concepts that are more often thought of in such nonmusical contexts as *bait guftan, lalai kardan,* and *sadā.*

Surprisingly, terms for genres of music are used more in Faizabad than Herat. This may seem somewhat inconsistent with other findings until one considers the fact that songs and pieces are identified differently in the three areas. In Herat, 49 out of a total of 112 songs were identified by specific title based on the song text; 28 were identified by genres which included poetic and melodic types; and 15 were identified by place names; however, all 15 were Kazakh songs, considered somewhat special and outside the cultural milieu of Herat (see Table 10). In Faizabad only 4 songs out of a total of 107 pieces were identified by a specific title, while 36 songs were identified by genre. Khadir, on the other hand, identified most of the songs by indicating location. Thus, the very fact that genres were considered as a category while titles and locations were not, biases the survey of generic terms in favor of Faizabad.

A relatively large number of technical terms are used in Herat because of the presence of a highly professional musical personnel. Besides the presence of professional musicians, the popularity of certain instruments affects parts of the technical vocabulary. The most classical and widespread of the Afghan instruments is the *rabāb.* Because of its classical implications, the terminology associated with the *rabāb* is highly systematized. The *dutār* has been the folk instrument of the Herat area for centuries, but has come under the influence of the *rabāb* within the last

TABLE 10
Identification of Pieces

	Herat	Faizabad	Khadir
Title	49	4	2
Genre	28	36	7
Melodic Mode		9	
Location	15	7	12
Unidentified or Identified by Other Means	20	51	38
Total:	112	107	59

twenty-five years. Thus, much of the *dutār* terminology is borrowed from and related directly to the *rabāb*. On the other hand, the *dambura*, a two-stringed, fretless, plucked lute of northern Afghanistan, has remained a folk instrument; thus, technique and terminology remain unsystematized. Faizabad musicians play both the *dambura* and the *rabāb*, as well as the folk fiddle, *ghichak*, while only the *dambura* can readily be found in Khadir. This may explain the relatively great hiatus one finds in the technical vocabulary of Khadir.

Tables 11, 12, and 13 represent the musical vocabulary common in the three areas of the study. From these tables, the following generalizations

TABLE 11
Musical Terms in Herat

	Category A	Category B	Category C	
General Terms	*Lalai Kardan*	*Khāndan*	*Zadan*	
	Sadā	*Āwāz*	*Naghma*	
			Sāz	
			Musiqi	
Genre Terms	*Bait*	*She^c r*	*Aushāri*	
	Lalai	*Fard*		
		Chār Baiti		
		Du Baiti		
		Ghazal		
		Shomāli		
		Sarhady		
		^c Ishqi		
		Mahalli		
		Keliwali		
Technical Terms		*Rez Dādan*	*Bāzi*	*Gushak*
		Pāzarb	*Atan*	*Sim*
		Tasnif	*Raqs*	*Tār*
			Geda	*Nākhonak*
			Dadra	*Sor*
			Mogholi	*Kuk*
			Dasta	*Sar Āwāz*
			Gardan	*Shakal*
			Post	*Maqām*
			Kāsa	*Rāg*
			Parda	*Tarz*
			Rutal	*Naghma*
			Kharak	

TABLE 12
Musical Terms in Faizabad

	Category A	Category B		Category C
General Terms	*Lalai Kardan*	*Khāndan*		*Zadan*
	Sadā			*Sāz*
Genre Terms	*Bait*	*Zahiri*	*Kurdaki*	
	Lalai	*ᶜIshqi*	*Gharibi*	
		Sheᶜr	*Chopāni*	
		Chār Baiti	*Mahalli*	
		Rubāᶜi	*Falak*	
		Ghazal	*Shomāli*	
		Rustāyi	*Gorgholi*	
Technical Terms			——— *Zarb* ———	*Bāzi*
			——— *Paron* ———	*Raqs*
				Kuk Kardan
				Sor Kardan
				Rāg
				Post
				Kāsa
				Gushak
				Kharak
				Tār
				Parda

can be made: the more urbanized the area the more terms are in that area's musical vocabulary. Not only is there a difference in the quantity of the vocabulary, but the quality is affected as well. Therefore, the bulk of Herat's vocabulary is technical and almost always used in reference to music; that is, most of the vocabulary falls into Category C. Faizabad's vocabulary is heavily based on generic terms and falls equally into Category C, terms that are almost always considered in the musical context, and Category B, terms that are sometimes considered in the musical context. Khadir, on the other hand, has very few terms in any of the groups— general, generic, technical—and the terms fall evenly into all three categories. Although the greatest percentage of each area's vocabulary falls into Category C, if all three areas are compared, the percentage of Herat's vocabulary that falls into Category C is the highest; the percentage of Faizabad's vocabulary that falls into Category B is the highest; and the percentage of Khadir's vocabulary that falls into Category A is the highest (Table 14). This suggests that professionality, instrumentality, formality, and specificity of the terms are directly proportional to the degree of urbanization of an area.

The forms of identification of pieces also give strong support to the contention that urbanized vocabulary is more specific than rural vocabulary. Titles based on song texts are references to specific songs, and almost as often, to specific melodies. References to genres can include a number of pieces based on certain subject matters, melody types, or even poetic forms. References to locations are even less specific, in that a dance form, love

TABLE 13
Musical Terms in Khadir

	Category A	Category B	Category C
General Terms	Lalai Kardan Bait Guftan Sadā	Khāndan	Zadan Sāz
Genre Terms	Bait Lalai	She^cr ^cIshqi Chār Baiti Mahalli	
Technical Terms			Bāzi Raqs Kuk Kardan Tār

TABLE 14
Percentage of Vocabulary That Falls into the Three Categories

Category	Herāt	Faizābād	Khadir
A	9	12	31
B	35	42	31
C	56	46	38

song, lullaby, or certain poetic forms can all be identified by the same location. As previously discussed, a majority of the Herat pieces collected were identified by titles based on song text; the majority of the Faizabad pieces were identified by genre; and the majority of Khadir pieces were identified by location. Even more pertinent is the fact that 64 percent of the Khadir pieces were left unidentified, or were identified by some other means, while 48 percent of the Faizabad pieces and only 18 percent of the Herat pieces were left unidentified or identified by other means.

Summary

It is clear that the concept of music that exists in Afghanistan does not parallel the Western notion of music. In examining the term *musiqi* and all its implications, the formal and informal aspects of this term have to be considered. Although basically a formal word and not readily used by everyone, most Afghans have some notion about its meaning when the term *musiqi* is heard. The formal meaning of *musiqi* can be glossed as "secular music." The colloquial or informal meaning can be glossed as "professional music" or "instrumental music," equivalent to the meaning for the term *sāz*, and it is with this definition that this chapter is most concerned, for it is with respect to this colloquial notion that all other terms are viewed.

The common musical terms can be divided for expediency into general terms relating to music, terms relating to genres of music, and technical terminology. The meanings and usages of these words were examined in several different contexts, and whenever appropriate, facets of formality, specificity, instrumentality, and professionality were considered in relation to usage. The closer a term to the colloquial concept of music, the more professional, more instrumental, more formal, and more specific it tends to be.

A list of the musical vocabulary for each area was made. The vocabularies indicate that the more urban the area, the more terms are used and the more musical those terms are, that is, musical in the sense that the terms are more closely related to the colloquial concept of music. This phenomenon is linked to urbanism, but cannot be explained by it. Population, one of the greatest considerations of urbanism, nonetheless does not affect this particular segment of this study because the sample was not representative or proportional to the population of the areas. Also, the way of life, or character of the inhabitants, is an important factor of urbanism, yet the sampling was heavily dependent upon my informants, many of whom were musicians. Most of the Herat musicians were professionals, the Faizabad musicians semiprofessionals, and the Khadir musicians amateurs. The nature of the professionality of the musicians involved seems to be the greatest contributing factor in the outcome of the vocabularies. The meaning and implications of the different types of musicians will be discussed in the following chapter.

CHAPTER FIVE

The Concept of Musician

Just as some Afghan words are conceived as having more musical or professional connotations than others, some musicians are thought to be more musianly than others. It was suggested in the last chapter that at least three different classes of musicians were observed: professional, semi-professional, and amateur. The Afghans readily admit to two different types of musicians: professional and amateur. They make the distinction on the basis of exchange, that is, whether the negotiations for the musical performance are business or social in context. The nature of exchange also implies a degree of proficiency; those who are "in the business" are thought to be somewhat more proficient than those who perform music for pleasure. Still another distinguishing feature is covert, and yet seems to override the features of exchange and proficiency in the final analysis: the feature of birthright or ascription. This important feature is hardly ever mentioned by the Afghans, yet has been an integral part of their conceptualization of musicians since the beginning of Islam.

TRADITIONAL CONCEPTS

As seen in chapter 3, "Islam and Music," strict Muslims proscribe the art of music so that those who engage in music as a profession are looked down upon. Even before Islam, the profession of music was largely in the hands of singing girls called *qaina* who were, for the most part, foreign slave girls.[1] Although not entirely the profession of slaves, other musicians were usually only one step up the social scale—freemen, usually of Persian extraction. Musicians from the aristocracy were rare, and when it happened that nobles chose to be musicians, they faced harsh criticism from other aristocrats. It is said that an Abbasid caliph banished Ibn-Jami, a Quraish musician born in Mecca, by saying, "You, one of the Quraish, and following the profession of music! What a disgrace! Out of my sight! Leave Baghdad instantly!"[2]

Henry G. Farmer explains that many of the terms for singing girls and female musicians of the taverns were synonymous with courtesan and adultress. Musicians not connected with the taverns fared little better. Tuwais, a seventh-century freeman credited as the first male professional musician of Medina, was esteemed by the nobility for his musical abilities, yet he was a social outcast because he was a *mukhannath*, or male professional musician. "These people were an effeminate class who dyed their hands and affected the habits of women."[3]

There were, according to Farmer, three classes of court musicians: first, the virtuosi, of whom there may have been a dozen or so at court at the same time; second, the instrumentalists (*ālati*); and third, the singing girls (*qaina*). The virtuosi's fate was often dependent upon the whims of those in power at the court. These musicians could be elevated to great riches, and even to the position of caliph's favorite, or could be punished, imprisoned, banished, or put to death. The virtuoso was thus placed in an anomalous position. The instrumentalists and singing girls were freemen and slaves who acted as accompanists and assistants to the virtuosi. The singing girls were the most numerous of court musicians, sometimes numbering over one hundred, and were taught by the virtuosi.[4]

Birthright as an aspect of the concept of musicians is not dealt with directly in the Afghan culture, but rather must be approached via such negative case evidence as has already been cited. Most musicians were slaves and foreigners, an indication that a respectable native was not ordinarily a musician; in other words, a respectable native's birthright precluded his becoming a musician. The point was made even stronger in the case in which an aristocrat was in question. As a group, musicians have been traditionally characterized as amoral or perverted, and as such, traditional society always seemed able to acknowledge such deviant behavior more readily in the lower classes and in foreigners.

A specific reference to birthright was made by William E. Lane when he wrote in the early nineteenth century about the public dancing girls of Egypt known as *Ghazeeyeh*. He stated that they were from "a distinct tribe called Ghawazee," who, he said, were an endogamous tribe whose origin is marked with much uncertainty:

All of them are brought up for the venal profession. . . . The husband is subject to the wife; he performs for her the offices of a servant and procurer; and generally, if she be a dancer, he is also her musician, but a few of the men earn their subsistence as blacksmiths or tinkers. . . . Though some of them are possessed of considerable wealth, costly ornaments, etc., many of their customs are similar to those of the people whom we call "gipsies," and who are supposed, by some, to be of Egyptian origin.[5]

Gypsies in nineteenth-century Egypt were known collectively as *Ghagar* or *Ghajar*.[6] Although they were not known as musicians, they were similar to musician groups by way of their claimed descent and activities. Like the *Ghawazee*, they claimed to be descendants of the famous Barmakid family whose members had been viziers to the early Abbasid caliphs. They were blacksmiths, tinkers, or itinerant sellers of trinkets and other wares. The women told fortunes and performed circumcisions and blood-letting. Further, Lane notes another group of dancers called *khawals*, young men who impersonated women.[7] It is interesting to note that the term, as well as dancing boys of this description, are both met in Afghanistan today.

Musicians have long been viewed as outcasts of traditional Islamic societies. As will be evidenced in the contemporary musician terms used in Afghanistan, these views have changed very little through the years.

CONTEMPORARY TERMINOLOGY

A perusal of words referring to musicians in Afghanistan reflects a number of descriptive titles, names, and terms of address. Some terms are tribal or clan names; others are references to larger ethnic groups, and some refer to music or other occupations directly connected with music.

Dalāk, gharib zāda, jat, ustā, magad, moqaled, motreb, sāzenda, and *nawāzenda* are terms of reference for professional musicians in Afghanistan. The terms designate occupations and tribal names that imply heredity. Of all the terms, *dalāk* is the most widespread and is commonly used in all metropolitan areas and in the Pashtun-dominated areas of Afghanistan. *Dalāk* literally means "bath attendant" or "barber," but these occupations are held by a low class of musicians, dancers, and actors. No *dalāk* would ever identify himself as such. When asked about their profession, most *dalāk*s prefer to say they are *salmāni* (barbers), rather than identify themselves by any other occupation in which they may engage: "The word dalak is so approbrious that barbers in the city of Herat (who were probably dalaks themselves) asked us to use the more genteel term of salmani."[8] The term *dalāk* is defined by non-*dalāk*s as a *qaum* or tribe of barbers, musicians, actors, and dancers who are not regarded as members of the community they serve, but are looked upon as an endogamous, occupational group of outsiders or foreigners. They often live in segregated quarters of a city or village and their dead are buried outside the village cemetery walls.[9]

Barbers are professional circumcisers and many of their women practice blood-letting. Hafizullah Baghban elaborates the functions of traditional barbers: "In addition to shaving heads and whiskers, the barber circumcises children, pulls teeth, practices phlebotomy, operates on bumps, and makes a variety of organic and herbal medicines for curing diseases."[10]

Baghban adds that the barbers are sometimes veterinarians and livestock dealers as well.[11] The preferred terms for barber are *salmāni* and *sartarush*.

A Kabul musician pointed out to me an important feature which he could not explain; that is, all barber groups don't necessarily include musicians and all musician groups don't necessarily include barbers, but all *sāz-dohl* (*sornā* and *dohl*) players are barbers themselves or are related closely to barbers. Observations further indicate that the *sornā* and *dohl* are considered the most professional of all the instruments. Although amateurs could and would learn to play *rabāb*, *tabla*, and *dutār*, no amateurs play *sornā* and *dohl*. These instruments are left solely to those who are known as *dalāks*. Again, not all *dalāk* musicians play *sornā* and *dohl*, but those musicians who do are sure to be *dalāks*.

I suspect this strange alliance of *sornā* and *dohl* players and barbers has something to do with the ancient Indian caste system. Schurmann notes:

> It is possible that they (dalaks) are ultimately related to the Jats of Eastern Afghanistan. The Jats fulfill the same role as the Dalaks and are equally despised. Both groups show strong resemblances, as far as their social role is concerned, to the gypsies, and all three groups may ultimately derive from an Indian pariah group.[12]

Although my own observations have not supported the view that eastern Afghan *jats* and *dalāks* fulfill the same roles, both groups are despised. Perhaps the exclusion of *sornā* and *dohl* players can be explained by the instruments' supposedly polluting qualities. The double reed of the *sornā* is placed entirely within the mouth of the player; thus, the reed, and by extension, the whole instrument is contaminated by the player's own spittle. Spit is likened to semen by the gypsies,[13] an idea suggested by our own expression, "he is the spitting image of his father." This polluting attribute is supported and sustained by stories and notions of the evil, satanic origins of the *sornā*. It is considered by some to be the "penis of Satan," and the first maker, performer, and teacher of the *sornā* was supposed to be the devil himself.[14] According to a Herat folksong, the skin for the *dohl* is made from a donkey's stomach and the *sornā* is made out of its penis.[15] Evil and disreputable tendencies are attributed to the performers of these instruments as well. Baghban quotes a story about an act of incest ordered by Satan; no one would comply with his order except a *jat* (a derogatory term for a hereditary, barber-musician in Herat).[16]

The hair, teeth, and nails handled by barbers are also considered powerful and magical by the gypsies. Jean-Paul Clébert notes that these materials "have a life of their own, independent of the body: a notion whose origin must doubtless be seen in the fact that these elements continue to live, or at least do not die immediately, after the decease of the subject."[17]

Mohammed Omar, *sornā* and Khalifa Dohlchi Sarwar, *dohl*. Herat.

Charles G. Leland relates a number of gypsy beliefs and cures regarding hair including "an old belief, and one widely spread, that if the witches or the devil can get a lock of anybody's hair, they can work him evil."[18] Perhaps it is the magical and powerful by-products associated with musicians and barbers that relegates their handling to a certain class of people. An interesting aside is that *jat* in Armenia is the vernacular word for hair.[19] G. P. Tate attributes this meaning to the long hair of the emigrants from the east known as *jat*s who appeared in Armenia from A.D. 300 to 400.[20]

Sir Richard Burton supposes that the gypsies were originally outcasts rather than Hindu pariahs.[21] It is not the intention here to establish whether or not this is accurate, but instead to note that their occupations were basically hereditary. Fredrik Barth, in his study of the social stratification in Swat, northern Pakistan, has equated the word *qaum* (tribe) with "hierarchically-ordered social groups" which he calls "castes."[22] Among the various caste groups, he has categorized "musician and dancer," called *dom*,[23] "barber," called *nai*; and "thong and sieve-maker, dancer," called *kashkol*. All three of these groups, along with the washerman, *dobi*, occupy the lowest stratum of society:

> The indigenous polluted castes include Washermen, Barbers (who are concerned with shaving, nail-paring, and childbirth), and Thong- and Sieve-makers (who work with the guts of animals); these three groups are everywhere despised

and form the lowest stratum of society. The caste of Dancers also falls into this category, since they are associated with prostitution and other morally bad practices.[24]

I should mention here that the word *dom* is sometimes used for *dalāk*s in eastern Afghanistan. *Dom* in eastern Afghanistan, then, includes the *dom* and *nai* castes of Swat, but not the *kashkol*, who are generally known as *jat*s in eastern Afghanistan.

Barth recognizes the reason for the low social status of barbers in the services they render:

> These services include haircutting (of men by the barber, of women by his wife) and shaving, but they also include the organization of celebrations, the announcement of the event to appropriate outsiders, and the mobilization of the assistance from fellow association members to which each family is entitled. . . . The 'low,' 'taboo' status of the barber stems from this special role. Because it involves intimate contact with the domestic life of each family, in breach of the usual barriers of prudery and seclusion, the barber's status needs to be clearly segregated from that of other persons in the community.[25]

The *dalāk*'s services parallel those just mentioned and bring out another reason for the association of *sornā* and *dohl* players with barbers; the announcement of important events to outsiders is made by the playing of the *sornā* and *dohl*, thus breaching the same barriers of privacy that the professions themselves breach.

Gharib zāda (son of a poor man or foreigner) is said to be the tribal name (*qaum*) or ethnic group of professional musicians in Herat, the *dalāk*s of Herat. The musicians themselves, however, do not identify themselves as *gharib zāda*, but claim to belong to some Pashtun tribe such as Barakzai, reminiscent of the Egyptian *ghawazee*'s claim that they were descendants of the Barmakids. It is thought that the *gharib zāda* were once members of a ruling family who were forced to flee their home at a time of political strife and war. They eventually settled in different parts of the world and took to making music for a living; hence, "son of a stranger, foreigner or poor man."[26] The connection between being poor and foreign lies in the fact that most homeless wanderers are considered indigent in psychological terms as well as economic ones. Many Afghans expressed their pity when they found out my "family" (mother, father, siblings) lived thousands of miles away. Separation from family or home for even a short time is extremely painful and distressful to most traditional Afghans. One informant from Badakhshan expressed the belief that the best instrument-makers in the area of Badakhshan were *mahajir*s or emigrants and, in fact, a famous instrument-maker of Kabul is known simply as *gharib* (foreigner, poor man).

The *gharib zāda* are actors, dancers, barbers, and musicians. The women are also musicians and thought to be prostitutes as well. Some of the young boys perform as dancing boys who impersonate women; they are known as *bacha* (boy), *bacha bi rish* (boy without a beard), or *bāzigar* (dancer). Young *gharib zāda* boys perform this function until puberty, when as the Afghans express it, "the beard begins to show." An interesting use of the word *bāzingar*, supposedly from *bāzigar*, was cited by anthropologist Nazif Shahrani, a native of Badakhshan, who said that his grandmother used to call naughty boys *bāzingar*.[27] Shahrani stated that not all boy dancers came from these professional families, but outsiders were usually orphans or runaways who were enticed into the profession by procurers.

A pejorative term for *gharib zāda* in Herat is *jat*. *Jat* refers to a great number of groups living in Iran, Afghanistan, Pakistan (Baluchistan), and India. It is not known how the various groups are related. G. P. Tate supports the notion that the *jat*s and the *gujar*s of Upper India originally came from Central Asia around the first century B.C. and cites the *jat*s in Baluchistan and Afghanistan as evidence for this theory.[28] He notes a group known as *godar* in Mazenderan on the Caspian Sea who are pariahs, and surmises that *godar* is a corruption of *gujar*; he finally reports an account of a "Hindu colony" of *jat*s in Armenia.[29] Tate describes most of the *jat* groups as pastoralists or agriculturists, yet none of the groups in Afghanistan known by the name *jat* are agriculturists or herders.

In eastern Afghanistan, *jat*s refer to gypsy-like groups of itinerant traders, fortune tellers, animal trainers, and makers of *gharbāl* (coarse sieves) and *dāira*s (tambourines). They are reputed to be thieves, eaters of horseflesh, and their women are alleged to be prostitutes. They are distinguished from the more respectable nomads, *kuchi*s, by the fact that the *jat*s live in white A-frame tents as opposed to the black goat's hair tents of the nomads, and by the fact that *jat*s do not have flocks. Other terms for nomadic *jat*-like groups are *qawāl* (*khawal* of Egypt?), *kouli*, and *jogi*. The *jat*s of western Afghanistan, the *gharib zāda*, are settled and are mainly musicians.

Burton, in *The Jew, the Gypsy and El Islam*, claims a direct relationship between the gypsies and the *jat*s of India. He describes five tribes of *jat*s, one being "a wandering tribe, many of whom are partially settled in Candahar, Herat, Meshed, and other cities of the Persico-Afghan frontier. . . . They are held to be notorious thieves, occupying a low place in the scale of creation."[30] Other writers of the period also described the *jat*s as gypsies, stressing their notorious reputation as people with loose morals. Music is by no means pointed out as a consistent occupation among these groups. Bray describes the *jat*s of Baluchistan as camel drivers who earn their living "partly on their camels and partly on their women—their two

sources of livelihood to this day. . . . Being notorious evil-livers and ex-
pert camel-lifters, they are not allowed to camp close to a village unless they
have taken service with some big man."[31] W. Ivanov describes the gypsies of
eastern Persia: "By craft they are tinkers, first and last."[32] Two terms used
by the gypsies studied by Ivanov are related to those used by the western
jats in Afghanistan. First, Ivanov states "Many of them prefer to be dubbed
usta, short for (P.) *ustad*, master-craftsman."[33] In Herat, *ustā* is a title for
gharib zāda, which is often incorporated into their names, as in Usta Abdullah and Usta Ibrahim. The second term, *qurbati, qulwati,* or *khulwati,* is
applied to gypsies and especially to their language. According to Ivanov,
the word comes from *ghurbat* or *gharibi* meaning "to be a stranger," or "to
live in a foreign country."[34] The *gharib zāda* of Herat refer to themselves as
magad in their secret language *magadi,* and to non-*magads* as *bikar.*[35] It is
not my intent to prove or disprove any real relationship between the various groups known as *jats,* or to show a relationship between professional
musicians in Afghanistan and gypsies, but simply to point out the criss-
crossing similarities between terms, occupations, and notions held about
these groups.

Moqaled (actor) is sometimes used to refer to a member of the *gharib
zāda* who participates in the folk plays of the Herat area. *Motreb* and *sāzenda* are terms which specifically refer to musicians. *Motreb* literally
means "minstrel" and comes from the Arabic *tarab* (joy, mirth), while *sāzenda* comes from *sāz* (instrument). Perhaps because of their specific reference, these terms are preferred over the terms *gharib zāda* and *dalāk,* which
imply birthright. The more formal appellations for *sāzenda* are *nawāzenda*
and *sāz nawāz,* both from *nawākhtan* (to play an instrument).

Two terms of address associated with hereditary musicians are *khalifa*
and *ustād. Khalifa,* usually spelled "caliph" in the West, means successor.
Ustād means "teacher." These terms, when applied to musicians, signify a
degree of professionality which amateur musicians cannot attain, nor care
to. Otherwise, they are terms of address for master workmen who are quali-
fied to teach apprentices such as blacksmiths, tailors, and truck drivers.
For musicians, the title *khalifa,* like the title *ustā,* denotes a *dalāk* and is not
generally used for all musicians. *Ustād,* quite distinct from the connotation
of *ustā,* is a title reserved for those musicians who are urban-oriented, professional musicians who try to maintain their ties to the Hindustani musical
tradition.

According to Afghan sources, the music culture of Afghanistan was
dominated by Persian traditional music as well as Afghan folk music until a
century ago when the Amir of Kabul, Sher Ali Khan, invited Indian Muslim musicians to his court in Kabul. He gave them lands in Kabul (the
section of old Kabul now known as *kharābāt,* entertainment quarters) and

transported them back and forth to the court on elephants. From that time on, Indian classical music became established as the elite, classical tradition of Afghanistan. These transplanted Indian musicians gained a preeminent status among Afghan musicians. The descendants and students of these Hindustani musicians in Kabul are given the title of *ustād*. The musical ties to India and Pakistan remained strong, as such Hindustani musicians as Ustad Villayat Khan were regularly invited to Mohammed Zaher Shah's court for private performances and music lessons for individual members of the royal family. One of the most respected Afghan musicians is Ustad Sarahang, who is said to have come to Afghanistan from India in the 1950s. He is a singer of Hindustani *khyals* (Hindustani virtuosic vocal form) and Persian *ghazals*. He sang often in Mohammed Zaher Shah's court and is a recognized musician in India and Pakistan as well.

Often risking economic security for a higher status, some Afghan musicians seek to emulate the musical characteristics of the Hindustani musicians by learning their repertoire, by striving for technical virtuosity, by learning their theory and vocabulary, and finally by attaining the title of *ustād*. Specialization seems to be a path for many *dalāk*s to dissociate themselves from their ascriptive qualities; thus one could become a Western-style barber who owns a shop in the city. To further mask their birthright, they can attempt to substitute religious titles such as *haji* or *sufi* for their professional ones; thus Khalifa Abdullah becomes Haji Abdullah.[36]

Only one term, *shauqi*, definitely distinguishes the musician as a non-hereditary professional. The term denotes one who does anything because of a strong interest, inclination, or desire to do so, but is not economically dependent upon these acts.[37] In all cases, *shauqi* musicians encountered in this study stressed the fact that they had other occupations and were only dilettante musicians. Yet, when *dalāk* musicians made the same claim—that their main occupation was that of barber—they were not accepted as *shauqi*. The antonym of *shauqi* is *kesbi* or *maslaki*, both meaning "professional." *Shauqi* and *kesbi* are defined in terms of economic dependence and on the basis of exchange. *Kesbi*s are wholly dependent upon their musical earnings for a livelihood. The earnings are received on the basis of business transactions. *Shauqi*s are not dependent upon such earnings or gifts which result from social transactions. Yet, the facts fail to uphold these definitions. Many *shauqi* musicians are almost completely dependent upon their musical earnings. What the term *shauqi* does manage to signify is a kind of dedication which results from having an element of choice: "If I didn't want to be a musician, I wouldn't have to be one," and clearly dissociates the *shauqi* musician from the *dalāk* musician.

The remaining terms are neutral, in that they do not presume to transfer the information of birthright. Included are the terms *kesbi* and *maslaki*. Those musicians who are undoubtedly professional and associate with *dalāk* musicians, but who are themselves nonhereditary musicians, may choose to claim being *kesbi* or *maslaki*. Yet, even these musicians may claim to be *shauqi* with no apparent discrepancy. John Baily uses *kesbi* to signify "members of hereditary professional musician families" in Herat.[38] Strictly speaking, the definition is correct, but I found that the term was often used to refer to a *shauqi* musician who had publicly "gone professional."[39]

Khānenda and *sarāyenda* are terms for singers. These terms do not imply birthright, yet are most often used for nonhereditary singers. We are reminded that vocal talents are not considered as musical or professional as instrumental ones, nor for that matter, as disreputable. Other neutral terms are words based on the instruments involved, such a "violinist" or "drummer." These words consist of the instrument name, plus the Persian attributive suffix -*i* or the Turkish suffix -*chi*, or the word *nawāz* or *zan* (player). Examples of such are: *rabābi, damburachi, tabla nawāz*, and *dā-ira zan*. In Herat the only performer who is identified in another fashion is a *sornā* player who is called *sāzenda*.

The instruments involved also give a clue to the professionality of the performer. We have already discussed the implications of a *sornā* and *dohl*. Some instruments such as *dambura* (two-stringed, plucked lute), *chang* (jew's harp), and *nai* (flute) are hardly ever played by hereditary musicians. The *dambura* is a traditional *shauqi* instrument of the North. The *chang* and *nai* are sometimes not even considered legitimate instruments, but toys for the use of children, women, and shepherds.

The final neutral term is *onarman* (artist), used in Kabul and official circles elsewhere. This term is used to refer to a musician who has been recognized by the government, whether he is *shauqi* or an *ustād*.

Professional names are sometimes an indication of the status of musicians. Those names that include *khalifa, ustā*, and *ustād* are almost certain to refer to hereditary musicians. Those that include local place names are likely to be names of *shauqi* musicians. Others with the title *khān* attached to the end of their names are from Indian musician families, and those names that include kin terms are likely to be *shauqi*.

Some terms used to refer to musicians are more regional than others, and the interpretations held about various musician types are dependent on the setting in which they operate; thus, each area will now be discussed in terms of how and when the musician types operate and the views held about them by other inhabitants.

MUSICIANS IN HERAT

Herat is a metropolitan area where public entertainment and music abound. The two obvious places are the public theaters. In 1972–73 the Herat Nendarei was owned and operated by the Herat Information and Culture Department, and the Behzad Nendarei was privately owned and operated by Mohammed Alishah Olfat Herawi, a musician and dramatist. Olfat began working in the Herat Nendarei at the age of eleven and stayed there for twenty-six years, gradually working his way to the assistant managership. He finally became the owner of his own theater in 1968. Olfat is not only singer, actor, and director, but also a playwright. He has received official recognition from the central government by being awarded the Third Degree from the Ministry of Information and Culture, the highest degree ever awarded to anyone in Herat. Olfat is a Tajik, a fact which absolves him from ever being considered a hereditary musician by others, even though he works with *gharib zāda*. Thus, although he is not, strictly speaking, an amateur, he is not a true professional in the sense of birthright. He may be considered *kesbi*, but a more appropriate term would be *onarman*.

The leader of the Behzad Nendarei Orchestra in 1972 was Ghulam Mohammed Shabahang, an Ali Kuzai, a Pashtun tribe settled in Herat. The Ali Kuzais no longer speak Pashtu. My *dutār* teacher, Ghulam Haidar, informed me that Shabahang's mother is a *gharib zāda*. This bit of information confuses Shabahang's true identity, as it is understood that *gharib zāda* do not marry outside their group. Most leaders of ensembles or orchestras play the harmonium, which Shabahang does; he also sings. He is considered an *ustād* or *khalifa* because, I was told, he is leader of the orchestra.

Other members of the orchestra also were Pashtuns. No other information concerning their background was given. The only Tajik member of the orchestra was Ghulam Haidar, my *dutār* teacher, who is a *shauqi* in the true meaning of the word. He started to play the *dutār* when he was a young boy. Although he had no formal musical training, he picked up whatever knowledge of music he could by watching others. When he was older, he started to work as a mason, but his interest in music did not diminish. He spent his spare time with professional musicians, learning whatever they had to offer. A year or two after the opening of the Behzad Nendarei, he took a job as a member of their orchestra and now plays with the orchestra for private engagements as well. His father, a cook by profession, only recently became resigned to the fact that his son had become a professional musician. Ghulam Haidar now considers himself a *kesbi*. He lives in the

Orchestra members of the Behzad Nendarei in Herat. Musicians left to right are: Ghulam Haidar, *dutār*; Mohammed Karim, *tabla*; Ghulam Qadir, *delrobā*; Abdul Ghani, *rabāb*; Ghulam Mohammed Shabahang, harmonium; Sultan Mohammed, *rabāb* (back to camera).

musician's quarters of Herat, but says that he will never marry into a musician family.

The male singers at the Behzad Nendarei were all Tajik and considered amateur musicians. The females were quite another matter. Although I did not receive any specific information concerning them, they are all considered professional prostitutes; the fact that they sing, dance, and act in public for a primarily male audience is reason enough in the Afghan mind to label them thus. In the theater they dress in an ostentatious manner, in brocade or sequined dresses and Pakistani-style bloomers with wide ankle cuffs; they wear no veil, and often have a cosmetic gold tooth. Outside the theater, they wear the modest *chāderi* like other women. It was extremely painful to our servant, a pious Tajik who was sometimes known as Mulla Khairuddin, that my work had anything to do with these notorious people and places.

The composition of the Herat Nendarei is very similar to that of the Behzad Nendarei. Much information about the theater was supplied by John Baily, who did research in Herat.[40] Until a decade ago, Baily notes, the Herat Nendarei's primary offering was drama. No women worked at the theater and women's parts were played by males. Following Kabul's example and in an effort to improve the status of women in music, dance,

Professional singer at the Behzad
Nendarei, Herat.

and theater, the Herat Information and Culture Department introduced
female actresses, singers, and dancers, with the result that they became the
main attraction. The talents of these females were questionable and the
theater became an advertising arena for local prostitutes. Two of the female
stars of the Herat Nendarei were introduced to me as the wives of a "rich
Herati," who turned out to be a famous local procurer. Although the male
personnel were quite stable, the females changed periodically, going from
one theater to the other. Sometimes famous actresses or singers from
Kabul were contracted for an extended period.

The most famous musicians of Herat are the *motreb*, surreptitiously
called *gharib zāda*. Among them is the Golpasand family. Zainab, the
daughter of Golpasand, enjoys the reputation as being the best female singer in Herat today. Her fame is based upon her family background and her
repertoire. She was taught old local Herati songs from her *'amma*, paternal
aunt, who is also her mother-in-law. Zainab's husband is a barber and her
nephew, Amir Mohammed, used to be a *bāzigar*. Now that Amir Mohammed is no longer a dancer, he plays the *tabla* and sings a little. Zainab,

her nephew, and her cousins came to our home to record songs. Ghulam Haidar, who lives with them, came and played the *dutār* for them. It was only after the recording session that Ghulam Haidar talked about the *gharib zāda*, about their background, their secretiveness, their own language, which is called *labs-e magadi*, and how they claimed to be Barakzai.[41] Although Zainab did not sing at the local theaters, the Golpasand family is somehow associated with the Behzad Nendarei.[42]

The *sāz-dohl* players of Herat are all from *moqaled* families. These musicians are residents of the city or villages and during the summer travel about the area performing their services whenever called upon. The *moqoladi* folk dramas are special performances put on for big celebrations like weddings.[43] During New Years, *sāz-dohl* musicians play from house to house for a small fee. They are also hired to play for work crews when they clean out ditches or harvest wheat. The two musicians I recorded were from a village just outside of Herat City. They were cousins, Mohammed Omar and Khalifa Dohlchi Sarwar.

The other public musicians perform in teahouses, *samowar*s, or restaurants known as "hotels." Ghulam Mohiuddin, *dutār* player and Baidola, *zirbaghali* player, are owners of a *samowar* at *Darwāza 'Irāq*. They serve and entertain in their teahouse, but also hire themselves out to play for private parties. During the New Years festivities, they close their teahouse and go to the parks where they serve tea and entertain. Both are Pashtuns and insist that they are *shauqi* musicians. Baidola has strong ties with Kandahar, the principal Pashtun city in southern Afghanistan. Although a *shauqi*, his life is enmeshed with professional musicians. He fell in love with a Kandahari dancing boy whom he proceeded to kidnap and bring to Herat. He finally served a jail sentence for fighting the dancing boy's Kandahari lover, but he managed to keep the boy with him in Herat.

Other *shauqi* musicians do not perform in public, but are true amateurs who perform for friends. One such musician is Mohammed Sharif, a student at the Herat Teachers' College, who learned to play the *dutār* on his own, without the benefit of professional training. Like Ghulam Haidar, he learned by watching others and much of his repertoire is based on songs heard on the radio. Professional musicians who heard him play belittled his ability. As a true *shauqi*, he could not ask for a fee; thus he took whatever was given to him as a gift.

Finally, there are those who are not considered musicians at all and, therefore, do not feel the need to designate themselves as *shauqi*. Since there is no special terminology associated with these people, I apply the term "nonmusician" to them. Nonmusicians are never considered to be musicians of any type, amateur or professional. Two of the nonmusicians I

Left to right: Ghulam Mohiuddin, *dutār*, Baidola, *zirbaghali*, Mohammed Zaher
Charikari, *dutār*.

recorded were female singers, another played the *chang* (jew's harp), and
another played the *nai* (shepherd's end-blown flute).

One woman, who was a friend of our servant, consented to sing some
old Herati songs for me. For this recording session, I was invited to our
servant's home for a luncheon and there, among the women and children,
she sang for me, accompanying herself on a *dāira* (tambourine). This was
done in the strictest secrecy from her husband who would, I was assured,
beat her if he knew what she was doing. Another was a young Jamshedi girl
who found it necessary to leave her nomadic family and find work as a
servant in Herat. She came to my home to record, bringing her young
charge with her. Another was a young Kazakh girl, a friend of mine, who
came to visit and incidentally played the *chang* for me as a favor. The *nai*
player was brought to our home by a friend of ours and introduced as a
malang, a religious enthusiast with eccentric appearance and behavior. In

this case, the title was a euphemism for his appearance and actions rather than for his religious convictions. As previously discussed, *nai* players are hardly ever considered professional musicians, and the fact that he was a *malang* erased all thoughts of this nature.

From the observer's point of view, then, there are four types of musicians in Herat:

—the hereditary, professional musician,
—the nonhereditary, professional musician,
—the amateur,
—the nonmusician.

The most obvious musicians in the public's view are the hereditary musicians, the *motreb*. There is no question about their professionality. Even the women *motreb* perform in public for a predominantly male audience. Most of these musicians claim descent from a Pashtun tribe. As mentioned in the discussion of the overview of Herat, many Pashtuns from the Kandahar area settled in the predominantly Tajik Herat area hundreds of years ago and now consider themselves native to Herat. To the Tajik inhabitant, however, there must be some consolation in thinking that these low-caste musicians were originally outsiders.

The nonhereditary, professional musicians such as Ghulam Haidar, Ghulam Mohiuddin, and Baidola, are so closely associated with the *motreb*, that there is, again, no question concerning their professionality. They not only entertain the public, but also live in the style of and in close proximity to the *motreb*. There is little opportunity for these musicians to explain their nonhereditary background to the inhabitants of Herat. My presence created a unique situation where they were able to dissociate themselves from the *motreb*. To my knowledge, there are no female, nonhereditary professional musicians.

The amateur *shauqi* musicians do not perform in public and do not make their livelihood as musicians. The nonmusicians most certainly do not entertain in public, with the exception of the *malang*, the *nai* player who carries his *nai* and plays in the streets of Herat. Because of the low public profile kept by these people, there is never a question that they are amateurs.

Basically, the division between amateur and professional is clear-cut in Herat. The nature of musical exchange is definitely businesslike for the professional and social for the amateur. The only exception may be people like the *malang* who get a few *afghanis* for playing in the streets. But the instrument involved and the character of the musician excuses them for much of their conduct. The public and private settings of the performances run parallel to the professional-amateur division, and the talents of the performers are also judged according to their professional-amateur status. Amateurs often make excuses for their performance on the basis that they are amateurs rather than professionals. Judgment of character and condemnation are also based on whether one is a professional or an amateur musician. Women are divided into the definitely professional and definitely amateur categories; there are no women in the intermediate groups. The only musicians who transcend this basic division are the male singers employed by the two theaters. They seem to have the sanction of a governmental agency, and if they are talented, may earn the title of *onarman*. This attitude may be held only by government officials, however; the lower classes probably wouldn't view these musicians with any distinction from other musicians.

The repertoire of Herat musicians is basically the same for all musicians. The theater musicians usually sing composed songs (*ghazal, du baiti*) with words by well-known poets. Many of these composed songs have been made popular by Radio Afghanistan musicians. The *motreb* have the largest repertoire, including popular composed songs as well as local folk songs. The amateur musician has a hodge-podge repertoire, depending on where and from what source he has learned the piece. The repertoire of the nonmusician is basically folk and topical, with little emphasis placed on poetic merit.

To most inhabitants of Herat one is either a musician or not a musician. The choice is clear and there are no complications to cloud the issue. This view is imbued in the minds of Heratis because the hereditary, professional musician has been a traditional part of the Herat scene for many centuries. On the other hand, Faizabad differs radically, mainly because the advent of hereditary, professional musicians is relatively recent.

MUSICIANS IN FAIZABAD

Although Faizabad is the administrative and economic center of Badakhshan Province, the town itself is relatively small and quiet with no provisions for public entertainment. The traditional teahouses called *kāfi* exist, but the entertainment is provided by radio, old phonograph recordings, or small tape cassettes. A *dambura* may hang on a teahouse wall for any customer to pluck, but occasions for live entertainment are rare. The majority of musical performances take place at private festivities: picnics, weddings, and parties.

The most prominent musicians in the Faizabad area are *shauqi* or nonhereditary musicians. This fact was made clear even before I went to Faizabad; some Badakhshis living in Kabul recommended I look up Dur Mohammed of Keshm, Faiz-e Mangal of Jurm, and Khan-e Baharaki of

Baharak, all *shauqi* musicians. Traditionally, the occupations of barber and musician have been considered mere avocations rather than vocations, with no stigma attached to them. In all cases I encountered, *shauqi* musicians stressed the fact that they had other occupations and were only dilettante musicians. Faiz-e Mangal is a government employee in charge of public forests, Khan is a small landowner whose sons are carpenters, and others are shopkeepers or farmers. The *shauqi* musicians conduct all transactions related to music in a social way, with an element of personal relationship and obligation attached. These social exchanges are treated as moral transactions which bring about and maintain personal relationships between individuals and groups. Thus, recording and interviewing these musicians posed a special problem.

Faiz-e Mangal was born in Badakhshan. Although his father was a Pashtun from Paktia Province, he considers himself—and more important, other Badakhshis consider him—Tajik. Tajik in Badakhshan implies, first, that one is a native of Badakhshan; and second, that one is a Persian-speaker. Faiz-e Mangal is a popular singer who accompanies himself on the *dambura*, the native instrument of that area, and is called upon to entertain at private celebrations throughout the greater Faizabad area. In fact, he seems to spend more time traveling and performing from one area to another than at his government post. At each gathering where I observed him, he was treated as a guest. Although he never outwardly refused to come to my house for the exclusive purpose of recording and talking about his music, he never came; probably he felt the situation would be too professional.

Khan-e Baharaki is an old man who sings and plays the *dambura* and *rabab*. Although he is treated with the utmost respect, he has reached the age at which he dismisses social niceties and artistic appreciation in favor of pecuniary appreciation, of which he feels he does not receive enough. Others consider him eccentric. At the time I went to meet him in Baharak, he made it known that he was "out of town." The *ᶜalāqadār* (minor district commissioner) of Baharak and another amateur musician from Faizabad, Naim, assured me that the Khan would come to a party that night which was given in our honor by the *ᶜalāqadār*. The Khan showed up late and moody, but as the evening wore on he became more friendly. Another younger musician, Islam, was also invited; the arrangement was between the *ᶜalāqadār* and the musicians, and the musicians felt a social obligation to appear.

Islam, the young *ghichak* (bowed, spiked fiddle) player and singer, had gone to school in Kabul, but returned to Baharak before graduating. Although a *shauqi*, he is eager to earn a reputation as a good musician, possibly to take the place of Khan-e Baharaki, who is old. Islam was the only *shauqi* to consent to come to our home in Faizabad to record. The Khan also came to visit us, but the occasion was purely social. Islam's thinking reflects a kind of urban attitude held by many young Kabulis who look to the music of the West and find nothing disgraceful about it.

Naim, the amateur *rabāb* player from Faizabad, known affectionately as Aka Naim (older brother Naim), does not share Islam's point of view. Naim plays only at small gatherings of his friends. He never allows people to see him carrying his instrument. He helped us tremendously by arranging social, musical gatherings at which we could be present as guests. He talked about other musicians, but never about himself. Naim owns a mixed-goods shop with his brother Akbar, who is also a musician. Akbar is not shy about his talents and often plays with hereditary, professional musicians on a professional basis. On one occasion, Naim was forced to admit that his brother was a *kesbi* rather than a *shauqi* because he conducted his musical affairs in a businesslike manner. Akbar himself still maintains that he is a *shauqi*, on the basis that he is mainly a shopkeeper, not a musician, implying that he is not a hereditary musician. It may be of interest to note that during the Independence Day celebrations of 1972 held in Faizabad, the only musicians to entertain at a school variety show were Akbar and his ensemble, and Islam. Although I am not certain, I feel that other musicians were probably asked to participate, but declined.

Dur Mohammed Keshmi is another famous *shauqi* musician. The only time I had a chance to observe him was at a wedding where he and some professional musicians were entertaining. Although there were hundreds of guests, only a few were invited to a special luncheon hosted by the groom and his family. I was surprised to see that Dur Mohammed was included among the luncheon guests. It should be mentioned here that I met most of these musicians at social gatherings where my husband and I were included among the honored guests by virtue of the fact that we were foreign visitors considered guests of the governor as long as we lived in Faizabad. These occasions were never ideal for recording and interviewing, but were right for observing music and musicians in their natural settings. As mentioned before, other *shauqi* musicians were guests, but usually were not included among the honored guests.

Independent as these musicians seem, they are, nevertheless, unofficial servants of the government and are constantly asked to make "command performances" at important functions. Dur Mohammed Keshmi, Akbar, Khan-e Baharaki, Islam, and Faiz-e Mangal have been asked in the past to represent Badakhshan at concerts in Kabul and Kunduz. At one rather large and conspicuous wedding in Faizabad—the groom was studying medicine in Germany and had returned to Faizabad for a bride—every important official from the area was invited. Each official brought along

Singer, Dur Mohammed Keshmi with *ghichak*, accompanied by Mohammed Za-hir, *rabāb*, and Mohammed Ibrahim, *zirbaghali*. Chata, Badakhshan province.

the best musicians he could find in his own village or district and referred to them as "his boys." The groom's brother from Kabul brought a famous Radio Afghanistan singer who was treated with more reverence than some local guests.

With the establishment of a government radio station in Kabul in the 1940s, administered through the Ministry of Information and Culture, a new type of musician emerged.[44] Like government bureaucrats, these musicians enjoyed official sanction and support; a majority of them began their musical careers at the radio. They were mainly young amateur musicians from socially established families (members of the extended royal family, or children of prime ministers, generals, or other officials), and their repertoire consisted of newly composed, popular songs. Their singing was accompanied by a large orchestra consisting of a conglomeration of Afghan and some Western instruments (piano, organ, trumpet). They developed a musical style that became distinctly associated with the radio and other government-sponsored institutions (theaters, concerts). These musicians represented a new, modern, and urban class of artists known as *onarman* who were supposed to lend their own respectable standing to music and musicians as a whole. In fact, this respect was limited just to these modern artists, and extended to them only by the urban, middle class. The rest of the society tended to view them as traditional entertainers of low character and status.

On a few occasions I was able to record and talk to *shauqi* musicians specifically. These occasions, however, had to be elaborately manipulated to make a show of a genuine social gathering. The musicians would never come to my house nor invite me to theirs; rather, they found a third party who would host a social gathering where the musicians and I were guests. What we did during the party was then interpreted as a social interaction rather than work. On two such occasions, I recorded Akbar, the *kesbi*, and Mardan, a shopkeeper and resident of Faizabad. Mardan subsequently came to our house on several occasions, but carefully hid his instrument (*dambura* or *rabāb*) under his coat on the way.

Another group of musicians in Badakhshan is the *dalāks*. Within the last century small numbers of Pashtuns from southern and eastern Afghanistan have resettled in parts of Badakhshan. Among these newcomers are a few *dalāk* families. Of the *dalāk* musicians in Badakhshan Province today, most are able to trace their families back to the Kabul and Logar regions within the last two or three generations. They are barbers as well as musicians and are addressed as *khalifa* or *ustād*. Dost Mohammed, for example, is a barber (*salmāni*) in Jurm. Although he was born in Faizabad, his parents were from Logar. He learned to play the *rabāb*, *tambur*, and harmonium from the late Khalifa Yasim, a harmonium player from Faizabad. On the occasion of the governor's visit to Jurm, Faiz-e Mangal and Dost Mohammed were called upon to entertain the guests. Faiz-e Mangal, the *shauqi*, sang and accompanied himself on the *dambura*, while Dost Mohammed, the professional, accompanied Faiz-e Mangal on the *rabāb*. He never sang or played a solo, hardly ever talked, and was definitely placed in a subordinate position. Dost Mohammed claims to be Tajik, but other Badakhshis are quick to point out that his parents are from Logar. Even though both Faiz-e Mangal and Dost Mohammed share similar backgrounds, the contrast between the two is great. The greatest distinguishing factor is Dost Mohammed's birthright as a barber and musician. Many of the *dalak*s are native to Badakhshan, but are still considered "outsiders" by the rest of the population. They continue to form an endogamous group maintained outside the mainstream of society.

Khalifa Gul Jan is another hereditary barber-musician in Faizabad whose father came from Logar. His teacher was also Khalifa Yasim, who was his *khesh*, a maternal relation. Khalifa Gul Jan operates a small barber shop in Faizabad and plays the *tambur* in Akbar's ensemble. Although he claims that the money earned by the ensemble is divided equally among the performers, Akbar or Kaka (uncle), another *shauqi* musician, is obviously the spokesman for the group. Other musicians who sometimes play with the group are hereditary barber-musicians. Khalifa Gul Jan claims to be Tajik. He at first thought that all the musicians with whom he played were *kesbi* because they got paid for their performances, but later he said they were all *shauqi* because each member of the ensemble had another profession besides music.

The other hereditary musicians I observed were the *sornā* and *dohl* players, a *rabāb* player, and a *bāzigar* from Keshm, who performed at the same wedding at which Dur Mohammed played. Although these musicians did not constitute a fixed ensemble in the way of Akbar's group, Dur Mohammed took the role as spokesman and lead musician for these people.

Successful *dalāk* musicians in Herat are proud and haughty; they sport watches, wear fine silk turbans or *karakul* hats, have at least one cosmetic gold tooth and at least until 1978, smoked American cigarettes. Though they are despised as a group, they are important for their exclusive services which are essential for certain rites of passage, and they are somewhat feared for their license publicly to criticize, as well as praise, through the medium of song. In Herat and other parts of southern and eastern Afghanistan, *dalāks* are true music specialists; however, transposed into northeastern Afghanistan, their situation becomes different. They are conservative in appearance and behavior, and they are robbed of their music specialist role by the nonspecialists. Even the frequency of performances by *shauqis* far exceeds that of *dalāks*. Whenever *shauqi* musicians perform with *dalāks*, it is the *shauqi* who displays the more dominant musical as well as social behavior. The reasons for this role reversal are twofold: social and musical. Socially, the services of *dalāks* are no longer exclusive. Musically, the *dalāks* in Badakhshan are mainly instrumentalists. The *dalāks* have lost the real strength of their profession, their exclusiveness and the power of words, the ability to manipulate through their songs.

In Badakhshan as well as in Herat, the hereditary musicians cannot escape their birthright. Notions held about musicians indicate that all *shauqis* are natives of Badakhshan, and *dalāks* are foreigners. Names of *shauqi* musicians emphasize local place names or indicate their personal, almost kin, relationship to others in society, while *dalāk* terms of address reinforce only the impersonal, economic aspect of their profession.

Nonmusicians—those people who were never considered to be musicians at all—in Badakhshan are very similar to the nonmusicians in Herat. There is never a question concerning their professionality. *Gorgholikhāns*, or singers of the *Gorgholi* epic sometimes known as *Kuroghli*, are consid-

ered storytellers rather than musicians. Although they require long and
arduous training in vocal technique and memory, and most accompany
their tales with the *dambura*, none of the *Gorgholikhāns* make their living
solely by singing these tales. Most are farmers living outside the greater
Faizabad area. They sing these tales either in Tajiki (the Persian of northeastern Afghanistan) or Uzbeki.

Other nonmusicians are the women and young girls who entertain at
women's celebrations by singing and playing the *dāira*. They are simply
expected to create a festive atmosphere in which other women can participate by singing and dancing. Coins of appreciation are dropped into their
*dāira*s, but this gesture is interpreted as part of the celebration rather than
as a form of payment.

There are no professional or *shauqi* female musicians in Badakhshan.
A unique situation occurred when Parwin, a famous female Radio Afghanistan singer, came to Badakhshan to arrange the sale of some land owned
by her family. Parwin has the distinction of being one of the first female
radio singers in Afghanistan. She was persuaded to sing for the radio because she has a good voice and because she is related to the royal family.
Her birthright was supposed to provide a bulwark against criticism, and
her decision to sing for the public was made with the hope of improving the
status of women in the entertainment world. In the beginning, a jeep provided by the station would transport Parwin to the studios. Still covered by
a *chāderi*, she would slip in by the back door of the station, tape her songs,
then return home in the same fashion. In 1959 when the mandatory wearing
of the *chāderi* was abolished, Parwin began appearing at the Pohan Nendarei, where her true identity first became known, and received both criticism
and acclaim. By 1972 female singers were no longer a rarity. Many of them,
including Parwin, had been awarded the King's Gold Medal in recognition
of their talents. Parwin was now older, not so beautiful nor so popular as
the younger singers; in Badakhshan, however, she was still a celebrity and
was included among the close associates of government officials. In a sense,
she was treated as a foreigner in much the way I was a foreigner, and was
thus able to deal with a predominantly male world. I was surprised when a
jeep in which we were riding refused to stop for Parwin. The driver, it
seems, didn't approve of women like Parwin and didn't want to have anything to do with her. The majority of the population who knew of her
presence felt the same way; thus, official recognition and acceptance does
not constitute acceptance by the community-at-large.

All musicians outside the greater Faizabad area are considered nonmusicians. Certain families, villages or areas are considered to have better
musicians than others, but there is never a question that they are professional, and no stigma is attached to their activities. Most Badakhshis, in-

Left to right: singers Mohammed Akbar with *daf*, Magul Beg with *daf*, and Adina.
Ishmurgh, a village in the Wakhan, Badakhshan province.

cluding those in the greater Faizabad area, proudly point to the area of
Sheghnan as having the best musicians, as well as the most beautiful
women. Although there may not be a direct relationship between the two
phenomena, women in these outlying areas are freer to mingle with men
than women in urban areas. As urban attitudes creep into these areas, the
women become less free and the musicians become more specialized. The
dambura, ghichak, Pamir *rabāb,* Sheghnan *nai,* and the *dāira* or *daf* are the
traditional instruments played by these nonmusicians.

There is little diversity among the repertoires of various Faizabad musicians. As mentioned previously, the professional musicians are mainly
instrumentalists, while the amateurs and nonmusicians sing local folk
songs such as *falaks* or *ghazals* composed by famous local poets. There is
less reliance on popular radio songs in Faizabad than in Herat.

The distinction between professional, amateur, and nonmusician is
less clear in Badakhshan than in Herat. Traditionally, there has hardly
been a distinction between *shauqi* and nonmusician in Badakhshan. Since
the coming of the hereditary, professional musicians to the greater Fai-

zabad area, the amateur musicians there have felt a need to dissociate themselves somehow from this very professional group through their own terminology and actions. Thus, one finds an almost paranoid behavior on the part of amateur musicians and the term *shauqi* has taken on the added covert meaning of non-*dalāk*. Outside the greater Faizabad area, the term *shauqi* is hardly ever used, simply because all musicians are understood to be amateurs and the question of one's standing is never raised.

MUSICIANS IN KHADIR

The musical situation of Khadir is similar to the situation in Badakh-shan outside the greater Faizabad area, with one exception: the relative scarcity of instruments in the Hazarajat as a whole. Although the *dambura* and *ghichak* are often thought to be Hazara instruments, I found no *ghichak*s and only a few *dambura*s during my 1966–67 and 1972 visits to the area. The few *dambura*s belonging to the Hazaras had been purchased outside the Hazarajat, suggesting that this instrument had recently been adopted from their northern neighbors, the Tajiks. Since the presence of a stringed instrument is a rare and special thing, it obliges the owner-player to function as a semiprofessional musician; however, conceptually, there is no difference between an instrumentalist-vocalist and a vocalist of the nonmusician category found in Herat and Faizabad. Therefore, the term *shauqi* is hardly ever used.

The occasions for musical events are less numerous in Khadir than in Faizabad or Herat. Our presence and the unusual turn of events, however, gave us opportunities to record musicians in an unnatural, unique situation. The nuclear town of Khadir has no physical provisions for visitors. There are no empty homes, or even rooms available for rent. The only way for an outsider to live in Khadir is as someone's guest. Unfortunately, Afghanistan had suffered a severe drought lasting three years and the Hazaras in particular were suffering considerably at the time of our visit. The only one able to care for us was the *wakil* (representative to Parliament) of Dai Kundi, who had returned to his home from Kabul to help distribute wheat to his starving constituents. All able-bodied men, women, and children from the district came to Khadir that autumn in order to get wheat, medical aid, and blankets. The *arbāb*s (village leaders) were in constant contact with the *wakil*, who found it necessary to host a great number of people nightly. The *wakil* took the opportunity to ask the various *arbāb*s to send those musicians present in Khadir to us. Thus, all examples of music from Dai Kundi were recorded in the *wakil*'s guest house under somewhat constrained conditions. Yet, at times, the setting seemed natural as the *wakil*,

Musician, Khadem, playing the *dambura*. Khadir, Hazarajat.

his family, and friends were entertained in their guest house, much as it might happen in other guest houses.

Of the twenty-two different performers recorded, only six were instrumentalists. Of these six instrumentalists, four played the *dambura*, while the other two played the nonlegitimate instruments, the *nai* and *chang*. The four *dambura* players performed on the two *dambura*s available in Khadir, one belonging to Ghulam Sauz and the other to Khadem.

Both Ghulam Sauz and Khadem are closest to being semiprofessional musicians in Khadir, mainly because they own *dambura*s. Ghulam Sauz repairs roads, but likes to entertain at parties, for which he receives gifts of clothing or money. He calls himself a *damburachi*, but is mainly a vocalist. Khadem is a landowner-farmer and had just begun to play the *dambura* when I met him in 1967. Since then his *dambura*-playing has improved tremendously, but his singing has not. This fact is a disadvantage in a place where all music is song-oriented.

The other two *dambura* players are from Dasht-e Nili, the southern part of Dai Kundi District. Arbab Ghulam is a music enthusiast who took

Musician, Bomand, playing the *dambura*. Khadir.

every opportunity to sing for us and arrange other musical performances for us. One of his farmers, Bomand, is a good *dambura* player and singer, and Arbab Ghulam jokingly referred to him as "his teacher." Since both were in Khadir to collect wheat, they had not brought along their instruments, so borrowed the *dambura*s of Ghulam Sauz and Khadem which were left at our disposal in the *wakil*'s home.

The *nai* player is the shepherd of Arbab Qasim, a relative of the *wakil*. He was sent down from the mountains where his sheep were grazing to play specifically for us, returning to his flocks immediately afterwards. His *nai* is an interesting innovation made from a brass tube. Traditional *nai*s are end-blown flutes made from reed pipes. *Tula*, fipple-mouth flutes or horizontal flutes, are often made of brass; thus, this particular instrument seemed to be a combination of the two: a brass, end-blown flute. The *chang* player is Gulu, the *wakil*'s sister. Her instrument was purchased in one of the shops in Khadir.

Since the repertoire of Hazara musicians is predominantly vocal—even the *chang* and *nai* melodies are based on songs—there is no stigma attached to singing songs or playing instruments. Further, men and women are quite free to mix socially. There is an aura of social openness in the Hazarajat not readily found elsewhere. There is no need to distinguish or segregate musician from nonmusician, and the absence of terminology in this aspect is evidence of this lack of concern.

The musician terms commonly used in the three areas are shown in Table 15:

TABLE 15
Musician Terms in the Three Areas

Herāt		Faizābād		Khadir	
Gharib zāda:	HP	*Salmāni/Sar tarush:*	HP	*Damburachi:*	A
Salmāni:	HP	*Ustād:*	HP		
Ustā:	HP	*Khalifa:*	HP		
Jat:	HP	*Bacha/Bāzigar:*	HP		
Magad:	HP	*Dalāk:*	HP		
Moqaled:	HP	*Kesbi:*	P		
Ustād:	HP	*Shauqi:*	A		
Khalifa:	HP	*Gorgholikhān:*	N		
Sāz dohl:	HP				
Bāzigar:	HP				
Dalāk:	HP				
Motreb:	HP				
Sāzenda:	HP				
Kesbi:	P				
Khānenda:	P				
Onarman:	P				
Shauqi:	A				

HP = Hereditary Professional	P = Professional
A = Amateur	N = Non-Musician

Thirteen of the seventeen terms used in Herat refer to hereditary, professional musicians (designated as HP), and three refer to professional musicians (P). Only one term refers to amateur musicians (A), and no specific terms were found for nonmusicians (N). The existence of a relatively large number of descriptive terms for hereditary, professional musicians is evidence that these individuals are clearly recognized as a separate entity or group, while the dearth of descriptive terms for amateur or nonmusician fails to distinguish them sharply from others.

The same may be said for Faizabad musician terms. Eight of the ten terms refer to professional musicians, one to amateur musicians, and one to nonmusicians. The absence of musician terms in Khadir is striking. Only one term, *damburachi*, refers to amateur musicians. Although I have already described the *damburachi* of the Hazarajat as semiprofessional by virtue of the stringed instrument he plays, he is closest in function to the *shauqi* musician of Herat and Badakhshan.

Summary

When comparing the three geographical areas in this study, it becomes obvious that the presence and number of hereditary, professional musicians is the largest factor in determining the number and types of musician terms used in each area. Herat supports the greatest number of hereditary, professional musicians and, therefore, has a great number and variety of corresponding terms. Faizabad has a few hereditary musicians, a fact which is reflected in the smaller number of descriptive terms. Hereditary musicians and corresponding terminology are completely lacking in Khadir.

The language community using these terms is not dependent upon the sophistication, sex, or occupation of the speaker as was the case in considering musical terminology, but upon the status of the speaker. Thus, the pejorative terms *gharib zāda, ustā, jat, dalāk, motreb*, and *sāzenda* are terms of reference used by nonhereditary musicians for hereditary musicians. The terms musicians use to describe themselves are *kesbi, salmāni, magad, shauqi, bāzigar*, and *damburachi. Ustād* and *khalifa* are terms of address and are often incorporated into musician names. All pejorative terms include a sense of birthright or are direct references to music. The other two terms which imply birthright, *salmāni* and *bāzigar*, are, for some reason, more acceptable to hereditary musicians. Perhaps *salmāni* outwardly has no connection to musician and is, therefore, more "respectable." On the other hand, there is no way one can separate *bāzigar* from musician.

Throughout the discussion of musical and musician terms, several features have consistently recurred. These features fall naturally into a system of binary oppositions which give insight into the relationship of the various conditions which influence the final conceptualizations of music and musician:

Music	Literature
Foreign	Native
Professional	Amateur
Instrumental	Vocal
Urban	Rural
Public	Private
Male	Female
Formal	Informal
Specific	General
Segregation	Nonsegregation
Censure	Praise
Variety of Styles	Lack of Variety of Styles
Terminology Abundance	Lack of Terminology

Although Afghanistan as a whole is predominantly Islamic and the people live by the precepts of Islam, the degree and the extent to which people adhere to the general principles of Islam are largely dependent upon the local institutions and mode of life within the setting. Thus, it appears that the more urban the setting, the more strictly the inhabitants view music and musicians, and deal with their view through formalized concepts, censure, and segregation. Musical terms are more numerous, specific, and formal in urban settings than rural ones. The musical performances in urban settings are basically public, executed by professional musicians who are predominantly male. Almost all these performances are purely instrumental or accompanied by musical instruments, and are based on a variety of styles, including classical, popular, and folk traditions. On the whole, there is more concern and stigma attached to the concept of music itself and to the musicians in urban settings; and segregation of females from males, of musician from nonmusician, is maintained in urban settings.

The following chapter presents examples of the setting, the music, and the musicians of the areas of study, with the intention of showing a clear and direct relationship between the cognitive organization of material phenomena and the structure of the material phenomena itself.

CHAPTER SIX

Musical and Conceptual Relationships

The previous chapters have relied mainly on verbal expressions as clues to cognition relating to music and musician. In this chapter, artistic expression in the form of music is examined in the context of the performance situations. Musical examples from each of the three areas concerned in this study are analyzed according to the conceptual categories discussed in chapters 4 and 5.

MUSICAL CONVENTIONS

The majority of the transcriptions that follow are based on examples recorded in the field during 1971–73. A few examples were recorded during 1966–67, and reference is made to that effect. Since the main concern of these transcriptions is to show structural relationships between concept and music, the emphasis is placed on the structure of the melodic and textual lines. Instrumental accompaniment or styles are not transcribed unless they are pertinent to the structure of a piece. Repetitions of melodic or textual units are acknowledged, but not transcribed. The song texts included in the musical transcriptions may differ slightly from the actual transcriptions of poems because the texts included in the musical transcriptions are approximations of the text as sung, and the transcriptions of poems represent the text as spoken.

There is no concept of absolute pitch in these areas of Afghanistan; each individual sings in the range most comfortable for him. Of course, when the voice is accompanied by an instrument, the voice must match the instrument. The harmonium is the only instrument with a fixed pitch in most ensembles, and other instruments usually adjust to the harmonium tuning. But the harmonium itself is not intentionally tuned to any standard pitch.

None of the musicians I recorded read or played from written notes; therefore, no standard notations upon which the transcriptions in this chapter are based exist. The notations in this chapter represent relative rhythm and pitch. Keeping in mind the relative nature of the notation and the arbitrariness of the beginning pitch, the following conventions are used:

Pitch: Examples are written in a way which utilizes the fewest accidentals. For the most part, examples from Herat and Faizabad are based on e'. All examples from Khadir are based on a'. Accidentals placed at the beginning of the staves are for convenience and are not meant to imply a key in the Western sense. All transcriptions of scales are based on c' for easy comparison.

Units: Dotted bar lines represent repeated rhythmic patterns in fixed rhythm sections. Solid bar lines represent the poetic unit of a *misrāᶜ*, or the smallest unit of text that is repeated.

Symbols: ↓ Lower than written.

↑ Higher than written.

♩ ▬ Held beyond the concept of meter.

ŗ ˣ Falsetto.

♪ₓ Spoken, or pitch not clear.

⌒ŗ ŗ ˣ Slide, portamento.

ʊɯɾʊ Incomplete transcription.

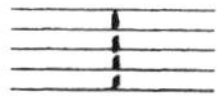

Division of repeated rhythmic patterns.

Division of *misrāᶜ*, or smallest unit of text that is repeated.

Division of stanza.

(wo −) Words or syllables included in parenthesis are not part of the poem.

[+]   Basic pitch.

(• ‾)   Drone string pitches, or notes not part of melodic
                         line.

Notes without rhythmic implications, except for
whole notes which are longer than the other notes,
are used mainly in performances of *shakal*.

Weighted notes of scale:
        ☐   Most important pitch.
        ⊓⊔   Secondary importance.
        •   Others.
        (•)   Ornamental.

MUSICAL EXAMPLES FROM HERAT

Without using special terms, Heratis make a distinction between composed songs and folk songs by indicating the type of poem involved. *Ghazal, du baiti,* or *tasnif* imply composed songs written by known poets or
songs performed by professional musicians in a popular style with instrumental accompaniment. *Chār baiti* indicates folk songs performed by all
types of musicians, with or without instrumental accompaniment.

The *du baiti* is similar in form to the folk *chār baiti*. However, being
the product of a single poet, the quatrains in a *du baiti* follow one another
in a sequence. *Gul-e Zard* is a *du baiti* written by Turābi and sung here by
Mohammed Alishah Olfat Herawi, the owner of the Behzad Nendarei in
1972. He was accompanied by the Behzad Theater Orchestra, consisting of
harmonium, two *rabāb*s, *dutār, delroba,* and *tabla.* The song is in the *Bairami* mode:

Example 1: Mohammed Alishah Olfat Herawi, "Gul-e Zard," *du baiti.*

zard ai gu le   zar de setam gar   de lam- ra ze re pa   kar de kha bar- dar(wo gu le

man)   de lam ra ze re pa   karde khabar- dar (wo gu le man)   ma ba da bar ke shad

a he ji gar   suz -   ma ba   da bar ke shad   a he ji gar   suz   de le   di wa   na am

- dar shahr ba-   zar (wo gu le   man)   de le   di wa na am-   dar shahr ba-   zar (wo gu le

man)   Inst.

Gul-e Zard

Gul-e zard ai gul-e zard-e setam gār
Delamrā zir-e pā kardi khabar dār   (wo gul-e man)
Mabada barkeshad ahe jiggar suz
Del-e diwāna am dar shahr o bāzār.   (wo gul-e man)

Ba del darde ke man dāram ki dāra
Be rokh garde ke man dāram ki dāra   (wo gul-e man)
Musulmānā namidānid bedānid
Gul-e zarde ke man dāram ki dāra.   (wo gul-e man)

Gul-e zarde emshab az yād-e tu mastam
Du chesmāne tu karda mai parastam   (wo gul-e man)
Tu zālem tork-e kāfir pishe kardi
Ghalat kardam ke del dādam be dastam.   (wo gul-e man)

Be yād-e qad-e shamshād-e gul-e zard
Hami nālam ze bidādi-ye gul-e zard   (wo gul-e man)
Newisam daftare bā yād o gāri
Sarāsar dād o bidād be gul-e zard.   (wo gul-e man)

Yellow Flower, oh cruel Yellow Flower
Be informed, you stepped on my heart   (oh, my flower)
I'm afraid lest a liver-burning sigh is released
By my crazy heart in the city and bazaar.   (oh, my flower)

The pain that I have in my heart, who else has it?
The dirt that I have on my face, who else has it?   (oh, my flower)
Muslims, you don't know, you should know
Yellow Flower that I have, who else has her?   (oh, my flower)

Yellow Flower, tonight I am intoxicated thinking of you
Your two eyes made me worship wine   (oh, my flower)
Oppressor, you turned me into a Turkish infidel
I made a mistake when I put my heart in your hands.   (oh, my flower)

Remembering the graceful stature of Yellow Flower
I cry about the unjustness of Yellow Flower   (oh, my flower)
I am writing in a diary as a memoir
All devoted to the injustices of Yellow Flower.   (oh, my flower)

This song is a love song. *Gul-e Zard*, or "Yellow Flower," is a reference to a lover, yellow being for Afghans the symbolic color of lovers. The title consistently appears in all four quatrains consisting of two *bait*s, and the refrain, *wo gul-e man* (Oh, my flower) follows every *bait*. Both these phrases tie all quatrains into a tightly knit whole.

The melodic structure is inextricably tied to the form of the text. The text consists of four quatrains, each with the rhyme scheme *aaba*. The melodic phrase corresponds to the *misrā^c* with the form *abcb*. Both melodic phrases A and B share a downward movement, while the C phrase moves upward. This distinguishes the C phrase from the other phrases and emphasizes the uniqueness of the third *misrā^c*, which does not rhyme with the other *misrā^c*s. Further, melodic phrase B is one measure longer than phrases A or C, and corresponds to the phrase length of the instrumental introduction and interludes (*naghma*). The extra measure is sung to the short textual refrain, *wo gul-e man*, which is not an integral part of the poem. This extra measure serves to accentuate the basic unit of the poem, the *bait*. The *naghma* is heard after every quatrain.

The entire song consists of an alternation between instrumental *naghma* and vocal *khāndan* consisting of four *misrā^c*s:

>   *Naghma*
>   *Khāndan*   (2 *bait*s)
>   *Naghma*
>   *Khāndan*   (2 *bait*s)
>   *Naghma*
>   *Khāndan*   (2 *bait*s)
>   *Naghma*
>   *Khāndan*   (2 *bait*s)

The last *misrā^c* of the last *khāndan* is repeated three times, and the orchestra ends the piece by suddenly changing from a triple accent to a duple accent:

Both the devices of repetition and the triple to duple accentual change in the closing phrases are stylistic features of the popular radio and theater style.

An instrumental version of *Gul-e Zard*, which was recorded in Kabul, is used here as a comparison to Example 1. The performer, Abdul Rahman Saljuqi, was a high school English teacher in Kabul. Originally from Herat, he is a member of a famous literary family who are descendants of the Saljuqs, a Turkish dynasty which ruled territories in Central Asia in the eleventh and twelfth centuries. Abdul Rahman is a dilettante in the finer sense of the word. He is a knowledgeable and talented musician who is far from being a professional, yet he is too learned to be called a folk musician. He performed for family and friends at informal social gatherings on the *chārtār* (a plucked lute) known as *tār* in Iran.

Abdul Rahman gave the title *Gul-e Zard*, but called it a *tasnif*. Although the example is purely instrumental, the piece itself is based on a song. He also identified the mode as *Bairami*:

Example 2: Abdul Rahman Saljuqi, *chārtār*, "Gul-e Zard," *tasnif*.

The example begins with a short introductory prelude known in Herat as *shakal*. The *shakal* outlines the melodic mode and emphasizes the altered second degree used in ascending passages, a characteristic of the *Bairami* mode.

The melody follows the melody of Example 1 quite closely and even coincides with the length of the melodic phrases of Example 1 (Table 16). Therefore, it can be assumed that *Gul-e Zard* has developed a standard form involving four quatrains. Even the repetition of each *misrā^c* is mirrored in the instrumental example, except for the repetition of the second *misrā^c* in each quatrain which is lacking in the instrumental example. The instrumental example marks each section, the *naghma* section and the *khāndan* section, by extending the melodic phrase one or two measures. Such a device is not necessary in the vocal example because the sections are

TABLE 16
A Comparison of the Melodic Phrase Structures of *Gul-e Zard*

Example 1: Vocal			Example 2: Instrumental		
Section	*Phrases*	*Measures*	*Section*	*Phrases*	*Measures*
Naghma	. . .	4	*Shakal*	. . .	. . .
	. . .	4		. . .	. . .
Khāndan	A	3	*Khāndan*	A	3
	A	3		A	3
	B	4		B	4
	B	4		. . .	. . .
	C	3		C	3
	C	3		C	3
	B	4		B	4
	B	4		B′	6
*(left side: * line)*					
Naghma	. . .	4	*Naghma*	. . .	4
	. . .	4	*Naghma′*	. . .	5
*(right side: * line)*					
Khāndan	A	3	*Khāndan*	A	3
	A	3		A	3
	B	4		B	4
	B	4		. . .	. . .
	C	3		C	3
	C	3		C	3
	B	4		B	4
	B	4		B′	6
Naghma	. . .	4	*Naghma*	. . .	4
	. . .	4	*Naghma′*	. . .	5
Khāndan	A	3	*Khāndan*	A	3
	A	3		A	3
	B	4		B	4
	B	4		. . .	. . .
	C	3		C	3
	C	3		C	3
	B	4		B	4
	B	4		B′	6
Naghma	. . .	4	*Naghma*	. . .	4
	. . .	4	*Naghma′*	. . .	5
Khāndan	A	3	*Khāndan*	A	3
	A	3		A	3
	B	4		B	4
	B	4		. . .	. . .
	C	3		C	3
	C	3		C	3
	B	4		B	4
	B	4		. . .	. . .
	B′	6		B′	6

*Only the section above these lines has been notated.

easily identified by the presence or absence of the voice. However, the device of extension is used at the very end of the song.

The instrumental example of *Gul-e Zard* shows just how dependent most instrumental pieces are upon songs. Whether the text is sung or not, it plays an important part in determining musical phrases and repetitions.

The performance of a short introductory prelude is characteristic of instrumental solos played by performers with a classical orientation. Where a song is involved, a *fard* (a line of verse) is often sung in free rhythm. Even when the piece is strictly instrumental, but based on a song, the *shakal* is often developed on a theoretical *fard*.

Example 3 is an example identified as *du baiti* although the poet was not known to the performer, Ghulam Dastegir Sarud, a singer at the Behzad Nendarei at the time of the recording. This song is also accompanied by the Behzad orchestra and in the *Bairami* mode:

Example 3: Ghulam Dastegir Sarud, "Sarwe Gulpusham," *du baiti.*

Sarwe Gulpusham

Fard:

Sarwe gulpusham ghārat-e husham
Makon farāmusham biyā dar aghusham

As an ruzi ke bimārat shoda del   (nakoni yādam cherā)
Be sadhā gham gereftārat shoda del   (nakoni yādam cherā)
Be bāzār-e jamālat kaifare ruz   (nakoni yādam cherā)
Be naqde jān kharidārat shoda del   (nakoni yādam cherā)

Biyā ai mones-e shabhā-ye āsheq   (nakoni yādam cherā)
Biyā ai shukh-e biparwāz-e āsheq   (nakoni yādam cherā)
Du cheshman kur gashta az ferāghat   (nakoni yādam cherā)
Biyā ai didae binā-ye āsheq   (nakoni yādam cherā)

Biyā jānā dame dar khāna-ye del   (nakoni yādam cherā)
Ke gerdat parzanad parwāna-ye del   (nakoni yādam cherā)
Mai-ye del jān o del mai khāna-ye del   (nakoni yādam cherā)
Sar o jān del jānāna-ye del   (nakoni yādam cherā)

Cypress tree covered with flowers, robber
    of my senses
Don't forget me, come into my arms.

From that day my heart became ill   (why don't you remember me?)
My heart was seized by a hundred sorrows (why don't you remember me?)
In the bazaar your beauty, the reward of the
    day   (why don't you remember me?)
At the expense of my soul I'm willing to buy
    my love.   (why don't you remember me?)

Come O companion of my amorous nights   (why don't you remember me?)
Come O cheerful, careless one of mine   (why don't you remember me?)
My two eyes were blinded from separation (why don't you remember me?)
Come O sight, sight of my love.   (why don't you remember me?)

Come sweetheart for a moment into my heart's
    home   (why don't you remember me?)
So that the butterfly of my heart can fly around
    you   (why don't you remember me?)
Wine of my heart, heart and soul, tavern of my
    heart   (why don't you remember me?)
Heart and soul of my heart, sweetheart of my
    heart.   (why don't you remember me?)

Example 3 differs slightly from the *du baiti* in Example 1. The quatrains are held together by a single *bait* or *fard* which is employed as a refrain. The title is taken from the first words of the *fard* and does not appear in any of the quatrains. The overall organization of *Sarwe Gulpusham* is not so tight as *Gul-e Zard*, and may be the result of assembling a number of appropriate quatrains into a whole, an acceptable technique in folk songs.

The *fard* is perhaps taken from the *matla^c* of a *ghazal*, as both of its *misrā^c*s rhyme. The quatrains have the rhyme scheme of *aaba*. The melody does not seem to follow the rhyme scheme, but instead, each *misrā^c* is sung to the same melody, except for the last *misrā^c*, which is sung to a new phrase.

The added refrain, *nakoni yādam cherā*, follows each quatrain, thereby increasing the melodic phrase length by one measure (Table 17).

TABLE 17
Melodic and Textual Phrase Structure of *Sarwe Gulpusham*

Section	Phrase	Measures	Rhyme
Naghma	. . .	4	. . .
Naghma'	. . .	5	. . .
Khāndan (Fard)	A	4	a
	A	4	a
	B	4	a
	B	4	a
Naghma	. . .	4	. . .
Naghma	. . .	4	. . .
Naghma'	. . .	5	. . .
Khāndan	C	5	b
	C	5	b
	C	5	c
	D	5	b *
(Fard)	A	4	a
	A	4	a
	B	4	a
	B	4	a
Naghma	. . .	4	. . .
Naghma	. . .	4	. . .
Naghma'	. . .	5	. . .
Khāndan	C	5	d
	C	5	d
	C	5	e
	D	5	d
(Fard)	A	4	a
	A	4	a
	B	4	a
	B	4	a
Naghma	. . .	4	. . .
Naghma	. . .	4	. . .
Naghma'	. . .	5	. . .
Khāndan	C	5	f
	C	5	f
	C	5	f
	D	5	f
(Fard)	A	4	a
	A	4	a
	B	4	a
	B'	7	a

*The section above the line has been notated.

Sarwe Gulpusham was performed in the popular style with instrumental introduction and interludes. Each section ends with a measure extension and a rhythmic change from three to two. The end of the piece is extended three measures. The singer, however, does not repeat the last *misrāᶜ* three times.

The *ghazal* is one of the most popular composed song forms throughout Afghanistan. Example 4, *Rafiq Kārawān*, was sung by Mohammed Ibrahim Enayat, also a singer at the Behzad Nendarei. The mode is again *Bairami*, which seems to be the most commonly used mode for composed songs:

Example 4: Mohammed Ibrahim Enayat, "Rafiq Karawan," *ghazal*.

Rafiq Kārawān

Matla^c:

Rafiq-e kārawān gashtam, ke tai sāzam biābānrā
Kashidam andaren sahrā, setamhā-ye muqilānrā

Kharidāre mohabatrā, gereftāre junun didam
Sar-e diwāna khosh dārad, hujum-e sang-e teflānrā

Hekāyathā-ye shirinrā, shabi bā cheshme tar goftam
Be kuyi bisetun bordam, deli ghamgin wa hairānrā

Deli zar-e labibirā, be tār-e, zolf-e khod basti
Be kam-e dushmanān kardi, shekasti ahdo paimānrā

I became a friend of the caravan, in order to cross the desert
I endured in this desert, the cruelties of the Egyptian thorn.

I saw a buyer of love, going mad
His tortured head enjoys, the rush of children's stones.

One night I told sweet stories, with tears in my eyes
To a world without support, I carried my sad and perplexed heart.

You tied Labibi's poor heart, with a single hair of your locks
You fulfilled my enemies' desires, you broke your promise.

The title is taken from the first words of the *matla*[c] of this *ghazal*. The *matla*[c] is thereafter used as a refrain. Each *bait* ends with the rhyme -*ān rā*, and the *takhallus* (poet's pen name), Labibi, appears in the last *bait* or *maqta*[c].

Again, the musical structure is consistent with the poetic structure as shown in Table 18 (see p. 122). The piece begins with a *naghma* of six measures which is repeated and lengthened by one measure. This extension technique used to mark off important sections is a prominent device of songs in the popular style. The melodic refrain, based on the *matla*[c], consists of melodic phrase A, which is repeated three times and corresponds to half a *misrā*[c]. The final half of the second *misrā*[c], which corresponds to the end of the *bait* or *matla*[c], is a slight variation of A, indicated by A', which is repeated. The whole *matla*[c] refrain is repeated. The subsequent *baits* are sung to melodic phrases B and C, each corresponding to half a *misrā*[c], and ends with the return of melodic phrase A to emphasize the return of the rhyme scheme. The rhyme scheme of only the *misrā*[c]s has been indicated in Table 18; however, there are rhymes at the half *misrā*[c]s also.

The transcription is based upon the first two *matla*[c]s and verse of the performance, where halves of the first *misrā*[c] of the *bait* are not repeated; however, in the subsequent verses each half of each *misrā*[c] is repeated. The last phrase of the song is repeated three times and the orchestra ends with two extra measures of displaced rhythm.

The *ghazal* in Example 5 was sung by Mrs. Nafisa, a singer at the Herat Nendarei, where she had worked for seven years. Her teacher was Mohammed Alishah Olfat, who owned the Behzad Nendarei. She was accompanied by the Herat Nendarei Orchestra, which did not differ greatly from that of the Behzad Nendarei:

Example 5: Mrs. Nafisa, "Belā Ai Del," *ghazal*.

del- geshti ba ja nam- mis li ba la del- dar ko he khu

ban ba kho da raf ti che ra del dar ko he khu ban ba khoda rafti che ra

del Inst.

gu yam ha qi qat-

ai khu ba ru- yan- gu yam ha qi qat- ai khu ba ru- yan-

qad re na da ran- naz de sho ma del- qa dre na da ran (ba kho da)

nazde sho ma del geshti ba ja nam- mis li ba la del-

geshti ba ja nam- mis li ba la del- dar kohe khu ban ba kho da

raf ti che ra del dar kohe khu ban ba khoda rafti che ra del

Belā Ai Del

Matla^c:

Geshti ba jānam misle balā ai del
Dar kuyi khubān ba khodā raft cherā del

Guyam haqiqat ai khuba ruyān
Qadre nadārad nazde shomā del

TABLE 18
Melodic and Textual Phrase Structure of *Rafiq Kārawān*

Section	Phrase	Measures	Rhyme	
Naghma	. . .	6	. . .	
Naghma'	. . .	7	. . .	
Khāndan (Matlaᶜ)	A	2	. . .	
	A	2	a	
	A	2	. . .	
	A′	2	a	
	A′	2	a	
(Matlaᶜ)	A	2	. . .	
	A	2	a	
	A	2	. . .	
	A′	2	a	
	A′	2	a	
Naghma	. . .	6	. . .	
Naghma'	. . .	7	. . .	
Khāndan	B	2	. . .	
	B	2	b	
	C	2	. . .	
	C	2	. . .	
	A	2	a	
	A′	2	a	*
(Matlaᶜ)	A	2	. . .	
	A	2	a	
	A	2	. . .	
	A′	2	a	
	A′	2	a	
Naghma	. . .	6	. . .	
Naghma'	. . .	7	. . .	
Khāndan	B	2	. . .	
	B	2	. . .	
	B	2	c	
	B	2	c	
	C	2	. . .	
	C	2	. . .	
	A	2	a	
	A′	2	a	
(Matlaᶜ)	A	2	. . .	
	A	2	a	
	A	2	. . .	
	A′	2	a	
	A′	2	a	
Naghma	. . .	6	. . .	
Naghma'	. . .	7	. . .	
Khāndan	B	2	. . .	
	B	2	. . .	
	B	2	d	
	B	2	d	
	C	2	. . .	
	C	2	. . .	
	A	2	a	
	A′	2	a	
(Matla)	A	2	. . .	
	A	2	a	
	A	2	. . .	
	A′	2	a	
	A′	2	a	
	A′	5	a	

*The section above the line has been notated.

Bā tigh-e abru ān shukh badhui
Zad zakhme kāri ākher turā del

Koshti marā del ba khodā koshti marā del.

You became a devil to my soul, O Love
By God, why were you attracted by the beautiful ones, oh my heart.

O beauties, shall I tell the truth
A heart has no worth to you.

With the sword of her eyebrow, that playful, angry one
Finally gave you, O heart, a mortal wound.

O Love, you killed me, by God, you killed me!

The title is again taken from the *matla^c* of the *ghazal*. This *ghazal* differs from the standard form, in that it only consists of a *matla^c* and two verses; the *takhallus* is missing, and an extra line—a kind of commentary— is added. The extra line can be considered a *pāzarb*, in that it consists of a short repeated phrase which carries the rhyme scheme of the poem: *Koshti marā del ba khodā koshti marā del.*

The *matla^c* is sung to melodic phrases A and B and functions as a refrain, shown in Table 19 (see p. 125). The first *misrā^c* of each subsequent verse is sung to melodic phrase C, while the second *misrā^c* is sung to refrain melody, A and B. The second *misrā^c* of the second verse (excluding the *matla^c*) is sung to phrase A, but the *pāzarb* sung to phrase B is added; thus, each verse ends consistently. The last *misrā^c* of the song is repeated three times and the orchestra ends with a displaced rhythm pattern.

Another example of the *ghazal, Zabān-e Shekwa,* was sung by Mohammed Farhat of the Herat Nendarei. This singer is an amateur miniaturist, singer, and composer. The poem is by Wafa Saljuqi, the brother of Abdul Rahman Saljuqi, the performer in Example 2 above, and the *tarz* (or melody) was composed by the singer, Mohammed Farhat:

Example 6: Mohammed Farhat, "Zaban-e Shekwa," *ghazal.*

za ba- ne- shek wa gar dar- pish e ya rom- wa na mi- kar-

dam za ba- ne- shek wa gar dar- pish e ya rom- wa na mi- kar-

dam be baz- le- mo da hi raf- ti na kha ram- shah na mi- kar-

dam be baz- le- mo da hi raf- ti na kha ram- shah na mi- kar -

dam   Inst.

Naghma

Khandan B

na bud- a- gar a qeb e- ma- ka si- dar-

del ne han e man na bud- a- gar a qeb e- ma- ka si- dar

del ne han e man a gar- be- khake ku yat- del ba ra ghau

gha na mi- kar- dam a gar- be kha ke ku yat- del ba ra ghau

Naghma

gha na mi- kar- dam

Zabān-e Shekwa

Matla^c:

Zabān-e shekwa gar dar pish-e yārom wā namikardam
Be bazle modahi rafti na khāram shāh namikardam

Nabud agar aqeb-e man kasi dar del nehān-e man
Agar be khāk-e kuyat delbarā ghaughā namikardam

Khiāl-e zolf-e mushkin-e tu dishab borda khāb-e man
Che mikardam agar tā sob bedān saudā namikardam

Sereshk-e dida afshā kard o rāze sinaam warne
Be bāzār-e mohabat khisharā roswā namikardam

Wafārā bi wafā pandam shodand ai post-e jān-e man
Man az tu in gamān ai shukh-e māh simā namikardam

TABLE 19
Melodic and Textual Phrase Structure of *Belā Ai Del*

Section	Phrase	Measures	Rhyme
Naghma	. . .	4	. . .
Naghma'	. . .	5	. . .
Khāndan (Matla^c)	A	4	a
	A	4	a
	B	4	a
	B	4	a
Naghma	. . .	4	. . .
Naghma'	. . .	5	. . .
Khāndan	C	4	b
	C	4	b
	A	4	a
	B	4	a
(Matla^c)	A	4	a
	A	4	a
	B	4	a
	B	4	a
Naghma	. . .	4	. . .
Naghma'	. . .	5	. . .
Khāndan	C	4	c
	C	4	c
	A	4	a
	A	4	a
(Pāzarb)	B	4	a
(Matla^c)	A	4	a
	A	4	a
	B	4	a
	B	4	a
	B'	7	a

*The section above the line has been notated.

If I hadn't opened my complaining mouth in front of my love
You would have followed the enemy's advice; I would be neither poor nor a king.

If there wasn't anyone in back of my secret heart
If I hadn't cried in the dust of your alley

Thinking of your musky hair, I couldn't sleep last night
What else could I have done until dawn if I hadn't?

She revealed her tears and made me reveal my heart's secrets
I wouldn't have made a fool of myself among the society of lovers

I learned about loyalty from your inconstancy, O dear one
I wasn't expecting such things from you, O moon-faced coquette.

   Everything that has been discussed about composed songs can be applied to this example. The music follows the poetic form very closely. The basic rhyme scheme and the melodic material are contained in the *matla^c*. Thereafter, each time the rhyme reappears, it is sung to the melodic material from the *matla^c*. The only new melodic material coincides with *misrā^c*s that do not contain the rhyme. A feature which has not previously been discussed is the relationship of the poetic meter to the melodic rhythm. Here, in Example 6, the *hajaz-e musamman-e sālim* meter, ‿ - - - repeated eight times, is followed faithfully in the music:

   The popular style consists of alternating instrumental and vocal sections known as *naghma* and *khāndan*, respectively. The instrumental introduction and interludes consist of a phrase which is repeated and lengthened by one or two measures. If the song is a *ghazal*, as in this case, the first *bait* or *matla^c* is used as a refrain and is sung after each subsequent verse. The melodic material of the subsequent verses always contains melodic material from the *matla^c* in order to recall the rhyme scheme. The final *misrā^c* of the song is repeated three times and the instrumental ending of the song is characterized by an accentual change in meter.

   Example 7, *Sarhadi*, is a *dutār* solo accompanied by a *tabla*. The performers, Ghulam Haidar and Mohammed Karim, were members of the Behzad Nendarei orchestra. Ghulam Haidar became my *dutār* teacher a few months after this recording was made.

   This piece differs considerably from the other songs performed by theater musicians, in that, first, it is in the *Bairo* mode:

Bairo

and second, it consists of an alternation of a rhythmically free section with a rhythmically fixed section. It was not until later that I learned this piece is based on a regional song, *Sarhadi*, which is sung in free rhythm. The two

Example 7: Ghulam Haidar, *Sarhadi, dutār naghma.*

Naghma II

sections in fixed rhythm function as instrumental interludes, but take on added importance and individual characteristics in this instrumental performance, by including entirely different material in the two interludes, by their relatively long duration, and by the second interlude's position at the close of the piece.

The section in free rhythm is not as free as it first appears. Because the section begins the performance, one may think of it as a *shakal*, but the fact that it returns again without much alteration determines that it is not a *shakal*. A study of a vocal performance of *Sarhadi* (Example 8) led me to believe that the section in free rhythm is related to the classical Persian *āvāz*, a classical song performed in free rhythm, but realizing the poetic meter by relatively long and short durations.[1]

Example 8: Zainab, *Sarhadi*, *chār baiti*.

Sarhadi

Gham-e eshqat biāban parwaram kard
Hawāyat morghe-e bi bal o param kard (jān-e man wi)
Khodat migi sabrui kon sabrui
Sabrui khāk-e ālam bā saram kard (wi)

Fard:

Alā ai delbar-e man delbar-e man
Chi wāqhe shod ke rafti az bar-e man (wi)

Pāzarb:

Shirin dokhtar-e māldār be sar mezana kaldār
Hami khālā negindār khodā bāsha negahdār

Du abruyat marā diwāna karda
Majāwar bā dare bot khāna karda (jān-e man wi)
Ba abruyat qasam ai yār-e shirin
Marā az qaum o khesh bigāna karda (wi)

Fard:

Alā ai del nadārom del nadārom
Digar tāqat be zi manzel nadārom

Du dandānat telā bāshad gul-e man
Negahwānat khodā bāshad gul-e man (jān-e man wi)
Agar khun-e marā pāi māl sāzi
Hanuz az man wafā bāshad gul-e man (wi)

The sadness of your love drove me to the desert
Your love made me a bird without wings or feathers
You are telling me to wait, wait
This waiting has put the dust of the world on my head.

O, my love, my love
What happened to make you desert me?

Sweet nomad girl, she puts coins around her head
All her spots are like jewels, may God keep her.

Your eyebrows drove me mad
They have turned me into a doorkeeper of a temple
I swear to your eyebrows, O sweet friend
I am alienated from my family and friends.

O, I have no heart, I have no heart
I can't endure this house any longer.

Your front teeth should be gold, my flower
May God keep you, my flower
If you should step on my blood
I would still be loyal, my flower.

The poetic meter of the "apocopated hexameter hazaj" which Browne attributes to Persian dialect poetry is definitely realized in the vocal performance.[2] Referring back to the instrumental example, I found that it also loosely outlines the same rhythm. Further, the melodic phrase of the first and third *hazaj* patterns end on a half cadence, and the second and fourth patterns end on a full cadence. This corresponds to the vocal version which ends the first and third *misrā^c* on a half cadence and the second and fourth *misrā^c* on the full cadence. The end of each phrase is extended in both versions.

The vocal version was sung by Zainab, the daughter of Golpasand. She is reputed to be the best female *motreb* in Herat. She accompanied herself on the harmonium and was assisted by Ghulam Haidar on *dutār* and Amir Mohammed on *tabla*. *Sarhadi* was the last of three songs meant as a single performance. The first two songs are in the *Bairami* mode and sung by Zainab and her two nieces. The final song, *Sarhadi*, is a solo by Zainab. A short *shakal* is played by the harmonium and *dutār*.

Because *Sarhadi* is a folk song, there is some freedom in the choice of verses sung, as well as the addition of appropriate verses. The number of repetitions of a musical phrase is dependent upon the harmonium player. If the harmonium player wants to repeat a phrase, he simply does so and the other instruments follow. But on the other hand, if he wants to conclude the section, he holds the note for an extra measure and the drummer plays a cadential pattern. Therefore, the repetition of phrases or sections need not be consistent. In Example 8 the first *naghma* is repeated once, but the second *naghma* is played three times; the first two quatrains are followed by a *fard* before entering the *pāzarb* section; the last quatrain is not.

Textually, the *pāzarb* is composed of short rhyming phrases which do not necessarily fit the poetic meter of the verses. Musically, the *pāzarb* acts as a refrain in fixed rhythm. The *naghma* consists of a four-measure phrase which is repeated and extended. The song ends with an accentual displacement of the meter.

Although *Sarhadi* is a folk song, both performances (Examples 7 and 8) are in the popular style with a recurring *naghma*, extension of the last phrases of a section, and the use of rhythmic displacements at the end.

Another example with a similar name, *Sarhadi Ghoriāni*, is included here for comparison. The transcription is based on a performance by Ghulam Haidar. The recording was made for a 2-1/2 minute film; therefore, the number of phrases and repetitions is limited:

Example 9: Ghulam Haidar, *Sarhadi Ghoriāni, dutār naghma*.

Sarhadi Ghoriāni was the first *dutār* piece taught me by Ghulam Haidar. Although it was taught as an instrumental piece, Haidar called it a *chār baiti*. When I asked him why an instrumental piece is called *chār baiti*, he answered that *chār baiti* quatrains are sung to *Sarhadi Ghoriāni*, and he sang a quatrain to show its relation to the music.

The melodic rhythm corresponds exactly to the apocopated hexameter *hazaj* rhythm encountered in Examples 7 and 8, a pattern most appropriately realized in the *mogholi* rhythm of seven. The dotted bar lines are placed according to the *mogholi* pattern of 3+2+2 taught to me by Haidar:

The last syllable of the *misrāᶜ* is twice the length of other long syllables in this example. The last syllable of any *misrāᶜ* is consistently emphasized by an agogic accent which equals or exceeds the longest syllable in a *misrāᶜ*. Sometimes the end of a *misrāᶜ* is held beyond the concept of meter and is followed by a pause; the rhythmic pulse of the phrase then ceases at the end of such a *misrāᶜ* (see Example 8 above).

Another instrumental example called *Sarhadi* was recorded in Kabul. Abdul Rahman, the performer, called it "*chār baiti* or *sarhadi* in the *Bairami* mode." This example is also in the *mogholi* rhythm. The poetic meter is apparent, but a phrase corresponds to only four *hazaj* patterns instead of six. It is difficult to ascertain whether the performer had a quatrain in mind or whether this was an abstract performance. The latter supposition is based on the premise that Abdul Rahman Saljuqi is an amateur musician who does not sing or accompany others as Ghulam Haidar, a professional musician, does. It is, therefore, feasible that Abdul Rahman was not cognizant of the poetic implications in *Sarhadi*.

Example 10: Abdul Rahman Saljuqi, *Sarhadi* in *Bairami*, *chārtār*.

Besides the importance of the realization of the poetic meter in all *Sarhadi* melodies, they share enough similar melodic characteristics to be considered a single melody type. Although Examples 7 and 8 are in the *Bairo* mode and Examples 9 and 10 are in the *Bairami* mode, the *khāndan* or main melody in every example begins by stressing the fifth degree of the mode before descending to the first degree. The *naghma* section in every example begins by stressing the fourth degree before descending to the first degree. The two modes used in *Sarhadi* melodies may be related, in that only the third degree differs between the two. This relationship between the two modes will be discussed further in the following section on the *chār baiti* melody type.

Pure folk melodies called *chār baiti* also stress the apocopated hexameter *hazaj* rhythm of the quatrains. Saman Jan, a nomad girl who moved into the city to find work as a domestic servant, sang three examples of *chār baiti*, each consisting of a number of quatrains to the same melody and rhythm:

Example 11: Saṃan Jan, *chār baiti*.

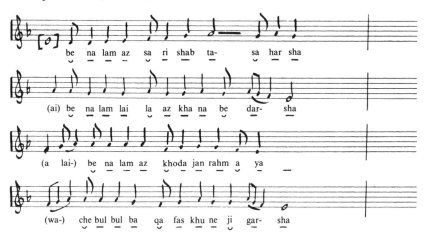

Chār Baiti

Be nālam az sar-e shab tā sahar sha
Be nālam lailā az khāna bedar sha
Be nālam az khodā jān rahm aya
Che bul bul bā qafas khun-e jigar sha

I will cry from dusk to dawn
I will cry until Laila comes out of the house
I will cry for mercy from dear God
Like a nightingale saddened by her cage.

The same melody was recorded in Neshin, Herat, in 1966. It also was called a *chār baiti*:

Example 12: Habibullah, *chār baiti*.

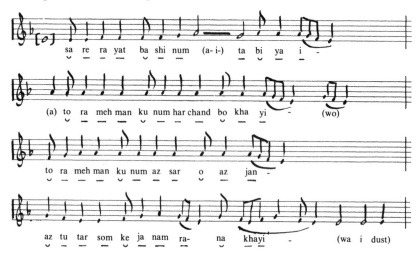

sa re ra yat ba shi num (a- i-) ta bi ya i -

(a) to ra meh man ku num har chand bo kha yi - (wo)

to ra meh man ku num az sar o az jan -

az tu tar som ke ja nam ra- na khayi - (wa i dust)

Chār Baiti

Sar-e rāhyat bashinum tā biyāi
Torā mehman konom har chand bekhāhi
Torā mehman konom az sar o az jān
Az tu tarsom ke jānamra nakhāhi

Until you come, I will sit and wait on your path
I will make you my guest whatever the cost
I will make you my guest with body and soul
I'm afraid you might ask for my soul.

The melodies are based on a diminished tetrachord of the *Bairami* mode, or on an intermediary tetrachord of the *Bairo* mode:

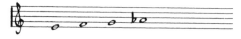

The melodies ascend to the fourth degree, stress the fourth degree as a reciting tone, then descend to the first degree again. Although both songs are unaccompanied and in free rhythm, the poetic meter is consistently outlined in a recitative style. The term *chār baiti*, then, signifies a melody type as well as a poetic form.[3]

Because *Sarhadi, Sarhadi Ghoriāni,* and *Chār baiti* are solidly based on the *chār baiti* quatrain and meter, they may have developed from the same source. Although the melody types are in three different modes, the modes do not differ radically:

The modes differ mainly in the size of one interval. The diminished fourth in *Chār Baiti* becomes a perfect fourth in *Sarhadi Ghoriāni*, while the minor third in *Sarhadi Ghoriāni* becomes a major third in *Sarhadi*. I am not suggesting that one melody type developed out of the other, but I am suggesting that a close relationship exists between the *Sarhadi* and *Chār Baiti* melody types, including the modes in which they are set.

Another Herati melody-type, *Aushāri*, is more problematical. Five different examples were identified as *Aushāri*, but they differed in modal characteristics. The first example (Example 13) is by Mohammed Omar on *sornā* and Khalifa Dohlchi Sarwar on *dohl*. The musicians were invited to our compound in Herat for the express purpose of recording traditional Herat songs. The musicians played two medleys, *Aushāri* being the second tune in the second medley. *Aushāri* was described as music for *chob bāzi*, a stick dance performed by a group of men. I had previously witnessed this type of dance in Gulran, Herat Province, and as far away as the Kama Valley in eastern Afghanistan. The dancers in Gulran were Baluches; those in Kama were Sikhs.

Melodically, the scale, transposed to e′, is as follows:

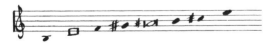

The melody consists of two motives, one emphasizing the first degree, and the other the fourth degree:

Example 13: Mohammed Omar, *Aushāri, sornā.*

Motive 1:

Motive 2:

Except for the augmented fourth degree which is used in an ornamental passage, Motive 1 seems to be in the *Bairo* mode, yet the second motive emphasizes this augmented fourth degree to a considerable extent. Many notes of the *sornā* are approximated or ornamented by the player; thus, it is difficult for me to ascertain whether the augmented fourth is meant or not. The rhythm, a fast six, is consistent with the other *Aushāri* examples.

The second *Aushāri* example (Example 14) was played on the *tula* by Abdul Rashid, a Turkmen silo worker who had been playing with the Herat Nendarei orchestra for a year. The motives of the *tula Aushāri* example are mainly based on the fourth degree of the mode and do not descend to the tonic until the end.

Example 14: Abdul Rashid, *Aushāri, tula.*

Motive 1:

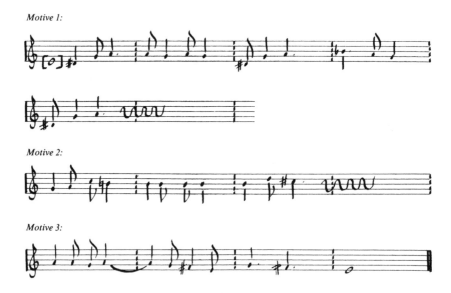

Motive 2:

Motive 3:

Again, the mode is in question, since the *tula*, like the *sornā*, plays many ornamented and altered tones that may or may not be part of the mode. The scale, transposed to e', is as follows:

The third example of *Aushāri* is the *naghma* section of a song, *Jāma Nārenji*. The singer was Amir Mohammed, accompanied by Ghulam Haidar on the *dutār*. The mode was first identified by Amir Mohammed as *Jog*, but Haidar corrected him by saying that I would not understand *Jog*, but would know *Bairo*. The two terms are apparently synonymous and I did not encounter the term again until Badakhshan.

The *naghma* sections are exactly the same as the *naghma* sections of Example 7. Both *naghma* melodies are similar to the *tula* example, in that the melody revolves mainly around the fourth degree of the mode and does not descend to the tonic until the end. Where the tonic does appear in the beginning motives, it acts as a dominant to the fourth degree rather than as a tonic.

The fourth *Aushāri* example is a *dutār* solo by Ghulam Haidar, accompanied on the *zirbaghali* by Amir Mohammed:

Example 15: Ghulam Haidar, *Aushāri, dutār*.

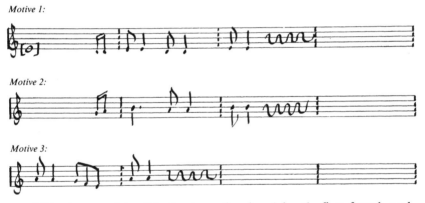

Motive 1:

Motive 2:

Motive 3:

This piece consists of rhythmic motives involving the first, fourth, and fifth degrees of the scale. The rhythm is again a fast meter of six, with an iambic rhythm (♪ ♩) characteristic shared by the other *Aushāri* examples. The mode is *Bairami*. It is interesting that both the previous example and this one are played by the same artist, yet the mode differs; thus, it is apparent that *Aushāri* is identified by its rhythmic motives and melody type rather than by its mode.

The fifth and final example of *Aushāri* is again played by Ghulam Haidar as an accompaniment to a dance by Amir Mohammed. The dance is not a *chob bāzi*, but the melodic motives are similar to the *naghma* sections of *Jāma Nārenji* in the *Bairo* mode. In every example of *Aushāri* the rhythm is in a fast meter of six with an iambic rhythm motive. The piece in all cases is purely instrumental and said to be an accompaniment for a dance. From an examination of the above examples, it can be said that the melody type consists of short repeated motives emphasizing the fourth degree of the mode. The movement is generally a descending one.

The evidence associating *Aushāri* with the Iranian mode of *Afshāri* is still inconclusive, yet a number of *Afshāri* characteristics can be seen in the *Aushāri* examples. First, Zonis[4] explains that *Afshāri* is an auxiliary mode of *Shur*, which has a scale like the Western natural minor scale, with a lowered second degree or a phrygian mode with a raised second degree: C, D♭, E♭, F♭, G♭, A♭, B♭, C.[5] This scale is close to the *Bairami* mode of Herat. Further, Persian theorists write the scale of *Afshāri* from the seventh degree of *Shur*: B♭, C, D♭, E♭, F, G, A♭, B♭, which corresponds to the lower tetrachord of the *tula* example when transposed to E: E, F♯, G, A. When the *Afshāri* scale is transposed from its stopping note: D♭, E♭, F, G, A♭, B♭, C, D♭, an interval slightly smaller than an augmented fourth becomes apparent. This interval is significant in the *sornā-dohl* example. Zonis describes the characteristic features of *Afshāri*: "Afshari opens on the fourth degree, stresses it heavily, and then descends."[6] Such a description fits the general description of the *Aushāri* melody type; thus, one can assume that *Aushāri* is a folk melody type based upon the classical Iranian mode of *Afshāri*.[7]

The remainder of the discussion of Herat folk songs will involve two popular songs which are more standardized than melody types. The two songs, *Heinā Ba Kārā* and *Mullā Mohammed Jān*, are claimed to be "old" Herat songs.

Heinā Ba Kārā is a wedding song about the henna used to color the hands of those in a wedding party. The title is taken from a line, *heinā ba kārā, peirahn gul-e nārā*, which follows every line of verse. Further, henna is the subject of a refrain section consisting of short rhyming phrases much like a *pāzarb*.

Two versions of *Heinā Ba Kārā* were recorded. One version was by Ghulam Mohiuddin, a nonhereditary, professional musician who sang and played the *dutār* in his *samowar* (teahouse). He was accompanied by his partner, Baidola, who played the *zirbaghali* and whistled bird calls. The other is sung by Khohar-e Sher Gul who accompanied herself on the *dāira*. She was a nonmusician who secretly sang a song for me while in the home of a mutual friend. Although the performers, performing style, and performance setting are quite different, the basic melody and words are similar.

Example 16: Ghulam Mohiuddin, *Heinā Ba Kārā*.

dar   ba me ba land-   kaf ta ra ba   shi-   ra zi   hei na ba ka-   ra - peh

ran gu li na - ra-

B

ma hei na na da- rem - az Ka bul bi a - rem

Heinā Ba Kārā

Dar bām-e baland kaftarakā-ye shirāzi
  Heinā ba kārā peirahn gul-e nārā
Āsheq nashodi cherā kolokh miandāzi
  Heinā ba kārā peirahn gul-e nārā
Āsheq nashodi ke āshuqi bad bakht ast
  Heinā ba kārā peirahn gul-e nārā
Gāhe bibini gāhe nabini sakht ast
  Heinā ba kārā peirahn gul-e nārā

Mā heinā nadārem az kābul biyārem
Bā heinā-ye kābul bā shasthā bemālem
Bā heinā-ye kābul por hel o qalamphor

Az ruze azal be eshq rāzi kardi
  Heinā ba kārā peirahn gul-e nārā
Lotfo o karam banda nawāzi kardi
  Heinā ba kārā peirahn gul-e nārā
Az ru-ye tu wafārā nadidam hargez
  Heinā ba kārā peirahn gul-e nārā
Ai dust bibin zamāne sāzi kardi
  Heinā ba kārā peirahn gul-e nārā

Muiyat be rokhat ajab perishān karda
  Heinā ba kārā peirahn gul-e nārā
Har kas ke āshuq noqs be imān karda
  Heinā ba kārā peirahn gul-e nārā
Dar mazhab-e āsheqi rawā kai bāsha
  Heinā ba kārā peirahn gul-e nārā
Albate torā kasi peshimān karda
  Heinā ba kārā peirahn gul-e nārā

Dar khāb didam khāb-e elahi didam
  Heinā ba kārā peirahn gul-e nārā
Pahlu geshtandam jā-ye tu khāli didam
  Heinā ba kārā peirahn gul-e nārā
Pahlu geshtandam jā-ye tu khāli nabud
  Heinā ba kārā peirahn gul-e nārā
Dar pahlu-ye khod yār khodāi didam
  Heinā ba kārā peirahn gul-e nārā

On the high roof Shiraz pigeons
    Henna is needed, the pomegranate flower shirt
You didn't fall in love, why are you throwing clods of dirt?
    Henna is needed, the pomegranate flower shirt
You didn't fall in love because it is difficult
    Henna is needed, the pomegranate flower shirt
Seeing sometimes, sometimes not seeing, it is hard.
    Henna is needed, the pomegranate flower shirt.

We don't have henna, let's bring it from Kabul
With the henna from Kabul rub the thumbs
With the Kabul henna full of cardamom and camphor.

From the first day of creation you agreed to be my lover
    Henna is needed, the pomegranate flower shirt
You were kind and generous and good to your slave
    Henna is needed, the pomegranate flower shirt
I never saw loyalty in your face
    Henna is needed, the pomegranate flower shirt
O friend, look, you were an opportunist
    Henna is needed, the pomegranate flower shirt.

How your hair falls in your face
    Henna is needed, the pomegranate flower shirt
Whoever is a lover damages his faith
    Henna is needed, the pomegranate flower shirt
In a religion of lovers it is not permissible
    Henna is needed, the pomegranate flower shirt
Perhaps someone has made you change your mind
    Henna is needed, the pomegranate flower shirt.

I saw in a dream, I saw a Godly dream
    Henna is needed, the pomegranate flower shirt
I turned on my side, I saw your empty place
    Henna is needed, the pomegranate flower shirt
I turned on my side, your place wasn't empty
    Henna is needed, the pomegranate flower shirt
On my side I saw a Godly friend
    Henna is needed, the pomegranate flower shirt.

Example 17: Khohar-e Sher Gul, *Heinā Ba Kārā.*

Heinā Ba Kārā

Mā heinā nadārem az kābul biārem
Bā heinā-ye kābul bā dasthā bemālem

Bālā balge pāyin o bālā balge
    Heinā ba kārā peirahn gul-e nārā
Nāzanin-e man shista ba pahlu-ye gabre
    Heinā ba kārā peirahn gul-e nārā
O man injā biqarāram
    Heinā ba kārā peirahn gul-e nārā
Musulmānā khoar-e yak barāram
    Heinā ba kārā peirahn gul-e nārā

Sar dastā safeda heinā balge beida
Sar dastā balura heinā balge gula

Barār jo bā safar parzo nadāram
    Heinā ba kārā peirahn gul-e nārā
Be jā-ye yak ke barār pā gozaram
    Heinā ba kārā peirahn gul-e nārā

We don't have henna, let's bring it from Kabul
Rub your hands with the Kabul henna.

The leaves are above, the leaves are above and below
    Henna is needed, the pomegranate flower shirt
My beloved is sitting beside an infidel
    Henna is needed, the pomegranate flower shirt
O, I am here, restless
    Henna is needed, the pomegranate flower shirt
O Muslims, I am the sister of only one brother
    Henna is needed, the pomegranate flower shirt.

The back of the hand is white, henna is the willow leaf
The back of the hand is bright, henna is the flower petal.

I don't want my brother to go on a journey
    Henna is needed, the pomegranate flower shirt
I would like to put my foot on my only brother so he'll stay
    Henna is needed, the pomegranate flower shirt.

All lines are sung to melody A, while the refrain line and the *pāzarb* section are sung to melody B. The text to melody A is not standard and it is up to the singer to supply poems which fit the melodic phrase. Ghulam Mohiuddin sang quatrains he had sung in other songs. Each *misrāᶜ* is followed by the refrain and each quatrain is followed by the *pāzarb*. Khohar-e Sher Gul improvised short biographical rhyming couplets followed by the refrain, then followed by the *pāzarb*. The song structure and much of the text is flexible and dependent upon the individual singer, yet the melody is standard. Both versions are remarkably similar in rhythm and phrase structure, the only major difference being a major third in Khohar-e Sher

Gul's version and an alternating major and minor third in Ghulam Mohiuddin's version.

Mullā Mohammed Jān had become popularized throughout the
country by Radio Afghanistan performers and had even been recorded in
Iran. Most listeners were not aware of the fact that this song is a folk song
from Herat. Two performances were recorded in Herat by Mohammed
Omar on *sornā* and Zainab on voice; yet, the melody is so standardized,
there is hardly a difference between the two.

Example 18: Zainab, *Mullā Mohammed Jān.*

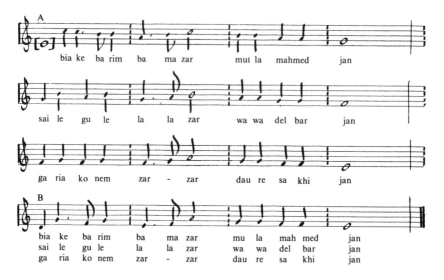

Mullā Mohammed Jān

Biyā ke berim bā mazār	*mullā mohammed jān*
Sail-e gul-e lālazār	*wā wā delbar jān*
Geria konem zār zār	*daur-e Sākhi Jān*
Az dur didam torā	*mullā mohammed jān*
Khosh nud didam torā	*wā wā delbar jān*
Akher migiram torā	*wā wā delbar jān*
Az dur miāyi	*mullā mohammed jān*
Khanda karda miāyi	*wā wā delbar jān*
Dar baghalam dar āyi	*wā wā delbar jān*
Az kurti qermez-e tu	*mullā mohammed jān*
Gul karda pāliz-e tu	*wā wā delbar jān*
Delakam kāriz-e tu	*wā wā delbar jān*
Rang-e shekariz-e tu	*wā wā delbar jān*

Biyā ke berim andaki	*mullā mohammed jān*
Piāla sar-e nalbaki	*wā wā delbar jān*
Chāi bekhorim sobaki	*wā wā delbar jān*

Come, let's go to Mazar,	Mulla Mohammed Jan
To see the wild tulips,	oh, dear sweetheart
We will cry around	Sakhi Jan's shrine.

I saw you from afar,	Mulla Mohammed Jan
I saw you were happy,	oh, dear sweetheart
At last I will get you,	oh, dear sweetheart.

You came from afar,	Mulla Mohammed Jan
You came laughing	oh, dear sweetheart
I wish you would come into my arms,	oh, dear sweetheart

From your bright coat,	Mulla Mohammed Jan
Your melon patch is in bloom,	oh, dear sweetheart
My heart is your aqueduct,	oh, dear sweetheart
Your sweet face,	oh, dear sweetheart.

Come, let's go a little way,	Mulla Mohammed Jan
The cup is on the saucer,	oh, dear sweetheart
Let's drink morning tea,	oh, dear sweetheart.

Like *Heinā Ba Kārā*, this song is held together by ending each line with a short standard phrase and the return of a refrain section. The verses, which consist of three phrases ending with short, set phrases, are sung to melody A. The refrain section is sung to melody B. The song is in the *Bairami* mode and consists mainly of three descending sequences. Like other folk songs, the melody and text are simple and repetitive. The simple setting gives singers the opportunity to improvise short, appropriate rhyming phrases without worrying about a difficult melody or strict poetic rhythm.

A perusal of the composed songs indicates that all are in the *Bairami* mode; all but two are in the meter of three; all are performed in the popular style; and all are songs by contemporary poets. These features point to a close relationship to the Iranian *tasnif*, which has a definite meter, is based on contemporary poetry, and often has an added "composed introduction and several orchestral ritornelli. In the tasnif-ha [plural] written today, after every verse or two is a section for instruments."[8] Although the term *tasnif* was hardly ever used by Herati musicians, this type of song represented a new trend of modern thought and epitomized the attitude held by these musicians and by the Information and Culture Office that music can be a respected art (see Table 20).

Folk songs are less uniform than composed songs and generalizations about the performers or performances are made with some reservations. Unlike the composed songs which are at the disposal of the often young,

TABLE 20
Examples of the Music of Herat

Example	Song	Mode	Rhythm	Style	Performer
1	*Gul-e Zard*	*Bairami*	3	Popular	Professional
2	*Gul-e Zard*	*Bairami*	3	Popular	Amateur
3	*Sarwe Gulpusham*	*Bairami*	3	Popular	Professional
4	*Rafiq Kārawān*	*Bairami*	3	Popular	Professional
5	*Balā Ai Del*	*Bairami*	3	Popular	Hereditary Professional
6	*Zabāne Shekwa*	*Bairami*	4	Popular	Professional
7	*Sarhadi*	*Bairo*	6	Folk	Professional
8	*Sarhadi*	*Bairo*	Free/3	Folk	Hereditary Professional
9	*Sarhadi Ghoriāni*	*Bairami*	7	Folk	Professional
10	*Sarhadi Ghoriāni*	*Bairami*	7	Folk	Amateur
11	*Chār Baiti*	?	Free	Folk	Nonmusician
12	*Chār Baiti*	?	Free	Folk	Nonmusician
13	*Aushāri*	?	6	Folk	Hereditary Professional
14	*Aushāri*	?	6	Folk	Professional
15	*Aushāri*	*Bairami*	6	Folk	Professional
16	*Heinā Ba Kārā*	?	7	Folk	Professional
17	*Heinā Ba Kārā*	?	7	Folk	Nonmusician
18	*Mullā Mohammed Jān*	*Bairami*	4	Folk	Hereditary Professional

literate, nonhereditary, radio-theater musicians, the folk songs are sung by every type of performer from the hereditary professional to the nonmusician. Only one melody type, *Aushāri*, is restricted to the repertoire of professional musicians because it is a purely instrumental dance melody which comes closest of all the genres to the concept of pure music designated to the realm of professional musicians.

Folk songs are much freer in structure than composed songs. The text for the most part is not standard; the rhythm is either free or in a parlando style, and even the modes of some pieces are not fixed. Two popular folk-song modes are *Bairo* and *Bairami*. The rhythms are either free, in six or seven, and more unlikely, in four. The style of performance depends upon the performers. Professional musicians include instrumental interludes based on thematic material from the song proper and use techniques borrowed from the popular style (see Table 20).

MUSICAL EXAMPLES FROM FAIZABAD, BADAKHSHAN

Composed songs in Faizabad are more traditional than in Herat. The performers are older folk musicians who are, for the most part, illiterate, but whose repertoires include a great number of composed songs. A Faizabad poet once lamented the fact that musicians learn songs by rote, never understanding the technicalities of the poems, thus never singing the poems correctly. This situation is in sharp contrast to Herat, where composed songs are sung by literate young men who have a different attitude toward music.

The performance style of these composed songs also differs markedly from Herat. In Herat a single performance consists of a single poem. In Faizabad a number of poems are sung in a series of gradually increasing tempi. Most musicians begin by singing a *fard* or two in free rhythm. Then they sing a poem (usually a *ghazal*) in slow, fixed rhythm called *zarb*. The *zarb* section is most often in duple meter, and sometimes in a slow meter of five. After the *zarb* section, another poem is sung in a faster rhythm, usually a rhythm of seven. This section is called *paron*. A fourth section with an even faster tempo is called *shamār* and is described as accompanying a circling or twirling motion of a dance, yet I have never heard an example of *shamār*.

The following two examples (19 and 20) are typical performances of composed songs. The first example, consisting of a *fard* (Example 19-a) and two *ghazal*s (Examples 19-b and 19-c) is sung by Aka Naim, the music enthusiast who performed only for small social gatherings of friends. This song was identified as *Jog*, which is a well-known mode name in Badakhshan, but is not an easily recognizable mode; therefore, it was given as the name of several songs in different modes. From the information subsequently received from Akbar, Naim's brother, I suspect that this song is in the mode of *Āsā*.

Nasir Khan, a teacher in Faizabad who helped translate the song text, identified the song as a *tasawwafi* or *sufi* song. It is composed of several different poems. According to Nasir Khan, the first *fard* is a line from Bedel, a late seventeenth-century poet who is thought to have lived in Badakhshan. It is sung in free rhythm:

Example 19-a: Aka Naim, *fard*.

man a zi zam zi gof tan o -   halq az   sho ni -   da nash

Fard:

Man gungi khāb dida wa ālam hama karānd
Man ājezam zi guftan o halq az shonidanash

Kāri makon ke rokhsat-e āhe sahar deham
Win tond bādrā ba cherāgh-e tu sar deham
Larzad delam ke khāna-ye khosnat konad siāh
Gar andak ekhtiār ba dud-e jigar deham

Gharaz az bāde gar mastist cheshmi yārham dārad
War az gul mudā rang ast ān rokhsārham dārad
Cherā gardun-e dun parwar ba kām-e man namegardad
Paraishāni agar aibast zolf-e yārham dārad

I am a mute dreamer and the rest of the world is deaf
I am incapable of telling it and others of hearing it.

Don't do anything to make me regret and release a sigh
To bring this gust of wind to your lantern
My heart trembles because your beauty's home would be darkened
If I permit a little smoke from my liver [anger] to escape.

If the purpose of wine is the state of intoxication, then so the eyes of a lover,
If the purpose of a flower is color, then so the cheeks;
Why does this world which buttresses the base not follow my wishes
If worrying is a misdeed, then so the lover's tresses.

The following two quatrains are unidentifed, but they are also sung in the free rhythm style of the first *fard*. The next section, known as *zarb*, consists of a *ghazal* by Anwar Badakhshi. The musical setting of the *ghazal* in Faizabad is similar to the *ghazal*s sung in Herat. The *matla^c* is sung to melody A. The following *misrā^c*s which do not rhyme are sung to melody B, while the *misrā^c*s which do rhyme are sung to melody A:

Example 19-b: Aka Naim, *ghazal, zarb.*

A
be gar dan ma hu az in   ai na da ghe khod na ka i ra

B
ta ra shuh   mo ya yi oj zam   khe ja

lat pe sha i sa man

Matla^c:

Begardān mahau az in āina dāgh-e khod namāirā
Karam farmā qabul-e khesh gardān āshnāirā

Tazaro^c māya-ye ojzam khejālat pesha-ye sāmān
Kodāmin sāya pahlu mezanad ājez nawāira

Tafākhor sarfarāzānrā ba pasti mekashad ākher
Ke nān-e sob bāshad dar baghal sham-e gadāirā

Dar in daftar ba joz hasrat nakardam noskhai inshā
....

Badardat nest dar māni chi bejā metapi anwar
Rahi tadbir masdud ast taqdir-e kohdāira

Wipe out any sign of vanity from this mirror
Be kind and accept this one you know.

My begging is a sign of weakness, and shame is my way of life
Who would push aside the weak ones.

Vanity leads to shame and unworthiness in the end
Like those who carry their morning bread and beg for the evening.

In this world I have never seen anything but disappointment
....

There is no cure for your illness, why are you running aimlessly, O Anwar?
There is no way out from God's will.

The *matla^c* functions as a refrain and is repeated after each *bait*. The structure of the song is as follows:

Melody	Text	Melody	Text
A A	Matla^c	A A	Instrumental
A A	Instrumental	B A	Verse
B A	Verse	A A	Matla^c
A A	Matla^c		

In actual performance, many lines are repeated, and at times, only the first half of the *matla^c* is sung; therefore, the number of A and B melodies are not heard in any regular order. The melody displays the following rhythmic pattern:

After the last verse and the repeat of the *matla^c*, the *rabāb* and *daf* immediately change into a lively rhythm of seven, the *paron* section in which a *ghazal* by Esmat Bokhari is sung. The structure of this *paron* section is similar to the structure of the *zarb* section and consists of two melodies:

Example 19-c: Aka Naim, *ghazal, paron.*

Matla^c:

Sar khosh az koyi kharābāt gozar kardam dush
Ba talabgāri-ye tarsa bacha-ye bada farush

Pesham āmad ba sar-e kucha pari rokhsāri
Kāfari eshwagari zolf cho zinār ba dush

Goftom in kucha chi koyist torā khāna kojast
Ai ma-he nau kham-e abru-e torā halqa ba gush

Goft tasbeh ba khāk afgan o zinār beband
Sang bar shishai taqwā bezan o bāda benush

Bad az an pesh biyā tā ba tu guyam sokhani
Sokhan in ast agar bar sokhanam dāri gush

Zud diwāna wa sarmast dawidam suyash
Ba maqame berasidam ke na din mānd o na hush

Didam az dur garuhi hama diwāna o mast
Waz taf-e bāda-ye eshq āmada dar jushājush

Bi daf o chang o sarāhi hama raqs o semāh
Bi mai o motreb o sāqi hama dar nushānush

Cho sar-e rishta-ye nāmus beshod az dastam
Khāstam tā sokhani porsam az u goft khamush

In na ka^cba ast ke be pā wa sar āyi badarun
In na masjid ke darān be khabar āyi bakharush

In kharābāt-e moghān ast darān rendānand
Az dam-e sob-e azal tā ba qiāmat madhush

Gar torā hast dar in shewa sari yak rangi
Din o duniyāt ba yak joroa cho esmat befarush

Last night I passed through the entertainment quarters
Looking for a wine seller, the son of a Zoroastrian.

On the street I ran into a fairy-like face
A coquettish infidel with locks like a girdle falling on her shoulders.

I asked her where is this street and where is your house
O new moon, your eyebrows would be my earrings.

She said throw your prayer beads on the ground and wear the girdle
Shatter the glass of piety and drink wine.

Then come to me and I'll tell you something
What I want to tell you is this, if you'll listen.

Hurriedly like a mad, intoxicated one, I ran toward her
I reached a point where I lost my faith, my senses.

I saw from a distance a group of mad and intoxicated people
Those who were happily mingling from the effect of the heat of the wine of love.

Without tambourine and harp and jug all dancing and singing
Without wine, musicians or wine bearer, all drinking

As soon as I came to my senses
I wanted to ask her something; she said silence!

This is not the Ka'ba where you can come barefooted and bareheaded
This is not a mosque where you can enter without permission, and roar.

This is a Zoroastrian tavern [place of *sufis*] and inside are rogues [*sufis*],
From the dawn of creation until resurrection, out of their senses.

If you agree to this way of life,
Then sell your faith and your world for a cup like Esmat.

Both melodies A and B have internal repetitions of parts of each *misrā^c*.
The *matla^c* section returns as a refrain.

The mode and format of Example 20 are identical to that of the
preceding example. The song, sung by Khan-e Baharaki, begins with a single quatrain and a *ghazal* by Shah Shujah in free rhythm. The second *ghazal*, also by Shah Shujah, is in a rhythm of five:

Example 20: Khan-e Baharaki, *ghazal, zarb.*

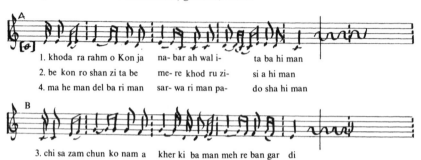

```
1. khoda  ra rahm o Kon ja    na- bar ah wal i-       ta ba hi man
2. be  kon ro shan zi ta be    me- re khod ru zi-     si a hi man
4. ma he man del ba ri man    sar- wa ri man pa-      do sha hi man
```

```
3. chi sa zam chun ko nam a    kher ki ba man meh re ban gar  di
```

The final *ghazal* is sung to the same melody as Example 20, but in a duple
meter. In each case, melody A is used for rhyming *misrā^cs*, while melody B
is used for odd *misrā^cs*.

Example 21 is a composed song performed in a less traditional manner
by the poet himself. Faiz-e Mangal had been a musician for twenty-eight
years and a poet for twenty-two years at the time of this recording. His
poems are sung in the greater Faizabad area by other young local musicians. Although Faiz-e Mangal is a respected local musician and poet, he
has been affected by outside influences; his instrument is the large northern
Afghanistan *dambura* instead of the small Badakhshani variety, and he
uses terminology that is not normally used in Badakhshan. For example,
he identified the mode of Example 20 as *Bairami*, but the term is not normally used in Badakhshan, and the mode does not correspond to the Herat
Bairami.

The *ghazal* is again based on two melodies, A and B, and the *matla^c* is
used as a refrain. Differing from Examples 19 and 20, this song consists of
only one *ghazal* sung in a rhythm of seven. Faiz-e Mangal does not identify
the piece as a *zarb* or *paron*, and there is no introduction to the poem:

Example 21: Faiz-e Mangal, *ghazal.*

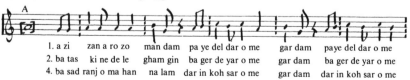

```
1. a zi    zan a ro zo    man dam   pa ye del dar o me    gar dam   paye del dar o me
2. ba tas   ki ne de le   gham gin   ba ger de yar o me    gar dam   ba ger de yar o me
4. ba sad ranj o ma han   na lam   dar in koh sar o me    gar dam   dar in koh sar o me
```

The next example is an interesting composed song from the view of its poetic form and content. The poem is a *tarkib-band*, a stanzaic form tied together by an internal rhyming *bait*. According to Browne, "the verses which form the *band*s of a *tarkib-band* must rhyme within themselves, and may, but need not, rhyme with one another."[9] The poem is a social commentary about the rich and dishonest. References are made to contemporary products and status symbols. The text is presented here for its textual content, and, incidentally, to clarify the structure of the *tarkib-band*:

Tarkib-band:

Ai setam paisha-ye bad kār turā migoyam
Khāin-e khalq o del āzār turā migoyam
Man ke reshwat khori ghadār turā migoyam
Ai daghal parwar-e tarāz turā migoyam

Az tu man khāteri por suz o malāli dāram
War jawābam bedehi chan o sawāli dāram

Padarat kuti parwān ba khodā dāsht nadāsht
Tamiri sorkh ba paghmān ba khodā dāsht nadāsht
Motar laine-ye laghmān ba khodā dāsht nadāsht
Hama shab yak labak nān ba khodā dāsht nadāsht

Pas turā kar o fari motar-e walgā zi kojāst
Qasri shash manzela-ye sar ba sar ya zi kojast

Gar tu reshwat nakhori but-e kerepsol zi chist
Paudar o sodar o in masraf bitol zi chist
Ba sari khānomat az shir o shekar khul zi chist
Rāst bogo ba man ke in pul zi chist

Qura-ye khāin dar dahr ba nāmat bādā
In maāshi ke migeri harāmat bādā

Rahm o ensāf o morowat tu nadāri chi konam
Pāi dar marka-ye jahl tu gozāri chi konam
Khuni mazlom zadai mast o khomāri chi konam
Dar sar-e shāna-ye iblis tu sawāri chi konam

Tā ke in dahri kohan dida-ye hasti bikushād
Chun tu qasāb hami mādar ayam nazād

Saif khodrā benegar qimat duniā dāri
Bāz ham dar shaqi chur dasti tawānā dāri
Zān sabab ārzo-ye sāghar o minā dāri
Sad chi nāmi o marā chi parwā dāri

Ai palang-e sahari jā-ye haiāho nang ast
Qālin khāna ast az hasta-ye mā khoshrang ast

O oppressor, I'm telling you
Traitor, offender of hearts, I'm telling you
O bribe-taker, I'm telling you
Deceitful one, I'm telling you.

I am distressed with you
If you'll answer me, I have a few questions for you:

Did your father have a building in Parwan, by God, or not?
Did he have a red building in Paghman, by God, or not?
Did he have a bus line to Laghman, by God, or not?
Did he have a morsel of bread every night, by God, or not?

Then where did you get your Volga car and splendor?
Where did the six-story building come from?

If you don't take bribes, where did your crepe-sole shoes come from?
Face powder, soda, and your infinite spending, where did they come from?
The gifts of milk and honey for your wife, where did they come from?
Tell me the truth, this money, where does it come from?

Traitor should be your name in this world
This salary you earn should be religiously forbidden.

You don't have mercy, justice, kindness, what should I do?
You always join the ignorant ones, what should I do?
You have tasted the blood of the oppressed and are intoxicated by it, what
    should I do?
You are riding on the devil's shoulder, what should I do?

Since the creation of this old world
The mother of time never gave birth to a butcher like you.

Look into your safe deposit, you have the price of the world
Yet you still have an able hand at stealing
Because of this, you seek after wine
You have a good name, what do you care about us?

O morning leopard, making all this noise is shameful
The carpet in your house is colorful with our wealth.

Like the *ghazals*, this *tarkib-band* is set to two melodies (see Example
22). The first stanza, except for the first half of the *band*, is set to melody A.
Thereafter, every stanza is sung to melody B, while the *band* is sung to
melody A. After each *band*, a line or two from the first stanza is repeated in
the manner of a refrain.

Example 22: Islam, *tarkib-band.*

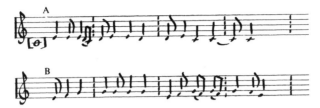

Other composed songs in Badakhshan are performed in a similar manner. The melody outlines the poetic form faithfully. The melodic material for all composed songs consists of two sections: A emphasizes the range from the first to the third degree; and B emphasizes the range of the third to the fifth degrees of the scale.

In each case the singer is the main instrumentalist; thus, he easily controls the tempo and mood. In the traditional performance style several poems are grouped into one performance, but distinguished by a different tempo and rhythm. Each song begins with a section in free rhythm. The more modern performers, however, concentrate solely on the metrical performances of single poems.

Generally, composed songs consist of poems by known poets, and folk songs are based on poems by unknown poets; yet some *fard*s and quatrains in the introductory section of composed songs are unidentified, and some lines in folk songs are taken directly from classical poems. Therefore, the distinction between composed and folk songs is made on the basis of musical style, as well as on the basis of text.

Example 23 is a folk song from the village of Ishmorgh in the Wakhan area of Badakhshan. For the most part, the text is unintelligible, but Enayatullah Shahrani, while transcribing the Badakhshani songs for transcription, recognized parts of the text as Hafez. Lines from Hafez are sung by folk musicians throughout Badakhshan, but seem especially popular in Wakhan and Sheghnan. The musicians are illiterate and do not recognize the poets.

This song is sung by a leader and chorus, accompanied by a *daf.* The leader begins the melody and the chorus joins in near the end of the phrase, then the whole phrase is repeated by the chorus, when the leader starts a new line:

Example 23: Wakhan Folk Song.

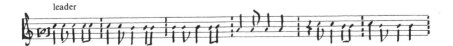

This melody is limited to an interval of a third and the rhythm is again in the meter of seven. Because the words are unintelligible, the relationship between music and text cannot be exhibited. It should be mentioned that although the inhabitants of these regions speak their own language, songs in Persian are more common than those in the native tongue.

A large class of folk songs is generally known as *falak, gharibi, rustāyi, kurdaki,* and *chopāni* in Badakhshan. In most cases, all the terms may apply to the same piece; however, of all these terms, *falak* is the most prevalent. Like *chār baiti* in Herat, *falak* denotes a number of things. The first definition one is likely to encounter is one most Badakhshis verbalize, concerning the subject of the song. *Falak* is a sad song of yearning; the second meaning of *falak* is the poetic form of *rubā^{c}i* or *du baiti*. The third notion is one of style. It is said that *falaks* can only be sung or played on the Sheghnan *nai*, the *dambura*, or *ghichak*. Example 24 is a *nai falak* performed by Jandar Shah from Sheduj, Sheghnan. The music is highly ornamented and noticeably chromatic with a limited range:

Example 24: Jandar Shah, *nai falak*.

accelerando

accelerando

The final notion, one of melody type, is rarely expressed. Two isolated incidents led me to believe that the term refers to melody type as well as style, poetic content, and form. In one case, Akbar played examples of different modes. One song was in the mode of *Jog* which he called *falak* (Example 25):

Example 25: Akbar, *falak*.

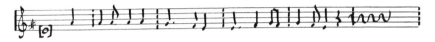

The scale of this example corresponds to Herat's *Bairo* which had once inadvertently been called *Jog*, the most obvious features being the minor and augmented second intervals. The second clue came when Enayatullah Shahrani heard a vocal piece called *chopāni*; he said it was a good example of the "sound" of *falak* (Example 26):

Example 26: Ramazan, *chopāni*.

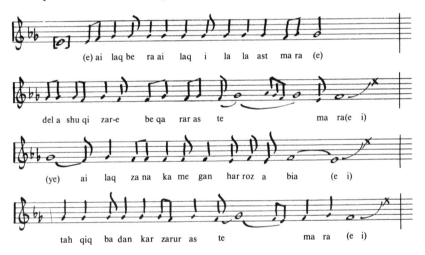

Chopāni:

Ailāq bera ailāq lāla ast marā
Dili āshuq zāre beqarār ast marā
Ailāq zanekā megan har roza biyāye
Tahqiq badān kār zarur ast marā

Go to *ailoq*, [summer pastoral encampments] *ailoq* is full of wild tulips
The distressed lover's heart is restless
The women say, come to *ailoq* every day
It is necessary for me to investigate this.

This unaccompanied melody sung by Ramazan of Khandud, Wakh-an, is very similar to the *nai* example. It is limited in range and chromatic, but the melody is not ornamented until the end of the phrases which are invariably lengthened. An interesting stylistic feature of this example is the portamento on the syllable "i" at the end of each phrase. This same effect is heard at the end of the first phrase of the *nai* example. Other vocal *falak*s end phrases on similar-sounding syllables. The only similarity between Akbar's *falak* and Ramazan's *chopāni* is the minor second interval between the first and second degrees, yet variations can be found in every aspect of the *falak*.

The vast majority of folk songs in Afghanistan are about unrequited love. Therefore, practically every song can be interpreted as sad. However, an ideal *falak* text is often biographical and melancholic as in the following lines from Jambi's song. Jambi is Ramazan's sister who had lived in the Khash Valley near Faizabad for seven years. This song is about the home and family she misses in Wakhan:

Dar shura zamin bulbul-e nālān māyom
Dam geria mislā-e abre bārān māyom
Khordek parik o musulman ba watan
Durāi wantan am jedā zi yārān māyom

In the salt flats, I am a weeping nightingale
In crying, I am like a rain cloud
Little one, little fairies, Muslims of my country
I am far from my country and friends.

Songs labeled *falak* are not always quatrains, but can be other popular forms such as a *mukhammas*, a five-line form with the following rhyme scheme:

    ——a ——a   ——b ——b   ——c ——c
    ——a ——a   ——b ——b   ——c ——c
      ——a   ——a   ——a

Example 27 is a *mukhammas* sung by Islam, who called it a *paron-e falak*:

Example 27: Islam, *paron-e falak*.

Like other *falak*s, the range is extremely limited and is characterized by a minor second and major second interval in melody A, and a minor second and a slightly narrow augmented second in melody B. All the *misrā^cs* with the *a* rhyme are sung to melody A, while all other *misrā^cs* are sung to melody B.

It is said that the *nai, dambura,* and *ghichak* are the only instruments which can play or accompany *falak*s, yet the example by Akbar (Example 25 above) is accompanied by the harmonium as well as the *dambura*. Further, the stylistic extended endings of phrases on the syllable "i" are not always apparent.

The final notion of "sound" or melody type is the hardest to refute, since it is the least verbalized and the least specific. In most examples of *falak* the minor second interval between the first and second degrees is immediately apparent. The interval between the second and third degrees, however, can differ from a minor second to a major second, or to an augmented second. The range of some *falak*s is limited to a second or third, while others extend to a fifth or more.

With such variant examples of *falak*, it is difficult to determine the distinguishing features of this form. The alternate terms, *kurdaki, chopāni,* and so on, suggest that the form has its origins in the rural hinterlands. Of the fifteen *falak*s I recorded, five of them were from the isolated Wakhan and Sheghnan areas, while ten were from the greater Faizabad area. An analysis of the five rural *falak*s results in a model showing a fairly consistent poetic content and form, style, and melody type (see Table 21 below).

The *falak*s of these regions comply with the definition of "poetic content and form," in that the text is expressive of the thoughts and lives of the people who sing them and is based upon folk poems of which the quatrain is the most common. Even in the purely instrumental *nai* example, the same emotions as *falak* texts can be expressed because the *nai* has traditionally been associated with nature and man's true feelings. The following song by Gulshan Begin of Ishmorgh, Wakhan, imparts these qualities to the instrument:

Logar dur ast o khat rawānat bekunam
Bari jān yak qabza-ye gul o basta rawān
Yak qabza gul o basta ba paishat narasid
In ast jāne khodam ba darone nai rawān

Logar is far for me to send a letter
A bouquet of flowers was sent to my Dear
The bouquet didn't reach you
This is my own life sent within the sound of the *nai*.

Two of the five *falak*s, F-1 and F-4, have already been discussed concerning their free rhythm and extended phrase ending style, and their narrow range and chromatic melody type (see Examples 24 and 26). The remaining *falak*s are performed by voice accompanied by *dambura* or

TABLE 21
Formal Analysis of Rural *Falaks*

No.	Artist	Instrument	Title	Sections	Place	Text	Intervals
F-1	Ramazan	Solo Voice	*Chopāni*	——	Wakhan	Quatrains	
F-2	Awaz	Voice and *Dambura*	*Falak*	Free/ Fixed	Sheghnan	Quatrains	
F-3	Nazar Mohammed, Gul Mohammed	Voice and *Ghichak*	*Falak Sheghni*	Free Fixed	Sheghnan	Quatrains	
F-4	Jandar Shah	*Nai* Solo	*Falak Shāh Mubārak*	Free Fixed	Sheghnan	——	
F-5	Ezrat Murad	Voice and *Ghichak*	*Falak She^{c}r*	Free Fixed	Sheghnan	Quatrains	

ghichak. They also are in free rhythm and have extended phrase endings on the syllables "i" or "e"; however, three more characteristics can be observed. First, the melodic range is extended, and in doing so, some of the chromaticism between the high degrees disappears, but the minor second interval between the first and second degrees is retained (see Examples 28, 29, and 30).

Example 28: Awaz, *falak* (F-2).

These three examples vary in range from a fourth to a minor seventh, although the seventh degree is used in F-5 (Example 30) only once as an upper neighboring tone to the sixth degree. The use of the augmented second interval between the second and third degrees, as in F-2 (Example 28),

Example 29: Nazar Mohammed, Gul Mohammed, *falak* (F-3).

Example 30: Ezrat Murad, *falak* (F-5).

is rare in rural *falak*s, but it is characteristic of more urban, developed *falak*s.

The second characteristic of the *falak* is an instrumental vamp in a rhythm of five, played between the vocal phrases in the following manner:

When the voice enters, the instrument follows the voice freely.

Finally, a melody or song in a fixed rhythm of seven follows the accompanied *falak*. The augmented second interval is conspicuous in these fixed rhythm sections. In two of the three rural accompanied *falak*s the section in fixed rhythm is given another name, clearly indicating that the section is not considered a *falak*. Awaz (F-2, Example 28), however, does not distinguish between the two sections as is often the case in urban *falak*s. This is the second time Awaz's performance differs from the other accompanied rural *falak*s. Perhaps it is through these slight deviations that the *falak* developed into its varied forms.

I suggest that the *falak* developed from the most basic folksong type of the Badakhshan countryside. Many songs sung by women were never identified as *falak*; however, every detail from text (see pages 158 and 159) to style and melody type is suggestive of the ideal *falak* model: unaccompanied, melancholic quatrains set to chromatic, narrow-ranged melodies in free rhythm with a general downward contour, characterized by length-

ened phrase endings with an upward glissando or yodel effect. Two examples of women's songs illustrate this. The first song is in Wakhi and the text
was not transcribed or translated. The lead singer, Haj Begin, is joined by
other women on the final syllable of a phrase, thereby emphasizing it. The
second song, a solo by Gulshan Begin, has already been cited on page 159.

Example 31: Haj Begin, Women's Song.

Example 32: Gulshan Begin, Women's Song.

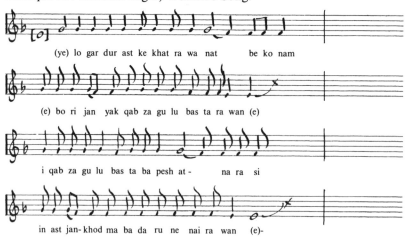

The *nai* and *chopāni* examples (Examples 24 and 26) are also consistent
with the original *falak* model.

In the hands of local semiprofessional musicians who accompany their
songs with instruments, the basic *falak* develops an instrumental style and a
wider range. Further, the *falak* becomes incorporated into a longer performance and functions as a prelude to a song in fixed rhythm.

The urban musicians; i.e., those in the greater Faizabad area, no longer distinguish between the *falak* prelude and the song in fixed rhythm which follows; both pass under the cover term of *falak*. Some musicians perform only the song in fixed rhythm without the prelude. Without exception, every *falak* in fixed rhythm is in seven, divided 3+2+2. The minor and augmented second intervals characterize a majority of the *falak*s. The urban *falak*, then, combines the elements of the rural accompanied *falak*s and the tunes in fixed rhythm which follow (see Table 22).

Besides these modifications made in urban *falak*s, the folk quatrain is sometimes substituted by composed forms (see F-8, F-11, F-13) and a qualifying vocabulary develops. The vocabulary signifies subject or rhythm. *Zahiri* (sad) or *gharibi* (poor) are descriptive of the text, but also indicate a style close to the rural *falak*. *Paron* always refers to a *falak* in the rhythm of seven. This vocabulary, however, is far from standard. Mardan sings two similar *falak*s (F-10, F-15); in one *falak* he calls the two sections *zarb* and *paron*, while in the other he calls them *gharibi* and *ʿishqi* (love).

*Falak*s, then, cover a wide range of folk songs and can be considered the most important genre of Badakhshani folk songs. They are sung by amateurs and semiprofessionals alike, by rural as well as by urban musicians. As different types of musicians sing *falak*, its style is modified, but the essence of *falak*—a song of and by the people—never changes.

A genre that is quite distinct from other Badakhshani folk songs is the Gorgholi epic. The Gorgholi tale is related to the popular Central Asian epic known by such various names as Kuroghli and Gurogli and told in a number of different languages including Azeri, Turkmeni, Turkish, Uzbeki, and Tajiki. The tale is loosely based on historical events in Azerbaijan during the sixteenth century and concerns the exploits of a Turkmen hero-bandit, Kuroghli, "Son of a Blind Man."[10] The Afghan cycle is known as Gorgholi, an adaptation of Gurogli, "Son of the Grave," a reference to the hero's posthumous birth in his mother's grave, mentioned in some versions. In Badakhshan, the tale is sung in both Uzbeki and Tajiki. The principal hero is Awaz Khan, the adopted son of Gorgholi, and involves also the adventures of his sons Nur Ali Khan and Sher Ali Khan, and his grandson, Jangir Khan.

The telling of the tale requires a specialist known as *gorgholikhān* (singer of Gorgholi) who accompanies himself on the *dambura*, sings in a particular, guttural vocal style, and sings loosely rhymed verses consisting of nine-syllable lines. As separate as this epic tradition appears to be from other musical genres in the area, the performance style is related directly to the most common folksong style of Badakhshan, the *falak*. By using the musical vocabulary of the *falak*, the singer uses information already familiar to his audiences, thereby expanding his own resources.

TABLE 22
Formal Analysis of Urban *Falaks*

No.	Artist	Instrument	Title	Place	Text	Sections	Rhythm	Intervals
F-6	Faiz-e Mangal	Dambura	*Sāz-e paron-e falak*	Jurm	Quatrains	Fixed	Seven	*(musical notation)*
F-7 a)	Faiz-e Mangal	Dambura	*Falak-e zahiri*	Jurm	Quatrains	Free	Five	*(musical notation)*
b)			*Falak-e zarbe-e zahiri*	Jurm	Quatrains	Fixed	Seven	*(musical notation)*
c)			*Falak-e farkhari*	Jurm	Quatrains	Fixed	Seven	*(musical notation)*
d)			*Falak-e qataghani*	Jurm	Quatrains	Fixed	Seven	*(musical notation)*
e)			*Falak-e sarghalami*	Jurm	Quatrains	Fixed	Seven	*(musical notation)*
f)			*Falak-e raqs*	Jurm	Quatrains	Fixed	Seven	*(musical notation)*
F-8	Islam	Ghichak	*Paron-e falak*	Baharak	*Mukhammas*	Fixed	Seven	*(musical notation)*
F-9	Islam	Ghichak	*Falak-e kohi*	Baharak	Quatrains	Fixed	Seven	*(musical notation)*

No.	Performer	Instrument	Title	Place	Text	Meter	Lines
F-10 a)	Mardan	Dambura	*Falak: Zarb*	Faizabad	Quatrains	Free	Five
b)			*Falak: Paron*	Faizabad	Quatrains	Fixed	Seven
F-11 a)	Dur Mohammed Keshmi	Ghichak	*Rubāᶜi*	Faizabad	Quatrains	Free	Six
b)			*Falak*	Faizabad	*Tarkib-band*	Fixed	Seven
F-12 a)	Nazir Mohammed	Ghichak	*Falak*	Khash	Quatrains	Free	Five
b)			*Falak*	Khash	Quatrains	Fixed	Seven
F-13	Islam	Ghichak	*Paron-e falak*	Faizabad	Quatrains [Poet—F. Mangal]	Fixed	Seven
F-14	Akbar	Harmonium	*Jog - Falak*	Faizabad	Quatrains	Fixed	Seven
F-15 a)	Mardan	Dambura	*Falak: Gharibi*	Faizabad	Quatrains	Free	Five
b)			*Falak: ᶜIshqi*	Faizabad	Quatrains	Fixed	Seven

In the following Tajiki example, Palawan Asil of Surun-e Yaftal, Badakhshan, begins with a rhythmic and rhapsodic *dambura* introduction. The melody, not unlike a *falak* melody, is restricted to a range of a fourth. The performer then sings two quatrains that are not related to the story. The quatrains are typical songs of separation sung in the same narrow range as the instrumental introduction. The end of each *misrā^c* is characterized by prolonged endings on pitches other than the final tone of the quatrain. The more important division of a *bait* is emphasized by the use of the syllable "wi," which is extremely lengthened and exaggerated. The first degree of the scale is not sung at the end of lines until the last line of the quatrain. Although the singer did not identify these quatrains as *falak*, the structure, the rhyme scheme, the subject matter, and the musical setting are identical to other examples of *falak*.

The *dambura* interludes which follow the quatrains include rhythmic vamps that are reminiscent of the vamps employed in *falak* performances. The story itself is sung within a limited range of a fifth, and to a scale involving a minor second interval between the first and second degrees, a characteristic of the *falak*. The interval between the second and third degrees fluctuates between a major and augmented second, reminding us that many rural *falak*s are also characterized by such fluctuating intervals while the urban *falak* has the distinctive feature of an augmented second degree between the second and third degrees of the scale.

Example 33: Palawan Asil, *Gorgholi*[11]

Dambura Introduction

Quatrain

a- mad jof-ta ka- bu- tara-(i) (ai) az khele je- da (ai)

(ai) yak sa- la qa- ti bu- dim (a) em- sa- la je- da (ai)

(a) yak sa- la qa- ti bu- dim yak ja me- gash tem (i)

(ai) em- sa- la (wa) je- da sho- da- im o por- gham dele ma (ya) wi —

(a) em- sa- la— je- da sho- de- im o por- gham de- le ma ya wi —

Dambura Interlude

Quatrain

(a) bul bul ba wa tan takhte su lai man khosh ta rai-

(a) khar ha i wa tan zi la-- he ra-i- han khosh ta rai wa wi — —

(ya) yu suf ki ba mis ra pa- du- sha- hi me kar da- i

(a) sad kash ki ge da me sho- u- do ke nan khosh ta- rai wi — —

(y) sad kash ki— ge da me sha du ke nan khosh ta rai — — —

Dambura Interlude

Story: Line Number 1

yak sha- bam   be- bu-   do   ni- mi shab

2

khof- ta- na   be- bu- do-   dade   shab

3

a- waz khan   ba- ehe gor-   ghli sul- tan

4

As- pe qir   bi- bi zi-   ri pash na

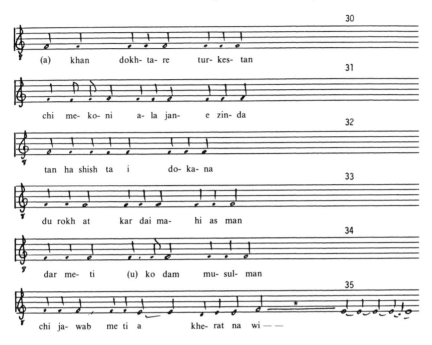

30

(a) khan dokh- ta- re tur- kes- tan

31

chi me- ko- ni a- la jan- e zin- da

32

tan ha shish ta i do- ka- na

33

du rokh at kar dai ma- hi as man

34

dar me- ti (u) ko dam mu- sul- man

35

chi ja- wab me ti a khe- rat na wi — —

Dambura Retunes

36

37

khal pa- ri (a) sho- nid i ga pa

38

sha- ran- gash ai ja jon- bid i dokh tar

39

ga na ha kham zad rui si- nash na

40

sa- lam dad in dokh tar a- waz a-

41

a- sa- lam- a leik goft sha- za- da

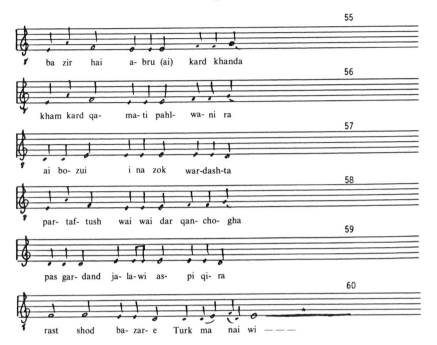

ba zir hai a- bru (ai) kard khanda

kham kard qa- ma- ti pahl- wa- ni ra

ai bo- zui i na zok war-dash-ta

par- taf- tush wai wai dar qan- cho- gha

pas gar- dand ja- la- wi as- pi qi- ra

rast shod ba- zar- e Turk ma nai wi — — —

Transcription

Quatrain

Amad jofte kabutar az khel jeda
Yak sal qati budim emsal jeda
Yak sal qati budim y yak ja megashtim
Emsal jeda shodim o porgham dele ma

Quatrain

Bulbul ba watan takhte sulaiman khoshtar ast
Kharhaye watan zilahe raihan khoshtar ast
Yusuf ke ba misr padshahi mekard
Sad kashki gada meshod o kenan khoshtar ast

Story	Line Number
Yak shabam bebud o nimi shab	1
Khoftan bebud dade shab	
Awaz khan bachaye gorgholi sultan	
Aspe qir zire pashna	
Tofang ham dara dar shana	5
Naizai guldar dast toshna	
Az jurai tanpasai gusheshna	
Kakal hai zariham dar gardaneshna	
Khanbid da rui bazarna	

Shauham amal bud no baja   10
Gozar kard rastai bazarna
Nazar kard dar labe dokan
Shishta yak nozok dokhtare nazian
Khodesh tanha shishta dar dokan
Du rokh dara mahi asman   15
Mesuza ba misli cheraghan
Awaz khan did o mand hairan
Pas gardan jelawi qira
Begirom guft az in surat khabar
Pas amad o dar labe dokan   20, 21
Nazar kard khal pari nazian
Khohare wazir ahmad khan
Wazir dokhtare turkestan
Tanha shishta dar labe dokan   25
Har du rokhash mahtabe asman
Awaz khan did kard khanda
Aferin guft ai kabutar
Sar kheli no o nim lak khana
Khane dokhtare turkestan   30
Chi mekoni ala jane zinda
Tanha shishtai dokana
Du rokhat kardai mahi asman
Dar meti kodam musulman
Chi jawab meti akheratna   35

Khal pari shonid i gapa   37
Sharangash ai ja jonbid i dokhtar
Ganaha khamzad rui sinashna
Salam dad in dokhtar awaza   40
Assalam aleik guft shahzada
Manda nabashi jane zinda
Chera tu porsidi hawale ma
Khabar nesti ke sare dele ma
In medat haft sal bud pora   45
Dar mushqab sokhtaudam i bachai
Na didam dar haft sal guft rutna
Shonidom hamin chand roz na
Tu raftai shekar zamina
Pa har shabost nami dukana   50
Na ai jin tarsidom na az deo
Pairadan usum dami rutna
Emshab khaleqam dad maqsadma
Awaz am shonid in gapa
Ba zir hai abru kard khanda   55
Kham kard qamati pahlawanira
Ai bozui nazok war dashta
Partaftush wai wai dar qanchogha
Pas gardand jalawi aspi qira
Rast shod bazare turkmana   60

Translation

Quatrain
A pair of pigeons flew away from the flock
One year we were together, this year apart
One year we were together and we went around
This year we parted and my heart is full of grief

Quatrain
The nightingale in its home is happier than (having) Solomon's Throne
The thorns of one's country are sweeter than basil
Joseph who was made King of Egypt
Had a hundred regrets, happier a begger in Canaan

	Line Number
Story	
One night, perhaps at midnight	1
It might have been during the late evening prayers	
Awaz Khan, son of Gorgholi Sultan	
Mounted on his horse Qir	
His gun slung over his shoulder	5
A decorated lance in his hand	
A pair of Tanpasai jewels in his ears	
His hair falling on his shoulders	
He dismounted in the bazaar	
It was nine o'clock in the night	10
He passed along the bazaar block	
He looked into a shop	
A slender coquette was sitting	
Sitting alone in the shop	
She had cheeks like moons in the sky	15
She glowed like a lantern	
Awaz Khan saw and was struck	
He turned back the rein of Qir	
I should learn more of this beauty he said	
He came back to the front of the shop	20, 21
He looked at beautiful Khal Pari	
Sister of Wazir Ahmad Khan	
Daughter of the Wazir of Turkestan	
Sitting alone in front of the shop	25
Both cheeks like moons in the sky	
Awaz Khan saw and laughed	
Bravo, my pigeon, he said	
The head of 950,000 households	
Daughter of the Khan of Turkestan	30
What are you doing, oh my dear	
Sitting alone in the shop	
Two cheeks like moons in the sky	
Which Muslim are you intending to burn	
How will you account for this on judgment day	35
Khal Pari heard this talk	37

Suddenly she moved from her place
All her jewelry fell upon her breast
This girl greeted Awaz   40
She said salam aleik, o prince
I hope you're not tired, my soul
Why are you asking about me
Do you not know who holds my heart
It has been exactly seven years   45
Since I fell in love with a boy
I haven't seen your face in seven years
I recently heard
You went to the hunting grounds
I sat every night in this shop   50
I did not fear *jin* nor *deo*
I hired men to watch on the other side
Tonight God gave me what I desired
Awaz heard all of this
He smiled lifting his eyebrows   55
He bent his wrestler's frame
He lifted her by her delicate arm
He threw her on his horse
He turned the rein of his horse Qir
And started off for the Turkmen bazaar   60

This Gorgholi example is but one of many examples indicating the far-reaching influence of the *falak*. Whether verbalized or not, the Badakhshis recognize and conceptualize the relationship of most Badakhshani folk songs to the essential *falak* model.

Musical Examples from Khadir, Hazarajat

When compared to Herat and Faizabad, the number of composed songs in Khadir is minimal. I had the opportunity of recording only two composed songs, both by the same singer, Mirza Husain, and both by the same poet, Hasan Beg of Takht-e Waras, Hazarajat, who died approximately thirty years ago. Five years previously, I recorded another composed song by the same poet.[12]

All three examples are remarkably alike in poetic form and presentation. The poetic form is a *musammat* in which a number of *misrā^c*s form a stanza. Each stanza has its own rhyme, except for the last *misrā^c* in a stanza, which rhymes with other final *misrā^c*s. Musically, each stanza is punctuated with a beginning pattern outlining important notes on vocables which I had previously termed "intonation."[13] The last *misrā^c* of a stanza is often repeated in whole or part, and is followed by a definite pause or break in the flow of the song. Mirza Husain does not always repeat the last *misrā^c* of a stanza, but he does end each stanza with a single note of long duration. Husain actually sings two *musammat*s to the melody of Example 34; however, only the first poem is given and only the first two stanzas of the first poem are transcribed:

Example 34: Mirza Husain, *musammat.*

Musammat:

> *Qadash harhar rokhash ahmar tanash sim o labash shekar*
> *Dahan ghunera zabān bulbul bowad dandān zi dur khostar*
> *Shekam qāq o gulu shisha du pistān por zi qanditar*

Ba har waqti ke u khodrā kherāmān karda meāyad

Ajab dast o ajab gardan ajab nāzok badan dāri
Ajab cheshm o ajab abru ajab zeiba ziqand dāri
Ajab qāsh o ajab mijgān ajab bu-ye khotan dāri
Ajab dor o ajab marjān ajab lal-e yeman dāri

Shabi daijur āsheqrā cherāghan karda meāyad

Fedā gardam ba estaghnā shewai raftārrā bandam
Du zolf-e anbar afshāni kaji tātārrā bandam
Ze del bordan nadāram chi rokh-e gulnārrā bandam

Siāh mārra be daure māh pechān karda meāyad

Her stature like a poplar, her rosy face, her wiry body, her sugar lips
Her flowerbud mouth, her nightingale tongue, her teeth prettier than pearls
Her trim stomach, her transparent throat, her breasts full with sugar syrup.

Anytime she comes, she comes strutting.

Wondrous hands, wondrous neck, wondrous delicate body you have
Wondrous eyes, wondrous eyebrows, wondrous beautiful chin you have
Wondrous eyebrows, wondrous eyelashes, wondrous smell of musk you have
Wondrous pearls, wondrous corals, wondrous rubies you have.

In the moonless night, my love comes like a lamp.

I sacrifice myself to her independence, I am a slave to the way she walks
I am a slave to her tresses with curls which give the scent of ambergris
I can't forget I am a slave to her pomegranate blossom face
She is coming with her black hair twisted around her moon face.

The vocal style which characterizes the three composed songs in question emphasizes open fourth intervals and employs falsetto voice on the high notes. This style had been identified as the *Jāghori* style;[14] Mirza Husain and those present, however, denied that the song or style has any special associations with the Jaghori area of the Hazarajat, or with any particular musical genre.

Although three out of the four composed songs I have recorded in the Hazarajat are in this vocal style—the fourth song is based on verses from the *Shāh Nāma* and was recorded in 1967—not all songs in this style are composed songs. Although the number of songs is too small to draw any fast conclusions about composed songs in the Hazarajat, a general observation is presented here.

A dichotomy between professional and amateur musicians exists in Herat. The same dichotomy in Badakhshan is represented by urban and rural musicians, while in the Hazarajat it is represented by instrumentalists and vocalists. Composed pieces in Herat and Faizabad are usually performed by the more professional or urban musicians because composed songs are more stylized and developed than folk songs. One would expect the same situation to occur in the Hazarajat—that composed songs are performed by those musicians who accompany their songs on the *dambura*—but, in fact, the opposite is true: every composed song is sung unaccompanied.

The reasons for this unexpected situation are not readily apparent. I can only think that composed songs in Herat and Faizabad differ greatly in musical style from folk songs, but there is little to distinguish musically the small number of composed songs from the vast majority of folk songs in the Hazarajat. The main distinction lies in the poetry itself which would be de-emphasized by the purely musical *dambura* accompaniment. Not only is the solo, unaccompanied voice used exclusively in rendering composed songs, but also a simple, almost declamatory vocal style accented by some disjunct motion of a fourth and falsetto voice is favored.

In 1968 I suggested a theory of gradual evolution of Hazara melody types.[15] Stating first that the interval of a fourth is important and apparent in most Hazara melodies, intonation patterns, and *dambura* tunings, I proceeded to point to a general tendency to increase in size and complexity ranging from the simple lullaby to the complex accompanied song. What I failed to notice at that time was the possibility that the so-called "*Jāghori* style" might, indeed, be the Hazara melody prototype.

Table 23 includes a brief description of the poetic and musical content of each prototype song I recorded during the two visits I made to the Hazarajat. The examples are in a variety of settings, including accompanied voice and solo *nai*, including folk couplets and quatrains and composed poems. The only consistent feature, then, is the melody type, which consists of a two or three-note conjunct melody characterized by skips up or down of an interval of a fourth.

The upward skip stems from the second degree and results in the highest note of the melody sung with a falsetto. Even when the actual skip seems to be only an interval of a third, starting from the third degree, the third degree is only functioning as a passing tone and is always preceded by the second degree. The skip down may or may not be present. When present, the relation of a fourth is established between the first degree and the lowest note of the melody. Sometimes the lowest note of the melody itself may be related to a note yet a fourth lower, but this happens only in some intonation patterns (P-9), or in the beginning of some lines (P-5), and is not part of the main melody but is completely at the discretion of the singer. The third degree is not always present in prototype melodies. When it is included, it can be either a major or minor third. In tunes other than prototype melodies, the third degree is often unstable and fluctuates between major and minor, or is at times neutral.

The only example that diverges from the above description is P-6 (see Table 23). Although the basic melody is contained in a three-note range

TABLE 23
Formal Analysis of Hazara Prototype Melodies

Ex.	Artist	Instrument	Place	Poem	Type	Poetic Meter	Intervals
P-1	Haidar	Solo Voice	Khadir	Couplets *Moghol Dokhtar*	Folk		
P-2	Ghulam Sauz	Voice *Dambura*	Khadir	Quatrains "lalai"	Folk		
P-3	Husain Ali	*Nai* Solo	Khadir	—	Folk		
P-4	Mirza Husain	Solo Voice	Khadir	*Musammat*	Composed		
P-5	Mirza Husain	Solo Voice	Khadir	*Musammat*	Composed		
P-6	Mirza Husain	Solo Voice	Khadir	*Naᶜt*	Composed		
P-7	Bejan	Solo Voice	Besud	Quatrains "lalai"	Folk		
P-8	Mohammed Asil	Solo Voice	Panjao	Quatrains	Folk		
P-9	Haidar	Solo Voice	Sangchelak	*Musammat*	Composed		

and the skip up of a fourth is maintained, the basic orientation of the melody differs; instead of being on the first, second, and third degrees, it is on the third, fourth, and fifth degrees.

Although realization of the poetic meter is not an integral part of the prototype melody, the melody is nevertheless easily adaptable to different phrase lengths and a variety of rhythms. Example 35 (P-8) is in the popular *chār baiti* rhythm:

Example 35: Mohammed Asil, Hazara Folk Song.

Folk Song:

Ma qorbān-e du cheshman-e ghazālesh
Agar kushta shawam khunam fedāesh
Agar kushta shawam khunam bereza
Tufāili jura zolfa kashālesh

I sacrifice myself to her two doe eyes
If I should be killed, my blood is sacrified for her
If I should be killed, spill my blood
For her two hanging tresses.

Songs P-1, P-4 and P-6 are in the *hazaj-e masamman-e sālim* meter in which the pattern ⌣ - - - is repeated eight times in a *bait*. Song P-4 has already been transcribed on pages 179–80 (Example 34). Perhaps it is this capability of being able to interpret poetic meter that makes the prototype melody attractive for singing composed songs.

With few exceptions, melody types other than the prototype melody share the same melodic contour; that is, a general downward movement from the highest note to the first degree. It is followed by a restatement or two of the downward movement on a smaller scale. A melodic line usually corresponds to a poetic *bait*:

misrā^c   *misrā^c*

The vast majority of the songs exhibit an opening melodic structure which approaches the highest degree conjunctly from below (see Examples 36 and 37):

Example 36: Ghulam Sauz, Hazara Song.

Hazara Song:

Darakhte lab-e dariā sāya dāra
Dutā bulbul miānesh khāna dāra
Kodami sangi zada dar pā-ye bulbul
Ke bulbul nālai sad sāla dāra

A tree next to the river has shade
Two nightingales have a home in it
Someone threw a stone at the nightingale
So the nightingale cries a hundred years.

Example 37: Bomand, Sakhidad, Yusuf, Anwar, Awaz, *Tamazāni.*

(o) sa daf wari dan dan dara   za li la   cheshem   da ra   az du   nia ma   ra ya   da

Tamazāni:

Du dandān yarma zaile muraka
Sadaf wāri dandān dāra zalila
Sadaf wāri dandān dāra zalila
Cheshm dāra az duniā marā yada

My lover's teeth are like pearls
Teeth like mother-of-pearl she has, Zalila
Teeth like mother-of-pearl she has, Zalila
She has eyes that I will always remember.

The conjunct line is sometimes preceded by a disjunct skip outlining an interval of a fourth (see Examples 38 and 39).

Example 38: Mahtab and Agha Gul, Hazara Song.

az   she ke bar sho da gam hai shi khosh khosh

hai hai du shan ma   mai   da gak   na shi   da na khosh

Hazara Song:

Az sheo ke bar shoda gam hāi shi khosh khosh
Hāi hāi da shanma maidagak nashida nakhosh
Hāi hāi qāsed budi rai kadi pesh-i yār
Hāi hāi hawāl-e maidagaga mikadi rosh

He came from below with slow steps
In my thoughts my little one was sick
If there were a messenger going to my love
The condition of my little one would be known.

Example 39: Arbab Ghulam, *Kisawi.*

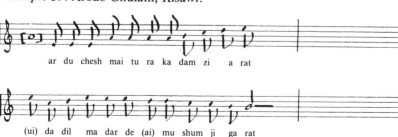

ar   du chesh mai tu ra ka dam zi   a rat

(ui) da dil   ma dar de (ai) mu shum ji   ga rat

da dil ma dar   de ai mu shum ji ga rat

i dagh a   mu ba rum ma ta qi   a mat

Kisawi:

Har du cheshma-ye turā kadem ziārat
Da dil ma dardi mushum jigarak
Da dil ma dardi mushum jigarak
In dagha muburom ma tā qiāmat

I made a pilgrimage to your eyes
In my heart it aches, my dear
In my heart it aches, my dear
I will carry this burden till Resurrection.

Example 39 is notable for a number of reasons: first, the approach to the highest note occupies the whole of the first *misrāᶜ*. Second, the melody for the second *bait* is slightly different from the first *bait* melody; thus, this is one of the few examples in which the melodic unit corresponds to two *baits*. Third, like Example 38, the *bait* ends on the second degree. After the initial reference to the lower tetrachord, the main melody is confined to the upper tetrachord. Fourth, the *dambura* introduction and interludes are in the meter of seven. When the voice enters, the rhythm loosens, but the feeling of seven is not lost. Finally, this and another similar melody were identified as *Kisawi* (an area south of Khadir), while two other similar melodies were unidentified. Though there may not be perfect agreement on the name of a melody, the melody itself can be identified as a special melody type. As is often the case in the Hazarajat as well as the other two areas, melodies constitute covert categories. Very little is verbalized about melody itself, yet people do discern melodies or distinguish between them.

Most Hazara folk songs are based on the quatrain or couplet form, with the melodic unit corresponding to a *bait*. The melodic line itself can be divided into two symmetrical halves corresponding to the *misrāᶜ*s. The line descends to the first or second degree at the end of the first *misrāᶜ*, giving a sense of a half cadence. The half cadence is often accentuated by a long note as in Examples 37 and 38, or accented by a large skip as in the following example by Baz Gul. As is quite common, she repeats the second *misrāᶜ*.

Other melodic lines like the one in Example 36 divide the line asymmetrically; that is, the first degree and agogic accent do not occur until well into the second *misrāᶜ*. It should be mentioned here that the singer of Ex-

Example 40: Baz Gul, Hazara Song.

(a)   sa rak tang a sto mo tar   tez   a   me raft

ke   del- bar jan   su   i   gar de-   za me   raft

(a) ke del-   bar jan   su i   gar de   za me   raft

Hazara Song:

Sarak tang ast motar tez meraft
Ke delbar jān sui Gardez meraft

The road is narrow, the car is speeding
Because my dear sweetheart is going to Gardez.

ample 36, Ghulam Sauz, uses the falsetto voice reminiscent of the prototype melody at the end of the line. Again, the falsetto voice is approached
and departed by disjunct motion.

The *Kisawi* melody type, Example 39, has already been mentioned in
terms of its melodic relationship to two *bait*s instead of one. The half cadence occurs at the end of the first *bait*, then after the third *misrā^c*; thus,
each section of the melodic contour is doubled in length.

bait   misrā^c   misrā^c

Most Hazara folk songs can be considered as coming from one melody
type, since they share so many common characteristics. Although a generic
term is lacking, parallels can be drawn with the Badakhshani *falak*. The
Hazara prototype melody reflects the same generative qualities as the rural
falak. The other Hazara melodies, like the urban *falak*, have developed into
divergent forms and are identified by qualifiers such as *Tamazāni* and
Kisawi.

The music reflects the homogeneous social setting of Khadir and the
rest of the Hazarajat. No distinctions exist between professional and ama-

teur music, between urban and rural styles. The same melodies are sung by both men and women, by both solo and accompanied voice, and used for both composed and folk songs. This is not to deny certain preferences or stylistic differences between songs of men and women, or between the accompanied or unaccompanied song, but on the whole, when compared with the other two areas, Khadir's music is the least complicated by different styles associated with professional musicians or urban music, neither of which has gained much importance in the Hazarajat.

Summary

The distinction between composed song and folk song is evident in all three areas. Composed songs are performed by specialized musicians, performed in a special style, and referred to in a special vocabulary. The degree of special treatment, however, differs from one area to the other.

In Herat composed songs are mostly sung by nonhereditary, radio-theater musicians in a popular style which includes orchestral accompaniment and interludes, and the characteristic devices of repetition, extension, and rhythmic displacement at the ends of sections. Composed songs often have a title of their own, the poet and type of poem are cited, and the name of the melodic mode is often given. Folk songs are performed by all musicians in any style. They are identified either by a specific title or by melody type.

Composed songs in Faizabad are most often sung by urban amateur musicians (*shauqi*) who accompany themselves on a stringed instrument. The traditional performances of composed songs include a number of poems sung in different rhythms and tempi. Composed songs do not have specific titles in Faizabad, but the poet and poetic form (most often *ghazal*) is usually known. Folk songs, on the other hand, are performed by urban and rural musicians alike, accompanied or unaccompanied. They are called *falak* or are unidentified.

In Khadir composed songs are sung unaccompanied, while folk songs are sometimes accompanied and sometimes not accompanied. Other than the fact that composed songs in Khadir are called *she^c^r* (poem) and the name of the poet is known, little distinguishes composed songs from folk songs. Some tunes are associated with certain areas, but the identification of folk tunes is far from consistent.

CHAPTER SEVEN

Summary

In the beginning, I attempted to write a book about the music of Afghanistan, but in the end, I hope I have written about the culture of Afghanistan. In order to discover, understand, and explain the relationships between musical concepts and the products of these ideas embodied in the musical sounds themselves, I looked to the sociocultural system of the people, because music is but one part of a reflection of the culture in which it is developed.

The three Persian-speaking areas of Afghanistan concerned in this work differ in geographic location, ethnic constitution, size, and historical orientation, yet a strong bond of unity exists between them. They share a religion and a way of life, Islam. As was shown in the Introduction, the Islamic religion is important in determining social as well as moral conduct. Further, it plays a large role in forming notions, categories, and definitions about all facets of Muslim life.

The concepts of "music" and "musician" in all three geographical areas are based on the assumption that music is religiously unpraiseworthy because of its associations with such activities specifically prohibited by religion as drinking intoxicating liquors, adultery, and gambling. The music associated with these forbidden acts, however, is specifically the music of professional musicians. Nonprofessional music is sometimes considered music, but the lines of demarcation are not always clear. Nevertheless, both professional and nonprofessional music are affected by each other.

Although these basic notions are shared by inhabitants of all three areas, the amount of professional music activity differs in each area and accounts for the diverse ways in which music and musicians are dealt with in these three areas. Professional musical activity abounds in Herat, the most urban and ethnically heterogeneous of the three areas. The inhabitants hold a variety of musical notions and identify different groups of musicians and musical styles, all of which are formalized into categories differentiated by special vocabulary and behavior. On the other hand, Khadir, the most rural and homogeneous of the three areas, has no professional music to speak of. As a result, its inhabitants have the least formalized musical categories, vocabulary or special behavior patterns. Faizabad lies somewhere in between these two poles.

Formalized concepts lead to strict segregation and censure of professional musician groups and identification of certain musical styles with certain musicians. In Herat a strict dichotomy exists between professional and amateur musicians. In Badakhshan this dichotomy is represented by the distinction between urban and rural musicians. In the Hazarajat it is represented by the distinction between instrumentalists and noninstrumentalists. In whatever way this dichotomy is represented, the basic distinguishing feature is one of professionalism, the urban musician being more professional than the rural one, the instrumentalist being more professional than the noninstrumentalist.

The musical styles of Herat are more separate and distinct than in the other two areas. The repertoire of professional musicians includes traditional, professional pieces such as *Aushāri*, as well as stylized folk songs. Modern composed songs are relegated to the few educated professional singers associated with the radio and theaters. In Badakhshan the composed songs are mainly sung by urban musicians, those from the greater Faizabad area. They also sing stylized folk songs. In the Hazarajat composed songs are always unaccompanied; otherwise, there is no distinction between the repertoire of instrumentalists and noninstrumentalists.

Formalized concepts are further reflected in the musical vocabulary used in each area. Heratis identify different folk melody types by such different names as *chār baiti, sarhadi,* and *sarhadi ghoriāni.* Badakhshani folk melody types are known simply as *falak*, and the Hazara melody type is not identified by a term at all.

If music is indeed a reflection of the culture in which it is developed, and if that culture is strongly influenced by the religion of Islam, then it can be assumed that the musical activities, the formalized concepts of music and musician, the musical styles, and musical terminology of other parts of Afghanistan as well as the Islamic Middle East will reflect the same structural principles and aesthetic values as those found in Herat, Badakhshan, and the Hazarajat.

This study gives strong evidence that most Muslims do think about musical sounds and musical functions as integral aspects of their lives. The chanting of the Koran is governed by the same aesthetic sense as that of other musical sounds. Some Sufis use music as a vehicle for mystical communion. Music theory or knowledge was at one time considered an Islamic science, and today, is still regarded as specialized knowledge. The important and festive events in a Muslim's life are punctuated with music. Practically no one remains untouched by music and musical notions.

Of all the artistic expressions of the Muslims, the verbal arts, especially that of poetry, reigns supreme. The importance of poetry in considering music and musicians is obvious in this study. Musicians are closely associated with poets as performers of poetry, or as performers of music based on structural principles of poetry. Much of the vocabulary relating to music is dominated by poetic terminology.

Finally, this study points to a close relationship between folk and classical musical genres, between rural and urban musical genres. By analyzing and comparing representative local forms to other musical expressions in the area, a developmental pattern appears, going from smaller and more fluid forms to larger and more fixed forms explicitly expressed by special terminology.

Although this work is based on verbal and musical expressions, it is an attempt to explore what is in the mind. Although the study focuses on music, it is also about culture. Although the data was collected and analyzed from three specific areas of Afghanistan, it is hoped the conclusions can lead to an understanding of the whole country of Afghanistan as well as of the Islamic Middle East.

APPENDIX A

Musical Instruments of Three Persian-Speaking Areas

A. Chordophones:

    1. *Dutār*

        a) Long-necked, plucked, Herati lute with three metal strings. An adaptation of the original two-stringed *dutār* with gut strings. Played with a metal plectrum, *nākhonak*. Length: 99 cm.

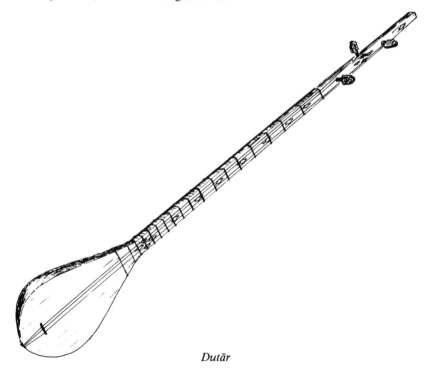

Dutār

b) A derivative of the three-stringed Herati *dutār* with additional sympathetic strings. Made of mulberry wood. Also played with a metal plectrum. Length: 138 cm.

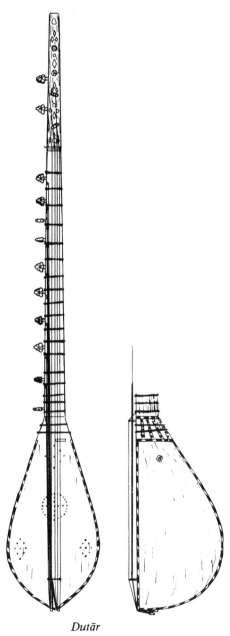

Dutār

2. *Dambura:*

a) Long-necked, plucked bowl lute with two gut or nylon strings, two fron-
tal pegs and no frets. The bowl is carved out of a single block of mulberry
wood and covered with a thick wooden soundboard. No plectrum. Played in
northern Afghanistan and the Hazarajat. Length: 106 cm.

Dambura

b) A smaller *dambura* made in Badakhshan. Usually the bowl and neck are carved from a single block of mulberry or apricot wood. Length: 78 cm.

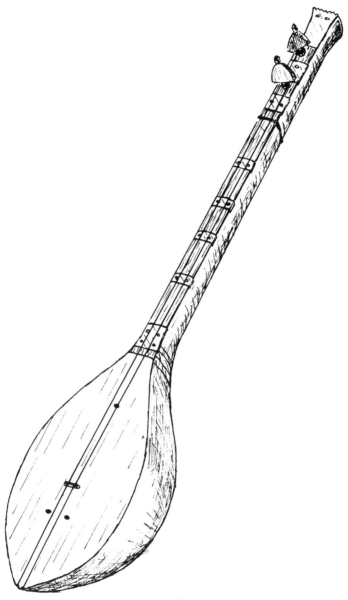

Dambura

3. *Tambur:* A long-necked, plucked lute with six metal strings and additional sympathetic strings. Made of mulberry wood. Sizes vary and some do not have sympathetic strings. Held upright and played with a metal plectrum. Also known in Badakhshan as *setar* (three strings). Length: 127 cm.

Tambur

4. *Rabāb:*

a) A short-necked, plucked lute with a membrane-covered waisted body. It has three main playing strings, two of nylon (*jalau, miana*) and one of gut (*kata*). The sympathetic strings are metal. Made out of mulberry wood. The *rabāb* is the predecessor of the North Indian *sarod*. It is considered the most Afghan of all the musical instruments. Played with a wooden plectrum (*shāhbāz*). Length: 93 cm.

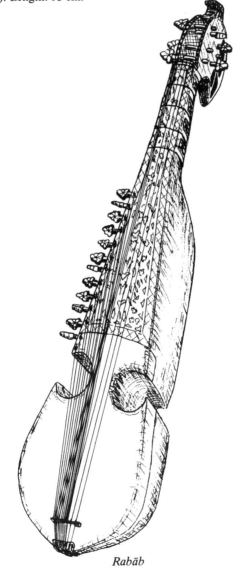

Rabāb

b) A long-necked, plucked lute with protruding spurs. The body is covered with a membrane. The *rabāb* has six nylon or gut strings. It is constructed of a single block of apricot wood. The lower part of the neck is hollow and covered with a sheet of wood which has sound holes. Played with a wooden plectrum. It is made in Sheghnan and played in the regions of Sheghnan and Wakhan. Length: 73 cm.

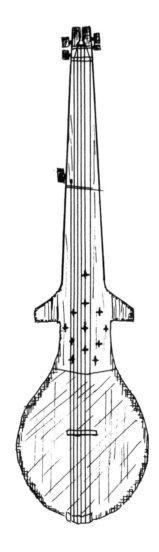

Rabāb

5. *Chārtār:* A long-necked, plucked lute with a membrane-covered body. Known in Iran as *tār*. Six metal strings grouped as two single courses and two double courses. Played with a metal plectrum. The name *chārtār* means "four strings" and may indicate that the original instrument had four strings, or may refer to the six strings which function as four. Not a popular instrument in Afghanistan. Length: 95 cm.

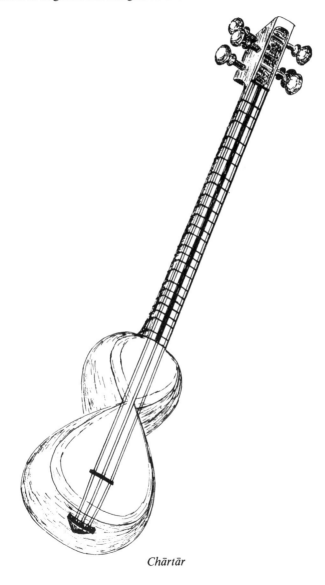

Chārtār

6. *Ghichak:* A two-stringed, spiked fiddle. The strings are metal and the res-
onator is made out of a tin can. Played with a horsehair bow, *kamān*.
Length: 75 cm.

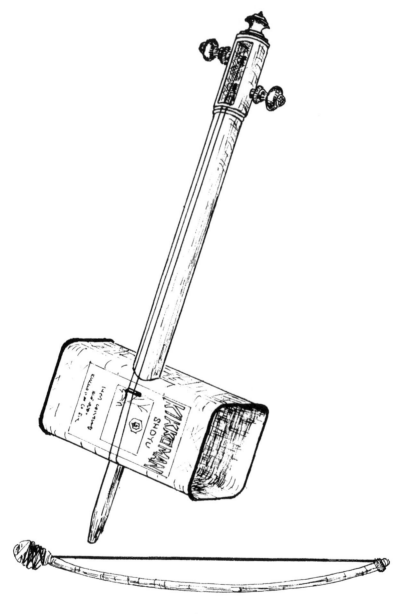

Ghichak

B. Aerophones:

1. *Nai*

a) The generic name for all flutes, but more specifically refers to the long, end-blown shepherd's flute. Length: 62 cm.

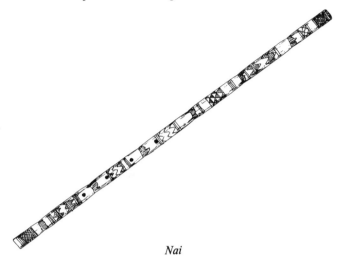

Nai

b) The *nai* of Badakhshan is a fipple flute made of either walnut or apricot wood. Length: 31 cm.

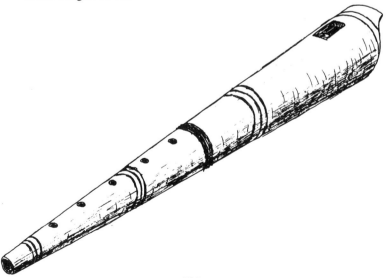

Nai

2. *Tula:* A transverse or fipple flute made of wood or metal. Length: 36 cm.

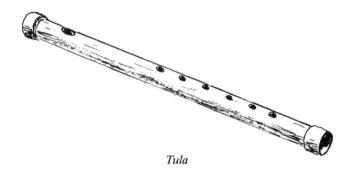

Tula

3. *Sornā:* A double-reed aerophone with a conical bore. The whole reed is placed in the player's mouth. The technique of circular breathing is often utilized in playing this instrument. The *sornā* is strictly a professional, outdoor instrument played with the *dohl*. Length: 46 cm.

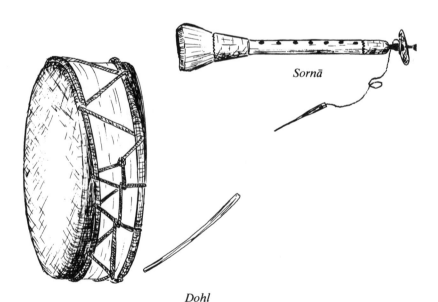

Sornā

Dohl

4. *Harmonium:* A portable reed organ with keyboard. An urban instrument.

Harmonium

C. Membranophones:

   1. *Dohl:* A large double-headed outdoor drum. The size, shape and construction varies. Played with sticks. Often played with the *sornā*. Diameter: 46
   cm. (For illustration, see *sornā*).

   2. *Tabla:* A pair of small kettle drums like the North Indian *tabla*. The body of
   the lower-pitched drum is metal and considerably taller than the North Indian variety. An urban instrument. Diameters: 25 cm. and 18 cm.

Tabla

3. *Zirbaghali:* A single-headed, vase-shaped drum related to the Iranian *dombak*. The size, shape, and material vary. Most drums are made from pottery, but some are carved out of wood. The name literally means "under the armpits." Diameter: 23 cm.

Zirbaghali

4. *Dāira* or *Daf:* A tambourine, with or without jingles. Size and construction vary. A nonprofessional drum often played by women and children. Diameter: 47 cm.

Dāira; Daf

D. Idiophones:

1. *Tāl:* Brass finger cymbals. Diameter: 5 cm.

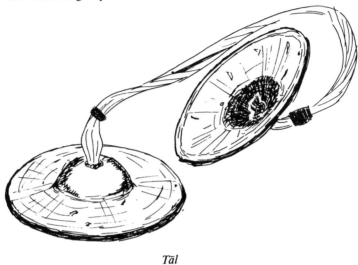

Tāl

2. *Chang:* Jew's harp. A nonprofessional instrument for women and children. Length: 9.5 cm.

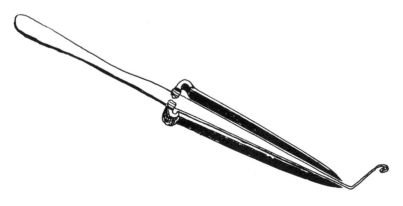

Chang

List of Musicians

The musicians are listed alphabetically according to the three areas in which they lived. All ages are approximate and tribal or ethnic affiliations, if known, are indicated according to the information given by the musicians themselves. All information refers to the time of this study.

HERAT

Abdul Rashid عبدالرشید
Male, 20s, Shekiban Turkmen. Plays *nai* for Herat Nendarei.

Abdul Rahman Saljuqi عبدالرحمن سلجوقی
Male, 31, Head of English Department, Habibia High School, Kabul. Moved to Kabul from Herat. Amateur *chārtār* player.

Amir Mohammed امیرمحمد
Male, 20s, Burakzai, Pashtun. Professional musician; former dancing boy. Nephew of Zainab's husband.

Baidola بیدالا
Male, 20s, Khaugani, Pashtun. Part owner of teahouse. Plays *zirbaghali*.

Ghulam Dastegir Sarud غلام دستگیر سرود
Male, 30s, Tajik. Singer at Behzad Nendarei.

Ghulam Haidar غلام حیدر
Male, 35, Tajik. *Dutār* player in Behzad Nendarei orchestra. My *dutār* teacher and main musical informant in Herat.

Ghulam Mohammed Shabahang غلام محمد شباهنگ

Male, late 30s, Ali Kuzai, Pashtun. Behzad Nendarei orchestra leader.

Ghulam Mohiuddin غلام محی الدین

Male, 25, Mohmand, Pashtun. Part owner of teahouse, *dutār* player, singer.

Ghulam Sarwar غلام سرور

Male, 30s, Tajik. Herat Nendarei orchestra leader.

Habibulla حبیب الله

Male, 30s, Tajik. Farmer in Neshin, Herat Province.

Khalifa Dohlchi Sarwar خلیفه دهلچی سرور

Male, 28, Timuri. Plays *dohl* with cousin Mohammed Omar, *sornā* player.

Khohar-e Sher Gul خواهر شیرگل

Female, 50s, Ali Kuzai, Pashtun. Originally from Ghorian.

Mohammed Alishah Olfat Herawi محمد علی شاه هروی

Male, 40s, Tajik. Owner, producer, director of Behzad Nendarei.

Mohammed Ibrahim Enayat محمد ابراهیم عنایت

Male, 25, Tajik. Singer at Behzad Nendarei.

Mohammed Farhat محمد فرهاد

Male, 40s, Kakar, Pashtun. Singer at Herat Nendarei.

Mohammed Karim محمد کریم

Male, 30, Tajik. *Tabla* player, Behzad Nendarei orchestra.

Mohammed Omar محمد عمر

Male, 25, Timuri. Plays *sornā* with cousin Khalifa Dohlchi Sarwar, *dohl* player.

Mohammed Sharif محمد شریف

Male, 20s, Ishaqzai, Pashtun. Amateur *dutār* player; student at Herat's teacher training school.

Nafisa نفیسه

Female, 20s, Tajik. Singer at Herat Nendarei.

Saman Jan سمن جان

Female, 20s, Jamshedi. Originally nomadic, came to Herat to get domestic work.

Zainab زینب

Female, 35, Burakzai, Pashtun. Professional musician; reputed to be the best female *motreb* in Herat. Daughter of Golpasand.

FAIZABAD

Awaz	عوض	Male, 19, Sheghni. From Sar Cheshma, Sheghnan.
Dost Mohammed	دوست محمد	Male, 52, Tajik (father from Logar). Barber-musician in Jurm.
Dur Mohammed Keshmi	در محمد کشمی	Male, 20s, Tajik, from Keshm. Singer, *ghichak* player.
Ezrat Murad	حضرت مراد	Male, 26, Sheghni from Sheduj, Sheghnan. Singer, plays *daf*.
Faiz-e Mangal	فیض منگل	Male, 37, Tajik from Jurm. Sings, plays *dambura*.
Gul Mohammed	کل محمد	Male, 50s, Sheghni from Bahshar, Sheghnan. Sings, plays *dambura* and Pamir *rabāb*.
Gulshan Begin	کلشان بیکم	Female, 35, Wakhi from Ishmorgh, Wakhan.
Haj Begin	حاج بیکم	Female, 30s, Wakhi from Ishmorgh, Wakhan.
Islam	اسلام	Male, 25, Tajik (Uzbek father) from Baharak. Sings, plays *ghichak*.
Jambi	جهان بیبی	Female, 20s, Wakhi in Kaj Gardan, Khash Valley.
Jandar Shah	جاندار شاه	Male, 25, Sheghni from Sheduj, Sheghnan. Plays *nai*, *ghichak*.
Kaka	کاکا	Male, 40s, Tajik. Faizabad merchant. Plays *rabāb*, harmonium in Mohammed Akbar's orchestra.
Khalifa Gul Jan	خلیفه کل جان	Male, 30s, Tajik (father from Logar). Barber-musician. Plays *tambur* in Mohammed Akbar's orchestra. Lives in Faizabad.
Khan-e Baharaki	خان بهاركی	Male, 80, Tajik from Baharak. Sings, plays *dambura* and *rabāb*.

Mardan	مردان	Male, 65, Tajik. Faizabad shopkeeper. Sings, plays *dambura* and *rabāb*.
Mohammed Akbar	محمد اكبر	Male, 40s, Tajik. Faizabad shopkeeper. Faizabad orchestra leader. Brother of Naim.
Naim	نعيم	Male, 55, Tajik. Faizabad shopkeeper. Amateur *rabāb* player, singer.
Nazar Mohammed	نظر محمد	Male, 50s, Sheghni from Bahshar, Sheghnan. Sings, plays *ghichak*.
Nazir Mohammed	نذير محمد	Male, 20s, Uzbek from Sarlula, Jurm. Sings, plays *dambura*.
Parwin	پروين	Female, 40s, Kabuli. Sings at Radio Afghanistan; one of first female singers on radio.
Ramazan	رمضان	Male, 20s, Wakhi from Khandud. Brother of Jambi.
Yasim	ياسيم	Male, deceased, family from Logar, lived in Faizabad. Teacher of Dost Mohammed and Khalifa Gul Jan.

KHADIR

Agha Gul	آغاگل	Female, late 20s, Hazara from Dasht-e Nili.
Anwar	انور	Male, 20s, Ekhtiari Hazara from Dasht-e Nili. Farmer for Arbab Ghulam.
Arbab Ghulam	ارباب غلام	Male, 35, Tajik Hazara from Dasht-e Nili. Sings, plays *dambura*.
Awaz	عوض	Male, 30s, Kalandar Hazara from Dasht-e Nili. Foreman for Arbab Ghulam.
Baz Gul	بازگل	Female, 20s, Hazara from Shish.
Bejhan	بيجان	Male, 60s, Hazara from Besud. Farmer.
Bomand	بهمن	Male, 30s, Ekhtiari Hazara from Dasht-e Nili. Farmer for Arbab Ghulam. Plays *dambura*.

Ghulam Sauz	غلام سبز	Male, 35, Osma Hazara from Khadir. Sings, plays *dambura*.
Haidar	حیدر	Male, 40s, Doda Hazara from Korga, Dai Kundi. *Wakil* of Dai Kundi's family steward.
Haidar	حیدر	Male, 30s, Neka Hazara from Sangchelak, Dai Kundi. Farmer.
Husain Ali	حسین علی	Male, 20s, Osma Hazara from Khadir. Shepherd. Plays *nai*.
Khadem	خادم	Male, 20s, Osma Hazara from Khadir. Plays *dambura* and sings.
Mahtab	مهتاب	Female, 18, Hazara from Dasht-e Nili.
Mirza Husain	میرزا حسین	Male, 63, Tajik Hazara from Korga, Dai Kundi. Farmer.
Mohammed Asil	محمد اصال	Male, 50s, Hazara from Akhzarat, Panjao. Farmer.
Sakhidad	سخیداد	Male, 20s, Ekhtiari Hazara from Dasht-e Nili. Farmer for Arbab Ghulam.
Yusuf	یوسف	Male, 30s, Ekhtiari Hazara from Dasht-e Nili. Farmer for Arbab Ghulam.

OTHERS

Ustad Mohammed Omar	استاد محمد عمر	Male, 50s. Famous *rabāb* player and orchestra leader at Radio Afghanistan. My *rabāb* teacher.
Ustad Sarahang	استاد سرآهنگ	Male, late 40s. Famous classical singer in Kabul. Radio Afghanistan artist.

Glossary of Persian Terms

The words are briefly defined according to the usage in the book.

Afghān	افغان	A citizen of Afghanistan. Commonly used to designate a Pashtun.
Āhang	آهنگ	Harmony, musical sound, melody.
Ailāq	ايلاق	Summer pastoral encampment.
Akhlāqi	اخلاقی	Song of morals, virtues.
Ala	اله	Lullaby.
Alai	الی	Lullaby.
Alap	آلاپ	Improvised exposition of melodic mode in free rhythm, from Hindustani tradition.
ᶜAlāqadār	علاقدار	Provincial district commissioner.
Ālat-e musiqi	آلت موسیقی	Musical instrument.
ᶜAmma	عمه	Aunt, father's sister.
Arbāb	ارباب	Village leader.
Āsā	آسا	A melodic mode.
Atan	آتن	Dance, men's line dance (Pashtu).

Aushāri	افشاری	Name of instrumental melody type from Herat; kind of dance.
Azān	اذان	Call to prayer.
Bacha	بچه	Boy; refers to boy dancers who impersonate female dancers.
Bacha bi rish	بچه بی ریش	Boy without a beard; refers to boy dancers who impersonate females.
Badakhshān	بدخشان	Province in Northeastern Afghanistan. Also refers to Faizabad.
Badakhshi	بدخشی	Native of Badakhshan.
Bahārak	بهارک	Town and district of Badakhshan province.
Bairami	بیرمی	Melodic mode. Hindustani *Bhairavi*.
Bairo	بیرو	Melodic mode. Hindustani *Bhairav*.
Bait	بیت	Verse or poetic line, stich. Commonly refers to song.
Bait guftan	بیت گفتن	To sing a song.
Baluch	بلوچ	Baluchi, inhabitants of southern Afghanistan, Iran, and Baluchistan, Pakistan.
Bam	بم	Lowest string on the *dambura*.
Bāzi	بازی	Dance.
Bāzigar	بازیگر	Dancer, especially boy dancer.
Besud	بهسود	Town and district in Wardak province.
Chāderi	چادری	Woman's veil.
Chakar zadan	چکر زدن	To take a stroll, walk.
Chang	چنگ	Jew's harp; the ancient Persian harp.
Chār baiti	چهار بیتی	Quatrain. Also refers to a melody type of Herat.

Chār shambe awal-e sāl	چهارشنبه اول سال	First Wednesday of the New Year.
Chār suq	چهارسوق	Four market places; main intersection in the old city of Herat.
Chārtār	چهارتار	Name of Iranian *tār* in Herat; long-necked plucked lute.
Chāriāri	چهاریاری	Followers of the Prophet's four Companions; reference to Sunni Muslims.
Chopāni	چوپانی	Pertaining to shepherds, a shepherd's song.
Daf	دف	Tambourine.
Dāi Kundi	دای کندی	District of Urozgan province.
Dāira	دایره	Tambourine.
Dalāk	دلاک	Hereditary, professional barber-musician.
Dambura	دنبوه	Two-stringed plucked lute.
Damburachi	دنبوهچی	*Dambura* player.
Dari	دری	Persian dialect spoken in Afghanistan.
Darwāza ᶜIrāq	دروازه عراق	West gate of the old city of Herat.
Darwāza Kandahār	دروازه کندهار	South gate of the old city of Herat.
Darwāza Khosh	دروازه خوش	East gate of the old city of Herat.
Darwāza Malik	دروازه ملک	North gate of the old city of Herat.
Dasta	دسته	Neck of lute.
Dāstān	داستان	A story.
Delrobā	دلربا	Bowed, stringed instrument.
Deo	دیو	A bad jinn, a demon.
Dini	دینی	Pertaining to religion.

Dohl	دهل	A large double-headed drum which accompanies the *sornā*.
Dom	دوم	Barber-musician (Pashtu).
Du baiti	دوبیتی	Quatrain.
Dutār	دوتار	Long-necked plucked lute.
Esnā ᶜAshari	اثنا عشری	Twelve-Imam form of Shiism.
Fahm	فهم	Knowledge.
Faizābād	فیض آباد	Capital of Badakhshan province.
Fakāhi	فكاهى	Comic song.
Falak	فلک	Folk song genre of Badakhshan.
Fard	فرد	Line or verse quoted from another poem.
Farkhāri	فرخاری	Pertaining to Farkhar, a district in Takhar province.
Fārsi	فارسی	Persian language.
Filmi	فیلمی	Pertaining to Indian movies.
Ganj	گنج	Animal bazaar in Herat.
Gardan	گردن	Neck of lute.
Gāz	گاز	Rope swing.
Geda	گده	Rhythm of four.
Ghamgin	غمگین	Sad, sorrowful; subject of many *falak*s.
Gharbāl	غربال	Coarse sieve.
Gharib zāda	غریب زاده	Hereditary, professional musicians in Herat.
Gharibi	غریبی	Song about a poor man or stranger; a folk song.
Ghazal	غزل	Love song; a poem consisting of four to fourteen rhyming stichs.

Ghichak	نیچک	Spiked-fiddle.
Ghol	غول	A bad jinn.
Ghoriān	غوریان	Town and district in Herat province.
Ghurbati	غوربتی	Gypsy.
Golrān	گلران	District of Herat province.
Gorgholi	گورغلی	Central Asian epic also known as *Kuroghli*, "Son of a Blind Man."
Gorgholikhān	گورغلیخوان	*Gorgholi* epic singer.
Gul	گل	Flower; decorations on musical instruments.
Gulun zadan	گلو زدن	To execute vocal ornaments, exaggerated vibrato.
Gushak	گوشگ	Tuning peg.
Hadith	حدیث	Traditions of the Prophet.
Hamāsi	حماسی	Song of bravery, heroic song.
Hari Rud	هریرود	River in western Afghanistan.
Hazaj	هزج	Poetic meter based on foot ⌣ - - -.
Hazāra	هزاره	Ethnic group, inhabitants of central Afghanistan.
Herāt	هرات	Province in western Afghanistan; capital city of Herat province.
Herāti	هراتی	Native of Herat.
Herawi	هروی	Name designating "of Herat."
Hindu Kush	هندوکش	Mountain range in Afghanistan.
ᶜIshqi	عشقی	Love song.
Ismāᶜili	اسماعیلی	Sect of Shiism sometimes known as "Seveners."

Jāghori	جاغوری	District of Ghazni province; name of a Hazara tribe.
Jalau	جلو	First or front string of *rabāb*, *dutār*.
Jamshedi	جمشیدی	Ethnic group living in Herat province.
Jat	جت	Gypsy; professional musician in Herat.
Jeshen-e Isteqlāl	جشن استقلال	Independence Day.
Jog	جوگ	A melodic mode.
Jogi	جوگی	A gypsy.
Jurm	جرم	Town and district in Badakhshan province.
Jush kardan	جوش کردن	To ornament, elaborate instrumental music.
Kābul	کابل	Capital of Afghanistan.
Kābuli	کابلی	Native of Kabul; pertaining to Kabul.
Kāfi	کافی	Teahouse.
Kāma	کامه	District in Nangrahar province.
Kamān	کمان	Bow of *ghichak*.
Kamand	کمند	Horizontal decorations around *dutār* neck.
Kandahār	قندهار، کندهار	Province in southern Afghanistan; capital city of the province.
Karbolāi	کربلای	Pilgrim to Karbala, Iraq, site of martyrdom of Husain.
Kāsa	کاسه	The bowl or main body of a lute.
Kata	کته	Large, third string of *rabāb*, *dutār*.
Kataghan	قطغن	Name of pre-1963 province that included existing provinces of Baghlan, Kunduz, and Takhar.
Kazākh	قزاق	Central Asian, Turkic ethnic group.

Keliwāli	كليوالى	Folk song (Pashtu).
Kesbi	كسبى	Professional.
Keshm	كيشم	Town and district in Badakhshan province.
Khadir	خدير	Administrative center of Dai Kundi district in Urozgan province.
Khadiri	خديرى	Pertaining to Khadir, a native of Khadir.
Khalifa	خليفه	Caliph; title for hereditary barber-musicians.
Khām	خام	Raw; unskilled.
Khāndan	خواندن	To read, sing; section of composition based on song text.
Khānenda	خواننده	Singer.
Khanjari	خنجرى	Arrow-shaped decorative design on *dutār*.
Kharak	خرك	Nut and bridge on lute.
Khesh	خيش	Name of decorative design on *dutār*.
Khiābān	خيابان	Central section of Faizabad.
Kisawi	كيسوى	Pertaining to Kisaw, area south of Khadir.
Khorāsān	خراسان	Area including eastern Iran and western Afghanistan; eastern Iranian province.
Kokcha	كوكچه	River in northeastern Afghanistan.
Kouli	كولى	Gypsy.
Kuchi	كوچى	Nomad.
Kuhi o dashti	كوهى و دشتى	Pertaining to hinterlands; mountains, deserts.
Kuk kardan	كوك كردن	To tune an instrument.
Kunduz	قندوز	Town and province in northern Afghanistan.

Kurdaki	کردکی	Pertaining to rural, from *kurd* meaning irrigation ditch; folk song.
Lailon	لیلون	Nylon string.
La*c*l Sarjangal	لعل سرجنگل	District in Ghor province.
Lalai	للی	Lullaby.
Lalai kardan	للی کردن	To sing a lullaby.
Lalu	للو	Lullaby.
Logar	لوگر	Province south of Kabul.
Madrasa	مدرسه	Religious school.
Magad	مگد	Actor, comedian of Herat folk drama. Reference to member of folk drama acting community in their own language.
Magadi	مگدی	Pertaining to *magad*s.
Magasak	مگسک	Small, round bone bridge for sympathetic string on *rabāb* or *dutār*.
Mahājir	مهاجر	Emigrant.
Mahalli	محلی	Local, regional folk song.
Maktab	مکتب	School.
Māldāri	مالداری	Pertaining to nomads, owners of flocks.
Maqām	مقام	Tune, melodic mode.
Maqta*c*	مقطع	Closing verse of poem.
Masjid -i Jāmi*c*	مسجد جامع	General mosque where Friday prayers are said.
Maslaki	مسلکی	Vocational.
Matla*c*	مطلع	Initiatory verse of poem.
Mazār -i Sharif	مزار شریف	Town in northern Afghanistan, capital of Balkh province.
Mela	میله	Picnic, outing.
Mela-ye chār maghz	میله چهار مغز	Walnut festival.
Miāna	میانه	Middle string of *rabāb*, *dutār*.
Mirzā	میرزا	Title indicating gentleman, educated person, a scholar; a scribe.

Misrā^c	مصراع	Hemistich, half verse.
Mogholi	مغلی	Rhythm of 7, divided 3+2+2.
Moqaled	مقلد	Folk actor, comedian.
Moqoladi	مقلدی	Folk drama in Herat.
Mosāla	ماله	Plastic material used for black, decorative pieces on *rabāb* or *dutār*.
Motreb	مطرب	Musician, entertainer.
Mukhammas	مخمس	Five-line poetic form.
Mullā	ملا	Person with religious knowledge.
Musammat	مسمط	Stanzaic poetic form.
Musiqi	موسیقی	Secular music, professional instrumental or art music.
Naghma	نغمه	Tune, instrumental music.
Nai	نی	End-blown flute.
Nākhonak	ناخنک	*Dutār* plectrum.
Na^ct	نعت	Song in praise of Mohammed.
Nawākhtan	نواختن	To play a stringed instrument.
Nawāzenda	نوازنده	Musician, instrumentalist.
Nendārei	ننداری	Theater (Pashtu).
Neshin	نشین	Town south of the city of Herat.
Nili	نیلی	Area south of Khadir in Urozgan province.
Onarman	هنرمند	Artist.
Panjāo	پنجاب	District of Bamiyan province.
Panjtani	پنجتنی	Followers of the "Holy Five," referring to Shias. In Badakhshan, refers to Ismaili Shias.
Parda	پرده	Fret.
Paron	پران	Dance rhythm, movement or section in a fast tempo.
Pashtun	پشتون	Speakers of Pashtu; commonly known as Afghan.

Pāzarb	با ضرب	Refrain in fixed rhythm, composed of short rhyming phrases.
Post	پوست	Membrane covering *rabāb* body.
Qāfia	قافیه	Rhyme; final consonant on which the rhyme of poem rests.
Qal^ca	قلعه	Fortress, citadel.
Qasida	قصیده	Ode, a long panegyric with rhyming verses.
Qaum	قوم	Tribe, family.
Qawāl	قوال	Gypsy.
Rabāb	رباب	Short-necked, plucked lute; also Pamir *rabāb*, a long-necked lute with spurred body.
Rāg	راگ	Melodic mode (Hindustani).
Ramazān	رمضان	Month of fasting.
Raqs	رقص	Dance.
Razmi	رزمی	Song of battle.
Rez dādan	رز دادن	To sing vocal trill, ornament.
Roda	روده	Gut string.
Roza	روزه	Fasting.
Roz-i bāzār	روز بازار	Market day.
Rubā^ci	رباعی	Quatrain composed of four hemistichs.
Rutāl	روتال	The lid or soundboard of *dutār*.
Rustāyi	روستایی	Pertaining to peasant, villager; folk song.
Sadā	صدا	Voice, sound.
Sadaf	صدف	Mother-of-pearl.
Saj^c	سجع	Rhymed prose (Arabic).
Salmāni	سلمانی	Barber.
Samowar	سماور	Teahouse.
Sar āwāz	سرآواز	Introduction of melodic mode in free rhythm.
Sarāyenda	سرآینده	Singer.
Sar Ghalām	سرغلان	Place in Badakhshan province.

Sarhadi	سرحدی	Pertaining to border or frontier region; melody type in Herat.
Sarhadi Ghoriāni	سرحدی غوریانی	*Sarhadi* melody type from Ghorian.
Sartarush	سرتراش	Barber.
Sāz	ساز	Music, instrument, melody.
Sāz nawāz	ساز نواز	Musician, instrumentalist.
Sāz-e bulbul	ساز بلبل	Bird calls.
Sāzenda	سازنده	Musician, instrumentalist.
Setār	سه تار	The *tambur*.
Shāhbāz	شاه باز	*Rabāb* plectrum.
Shahr-i Nau	شهر نو	New section of a city.
Shakal	شکل	Introduction of melodic mode in free rhythm.
Shākh	شاخ	Branch, an episode of Gorgholi epic.
Shamār	شمار	Fast dance; section of piece in fast tempo.
Shari^c*at*	شریعت	Islamic law.
Sharistān	شهرستان	District of Urozgan province.
Shauqi	شوقی	Amateur with strong interest in activity or thing.
Sheghnān	شغنان	District of Badakhshan province.
Sheghni	شغنی	Pertaining to Sheghnan, a native of Sheghnan.
Sher	شیر	Lion.
She^c*r*	شعر	Poetry, verse.
She^c*r khāndan*	شعر خواندن	To recite poetry.
Shi^c*a*	شیعه	Member of one of two sects of Islam who believe Ali is sole and rightful heir to the Prophet.
Shir o shekar	شیر و شکر	"Milk and sugar," refers to good mixture as a song in two languages.
Shomāli	شمالی	Northern, pertaining to the area north of Kabul; melody type.

Shoruwa	شروع	Corruption of word *shoro*; beginning; to designate melodic introduction in free rhythm.
Sim	سیم	Metal string.
Sor kardan	سورکردن	To tune an instrument.
Sornā	سرنا	Oboe, shawm-like instrument.
Sunni	سنی	Member of one of two great divisions of Islam who believes the first four caliphs are the legitimate successors to Mohammed.
Surah	سوره	Chapter of the Koran.
Tabla	طبله	Pair of kettledrums.
Tahrir	تحریر	Vocal ornamentation, a glottal trill.
Tājik	تاجیک	Person of Iranian descent. Commonly, a sedentary village-dwelling Sunni.
Tājiki	تاجیکی	Persian spoken by Tajiks.
Takhallus	تخلص	Pen name.
Tāl	تال	Finger cymbals.
Tamazāni	تمزانی	Pertaining to Tamazan, area south of Khadir.
Tambur	طنبور	Long-necked plucked lute.
Tār	تار	String; Iranian plucked lute.
Tārgir	تارگیر	Tail piece of string instruments, to which the string ends are fastened.
Tarkib-band	ترکیب بند	Stanzaic form of poetry.
Tarz	طرز	Style, melody.
Tasawwafi	تصوفی	Pertaining to mysticism, sufiism.
Tasnif	تصنیف	Ballad, vocal composition.
Tula	توله	Transverse or fipple flute.
Turkmen	ترکمن	Member of Central Asian Turkic ethnic group.
Urozgān	ارزگان	Province in central Afghanistan.
Ustā	استا	Professional barber-musician, actor-comedian of Herat folk drama.

Ustād	استاد	Teacher; title for professional, master musician.
Uzbek	اوزربک	Member of Central Asian Turkic ethnic group.
Wakhān	وخان	District of Badakhshan province.
Wakhi	وخی	Pertaining to Wakhan.
Wakil	وکیل	Representative to Parliament.
Woleswāl	ولسوال	District commissioner (Pashtu).
Woleswāli	ولسوالی	Major district of a province (Pashtu).
Yakāulang	یکاولنگ	District of Bamiyan province.
Zadan	زدن	To play a musical instrument.
Zahiri	زهیری	Sad, melancholy; subject matter of *falak*s.
Zarb	ضرب	Musical section or movement in slow, fixed rhythm.
Zāu	زاو	Cleft; name for part of decorative design on the *dutār*.
Zil	زیل	Upper string of *dambura*.
Zirbaghali	زیربغلی	Goblet-shaped, single-headed drum.

Notes

CHAPTER ONE: INTRODUCTION

1. Tyler, *Cognitive Anthropology*, p. 3.

2. Dumont, *The Headman and I*, pp. 4–5.

3. Afghanistan, Ministry of Planning, Department of Statistics, *Pocket-Book of Afghanistan: 1350*, pp. 3–4.

4. Farhadi, "Languages," in *The Kabul Times Annual: 1970*, pp. 121–24.

5. Sweet, *Peoples and Cultures of the Middle East* 2:xiii.

6. Caroe, *The Pathans*, p. xiv.

7. Elphinstone, *An Account of the Kingdom of Caubol* 2:102.

8. Schurmann, *The Mongols of Afghanistan*, p. 49.

9. Dupree, *Afghanistan*, p. xix, does not agree with the 1747 date assigned to the founding of a modern Afghan nation. Although the Afghan Republic was established under Daud in 1973, the Newells in *Struggle for Afghanistan* point to Daud's monarchistic tendencies and claim that his regime served as a transition between monarchy and Marxist dictatorship and marked "the definitive end of the Afghan monarch" (p. 46).

10. Schurmann, *The Mongols of Afghanistan*, p. 49.

11. Krader, *Peoples of Central Asia*, p. 74.

12. Schurmann, *The Mongols of Afghanistan*, pp. 73–74.

13. In describing the relationship between ethnicity and religion in the Bamiyan region of Afghanistan, Canfield, *Faction and Conversion in a Plural Society*, asserts, "There is a close correlation between ethnicity and sect affiliation. The ethnic categories 'Tajik' and 'Afghan' imply the sectarian category 'Sunni' . . . " (p. 4).

14. Elphinstone, *An Account of the Kingdom of Caubol* 2:258, 259.

15. For a discussion on the distinction between *Fārsi* and *Tājiki*, see Menges, *The Turkic Languages and Peoples*, pp. 65–66.

16. A number of neighboring groups such as Wakhi, Ishkashemi, and Sheghni are collectively referred to as Mountain Tajiks or Pamir Tajiks. For information on the Waskhi, see Shahrani, *The Kirghiz and Wakhi of Afghanistan*. Slobin, *Music in the Culture of Northern Afghanistan*, uses the term "Mountain Tajiks" to refer to the Tajiks of Badakhshan and "Pamir peoples" to refer to the various groups living on the upper Amu Daria; see pp. 20–21.

17. For a discussion on the origins of the Hazaras, see Bacon, "The Inquiry into the History of the Hazara Mongols of Afghanistan," pp. 230–47.

18. Canfield, *Faction and Conversion in a Plural Society*, p. 5, notes descriptions of Hazaras converting to Sunnism as having become "Tajiks."

19. Schact, *An Introduction to Islamic Law*, p. 1.

20. For an introduction to the historical data and basic principles of Islam, see Stewart, *Early Islam*.

21. Schact, *An Introduction to Islamic Law*, p. 56.

22. Stewart, *Early Islam*, p. 53.
23. Williams, *Islam*, p. 206.
24. Canfield, *Faction and Conversion in a Plural Society*, p. 8.
25. Ibid., p. 1.
26. In Afghanistan *madrasa* usually refers to religious colleges or to village mosque schools. The public schools are called *maktab*.
27. Baghban, *An Overview of Herat Folk Literature*, p. 1.
28. *Afghanistan Constitution*, Article 102.
29. Wilber, *Afghanistan*, p. 88.
30. Ibid., p. 93.
31. Ibn Khaldun, quoted in Sweet, *Peoples and Cultures of the Middle East* 1:12.
32. Ibid.

Chapter Two: Three Diverse Areas of Afghanistan

1. M. Jamil Hanafi lists six major Afghan cities, including the four listed, with the addition of Jalalabad in the southeast and Kunduz in the northeast. He estimates that these six cities account for 75 percent of the urban population of the country. *The Central Asian City and its Role in Cultural Transformation*, p. 1.
2. Ferrier, *Caravan Journeys and Wanderings*, p. 165.
3. Ibid., p. 182.
4. Fraser-Tytler, *Afghanistan*, p. 82.
5. Wolfe, *Herat: A Pictorial Guide*, p. 8.
6. Ibid., p. 12.
7. Ibid., p. 28.
8. Ferrier, *Caravan Journeys and Wanderings*, p. 179. The demolition was carried out with the help of the British army in anticipation of Russian's expected push toward India. See Dupree, *Afghanistan*, p. 318 and Fraser-Tytler, *Afghanistan*, p. 165.
9. Col. G. B. Malleson, in *Herat: The Granary and Garden of Central Asia*, contends that until 1717, when the Afghans conquered Herat, it was the prosperous commercial center of Central Asia.
10. English, "The Traditional City of Herat, Afghanistan," p. 83.
11. Ferrier, *Caravan Journeys and Wanderings*, p. 172.
12. Ibid., p. 453.
13. English, "The Traditional City of Herat, Afghanistan," p. 83.
14. Ibid., p. 84.
15. *Darwāza Malik, Darwāza ͨIrāq*, and *Darwāza Khosh* are mentioned in the early fourteenth-century manuscript on the history of Herat by Sayf Ibn Muhammad Ibn Yaqub al-Herawi, *Tarikhnama-i Herat*, p. 713.
16. Only Sundays and Wednesdays are mentioned as the traditional market days for Herat by both English, "The Traditional City of Herat, Afghanistan" in *From Madina to Metropolis*, p. 84, and Baghban, *The Context and Concept of Humor in Magadi Theater*, p. 90, but in 1971 and 72, Thursday was also market day.
17. Slobin, *Instrumental Music in Northern Afghanistan*, pp. 26–28.
18. Ibid., pp. 42–45.
19. English, "The Traditional City of Herat, Afghanistan," p. 78.
20. In Afghanistan the word for the Russian samovar is applied to the teahouse as well as to the metal tea urns.
21. The Iranians celebrate the last Wednesday of the old year, *Chahār Shambe Suri*, by lighting odd-numbered bunches of bramble bushes and accompanying the fire with tradi-

tional sayings. They also eat a special dish of dried fruits and nuts. On the thirteenth day after the New Year, many Iranian families make a traditional outing to the countryside. The Heratis seem to have combined the two special days into thirteen days. For more information on the Iranian New Year, see Satoodeh, *Persian for English-speaking People*, bk. 2, pp. 44–45.

22. Stewart, *Early Islam*, p. 36.

23. Ibid., pp. 36–37.

24. Ibid., p. 37.

25. The term *magadi* is used in place of *moqoladi* in Baghban's *The Concept of Humor in Magadi Theater*, the definitive work on folk theater in Herat; however, most Heratis refer to the folk theater as *moqoladi*, from *moqalid* meaning "imitator."

26. Dupree, *An Historical Guide to Afghanistan*, p. 261.

27. Elphinstone, *An Account of the Kingdom of Caubul* 2:441; Wood, *A Journey to the Source of the River Oxus*, p. 163.

28. Slobin in *Music in the Culture of Northern Afghanistan*, pp. 10 and 124, refers to the Tajiks of Badakhshan as "Mountain Tajiks." I do not make the distinction because the Tajiks of Badakhshan fit the general description of Tajik that most people of Afghanistan use, i.e., Persian-speaking, sedentary, Sunni Muslims.

29. See Slobin, *Music in the Culture of Northern Afghanistan*, pp. 148–51 for a discussion of Faizabad as a regional market center.

30. For a discussion of teahouse music of northern Afghanistan, see Slobin, *Music in the Culture of Northern Afghanistan*, pp. 64–66.

31. For a discussion of Hazara and nomad contact, see Ferdinand, "Nomad Expansion and Commerce in Central Afghanistan," pp. 123–59.

32. For a discussion of the Hazara tribes, see Bacon, "The Inquiry into the History of the Hazara Mongols of Afghanistan," pp. 230–47; Sakata, "Music of the Hazarajat," M.A. thesis, University of Washington, 1968; and Schurmann, *The Mongols of Afghanistan*.

33. Schurmann, *The Mongols of Afghanistan*, p. 153.

34. An example of choosing one's *arbāb* was made plain to me by a servant girl who was seeking a divorce. She felt that she did not have the support of her former *arbāb*; therefore, she sought another *arbāb* and worked for him as a household servant while waiting for approval for the divorce.

35. Elphinstone, *An Account of the Kingdom of Caubul* 2:250–51.

36. Amma Karbolai, for example, the maiden sister of an *arbāb* in Khadir, took over the *arbāb*'s duties whenever he would go to Kabul, where he would stay for periods of three or four months.

37. See Williams, *Islam*, p. 211 for more information on *mut^c a*, the institution of temporary marriage.

CHAPTER THREE: ISLAM AND MUSIC

1. Farmer, *A History of Arabian Music*, pp. 22–38.

2. Translation from Pickthall, *The Meaning of the Glorious Koran*, p. 271.

3. Ibid., p. 195.

4. Information on interpretations received in private communication from Niamatullah Shahrani, Professor of Islamic Law, Kabul University, Afghanistan; translation from Pickthall, *The Meaning of the Glorious Koran*, p. 294.

5. Farmer, *A History of Arabian Music*, p. 24.

6. Niamatullah Shahrani, private communication.

7. Hitti, *History of the Arabs*, p. 274.

8. Niamatullah Shahrani, private communication.

9. Farmer, *A History of Arabian Music,* p. 28.

10. Ibid., pp. 32, 33, 22.

11. Ibid., p. 32.

12. Nicholson, *A Literary History of the Arabs,* p. 159.

13. Ibid.

14. Ibid., p. 236.

15. Farmer, *A History of Arabian Music,* p. 100.

16. Nicholson, *A Literary History of the Arabs,* p. 181.

17. Ibid., p. 276.

18. Ibid., p. 284.

19. Farmer, *A History of Arabian Music,* p. 33.

20. Hodgson defines *ziker* in the following way: "Dhikr had presumably originated as a method for recalling a wandering attention and perhaps for controlling ordinary consciousness as part of a larger programme of self-awareness. In some circles, it now was turned into a method of achieving ecstasy directly—that is, the overwhelming euphoric state of consciousness which mystics had always regarded as a great grace, and often as a significant basis for mystical knowledge, but which sometimes now was felt to be an end in itself." *The Venture of Islam* 2:211.

21. Ibid. 2:213.

22. In referring to the religious stand on music in Afghanistan, both Slobin and Baily refer to music's links to disapproved behavior. Slobin states, "From the religious point of view, the most censurable aspect of music is perhaps its guilt by association with activities that are clearly offensive to public Islamic morals—specifically, loose sexual behavior, linked to music through the medium of dance, itself viewed with ambivalence" (*Music in the Culture of Northern Afghanistan,* p. 26); and Baily notes, "From the point of view of orthodox Islam, as interpreted in Afghanistan, music is generally considered somewhat undesirable, or even downright sinful, even though there is no clear Quranic prohibition on music. A mental association between music and other more clearly prohibited activities such as licentious dancing and drinking of alcohol is part of the rationale for this standpoint" ("Professional and Amateur Musicians In Afghanistan," *World of Music* 21 (2): 46).

23. Farmer, *A History of Arabian Music,* p. 35.

CHAPTER FOUR: THE CONCEPT OF MUSIC

1. Farmer, *The History of Arabian Music,* p. 14.

2. Ibid., p. 15.

3. Williams, *Islam,* p. 165.

4. Hitti, *History of the Arabs,* p. 311.

5. Farmer, *History of Arabian Music,* p. 152.

6. Nicholson, *A Literary History of the Arabs,* p. 283.

7. Ibid., p. 284.

8. Slobin, *Music in the Culture of Northern Afghanistan,* p. 26, also notes the close conceptual relationship between music and musical instrument: "The basic term for music throughout Afghanistan is *sāz.* . . . There is thus implied a close connection between the general phenomenon of music and the specific material object, or apparatus, of the musical instrument. This link is not accidental to the Afghan conception of music. Time and again it became clear through interviews that the layman, whose only word for music is saz (the learned term *musiqi* has highly specialized connotations and is not in general use), defines as music only those performances that include use of a musical instrument."

9. On one rare occasion, I had the opportunity to discuss the definition of *musiqi* with a

learned, renowned scholar from Herat who spoke no English. He defined it in terms of its sound. I pointed out that the reading of the Koran was music according to his definition. After a moment's thought and hesitation, he agreed with me. He was the only one to do so without feeling he had uttered blasphemy.

10. Burling, *Man's Many Voices,* p. 46.

11. Slobin, private communication.

12. Baghban, *An Overview of Herat Folk Literature,* p. 6.

13. Slobin, *Music in the Culture of Northern Afghanistan,* p. 26.

14. Nizami, "Chahar Maqala" in *Ganjina-ye Nasar Parsi,* p. 124.

15. For more examples of the use of *naghma,* see Baily, "A System of Modes Used in the Urban Music of Afghanistan," p. 30.

16. For more information on *shakal,* see ibid., p. 90. Here Baily transliterates the word as *shakl.*

17. For a discussion of *sarhadi* melody-type in Khorasan province, Iran, see Blum, "Persian Folksong in Meshed (Iran), 1969," pp. 86–114.

18. See Slobin, "Persian Folksong Texts from Afghan Badakhshan," pp. 91–103 for more information on *falak.*

19. Although *chār baiti* verses have been printed, the term "denotes songs which are assumed to be ancient and to have originated among the peasantry" (Blum, "Persian Folksong in Meshed," p. 86).

20. Forty-five examples of *falak* texts have been collected by Enayatullah Shahrani, "The 'Falaks' of the Mountains," pp. 68–75.

21. Ibid., p. 68.

22. Shahrani, *The Kirghiz and Wakhi of Afghanistan,* footnote on pp. 57–58, points out the different meanings attached to the term *gharib* in Iran and Afghanistan. He states that the primary meaning in Afghanistan is "poor and lowly" while in Iranian Persian it means "stranger." In fact, both these meanings may play an important part in *gharibi* songs, which are sad songs of loneliness and despair.

23. Slobin equates *qurtaki* (*kurdaki*) with *kilivali* (*keliwāli*) and *kuche-baghi* as " 'backwoods' music, i.e., music of peasants and nomads as opposed to urban styles" in a review of Hoerburger's *Volksmusik in Afghanistan, Asian Music* 4 (1) : 73.

24. For examples of the Persian *dastgahs* and their secondary modes, see Barkechli, *Les Systemes de la Musique Traditionnelle de l'Iran.*

25. Slobin has recorded an Uzbek example of *Gorgholi* in the record albumn, *The Music of Afghanistan, Vol. 1: Music of the Uzbeks.* Anthology AST 4001.

26. The Centlivres report that in Rustaq, Kataghan Province, the *Gorgholi* tale lasts three evenings in the telling and is divided into seven *shākh*s (Slobin, *Music in the Culture of Northern Afghanistan,* pp. 125–26).

27. Blochmann, *The Prosody of the Persians According to Saifi, Jami and Other Writers,* pp. 91–92, lists fifteen types of poems according to subject matter as specific as "Bahāriyah, a poem in praise of spring" or "Shahrāshob, an invective against the inhabitants of a town."

28. Ibid., p. 23.

29. For a detailed exposition of the poetic terminology, see Blochmann, *The Prosody of the Persians According to Saifi, Jami and Other Writers,* and Browne, *A Literary History of Persia* 2:22–27.

30. Blochmann, *The Prosody of the Persians,* p. 86.

31. Ibid., p. 91.

32. Farhadi, *Le Persan parlé en Afghanistan,* p. 150.

33. Arberry, *Classical Persian Literature,* p. 73.

34. Slobin, "Persian Folksong Texts from Afghan Badakhshan," p. 96.

35. Many of the folk quatrains are loosely rhymed or words are repeated rather than

rhymed, but both of these deviations will be considered "rhymed" for the purpose of this dicussion.

36. Farhadi, *Le Persan parlé en Afghanistan*, p. 10.

37. According to Michael Loraine, Department of Near Eastern Languages and Literature, University of Washington, personal communication.

38. Browne, *A Literary History of Persia* 2:259-60.

39. For a summary of scansion of Persian poems, see Blochmann, *The Prosody of the Persians*, p. 17, or Tsuge, "Rhythmic Aspects of the *Âvâz* in Persian Music," pp. 207-8.

40. Slobin, "Rhythmic Aspects of Tajik *Maqam*," p. 102.

41. Arberry, *Classical Persian Literature*, pp. 12-13.

42. Browne, *A Literary History of Persia* 2:27, 29.

43. Blochmann, *The Prosody of the Persians*, p. 86.

44. Arberry, *Classical Persian Literature*, pp. 12, 13.

45. Browne, *A Literary History of Persia* 2:34.

46. See Baily, "A System of Modes," for a discussion of musical modes in Afghanistan.

47. Ibid., pp. 8-9.

48. See Ibid., p. 9 for more on *shakal*.

49. See Baily, "A System of Modes," for references to Hindustani terminology and theoretical concepts used in Afghanistan.

50. Ibid., p. 9.

51. Slobin, *Music in the Culture of Northern Afghanistan*, p. 164.

52. I am most grateful to John Baily who gave me the information concerning *dadra*; it is a common term, but one which I failed to collect. He also pointed out that Popley, *The Music of India*, p. 76 states that *dadra* is sometimes called *pashto*.

53. Tsuge, "Rhythmic Aspects of the *Âvâz* in Persian Music," p. 22.

54. Steingass, *A Comprehensive Persian-English Dictionary*, p. 726.

55. Slobin, *Music in the Culture of Northern Afghanistan*, p. 223; Baily, personal communication.

56. Slobin, *Music in the Culture of Northern Afghanistan*, p. 214.

57. There seems to be some disagreement as to the spelling of *sor* since it is a colloquial term. The expression is sometimes used for machinery, as in the expression *motar bikhi bisor ast*, for something that is "out of tune" or "out of rhythm."

CHAPTER FIVE: THE CONCEPT OF MUSICIAN

1. Farmer, *A History of Arabian Music*, p. 7, discusses *qaina*; for slave girls as musicians see Nicholson, *A Literary History of the Arabs*, p. 236.

2. Farmer, *A History of Arabian Music*, p. 115.

3. Ibid., pp. 44-45.

4. Ibid., p. 102.

5. Lane, *An Account of the Manners and Customs of the Modern Egyptians*, pp. 377, 380.

6. Ibid., p. 387.

7. Ibid., p. 381.

8. Schurmann, *The Mongols of Afghanistan*, p. 227.

9. Baghban, *The Context and Concept of Humor in Magadi Theater*, p. 101.

10. Ibid., p. 71.

11. Ibid., p. 73.

12. Schurmann, *The Mongols of Afghanistan*, p. 277.

13. Clébert, *The Gypsies*, p. 202.

14. Baghban, *The Context and Concept of Humor in Magadi Theater*, pp. 84, 83.

15. Ibid., p. 99.

16. Ibid., p. 84.

17. Clébert, *The Gypsies*, p. 155.

18. Leland, *The Gypsies*, p. 24.

19. Tate, *Seistan*, p. 311.

20. Ibid.

21. Burton, *The Jew, The Gypsy and El Islam*, p. 213. For a discussion of pariahs, see Barth, *Ethnic Groups and Boundaries*, p. 31.

22. Barth, "The System of Social Stratification in Swat, North Pakistan," *Aspects of Caste in South India, Ceylon and North-West Pakistan*, p. 115.

23. Leland, *The Gypsies*, p. 334 draws a parallel between *dom* and *rom*, Romany for gypsy, the Hindi "d" becoming "r."

24. Barth, "The System of Social Stratification," p. 140.

25. Ibid., pp. 123–24.

26. For a version of the origin of the *Gharib Zāda*, see Baghban, *The Context and Concept of Humor in Magadi Theater*, pp. 83–84.

27. Nazif Shahrani, personal communication.

28. Tate, *Seistan*, pp. 302, 310. On page 313, Tate notes that some traditions preserved by the *jats* of Punjab indicate that some of them originally came from Herat or Ghazni. One story tells the tale of Tilak, a Hindu, possibly a *jat*, the son of a barber in the service of Mahmud of Ghazni who, with the help of *jats*, captures a rebellious governor.

29. Ibid., pp. 310, 311; also, could *ghajar* of Egypt be a corruption of *gujar*?

30. Burton, *The Jew, the Gypsy and El Islam*, p. 142.

31. Bray, "The Jat of Baluchistan," p. 30.

32. Ivanov, "On the Language of the Gypsies of Qainat," p. 441.

33. Ibid.

34. Ibid., p. 442.

35. Baghban, *The Context and Concept of Humor in Magadi Theater*, p. 120.

36. Ibid., p. 75: and yet, the religion of these low status groups is most often suspect by the dominant community. The community often questions the strictness of adherence to Islamic (Sunni or Shia) ritual or questions the sincerity of these Muslims. For a discussion of pariahs attempting to pass into the larger society, see Barth, *Ethnic Groups and Boundaries*, p. 31.

37. For a detailed discussion of the meaning of *shauq* or *shauqi*, see Slobin, *Music in the Culture of Northern Afghanistan*, pp. 23–24.

38. Baily, "Professional and Amateur Musicians in Afghanistan," p. 49.

39. For a discussion of the two concepts of payment and ascription involved in the meaning and usage of the term *kesbi*, see Slobin, *Music in the Culture of Northern Afghanistan*, p. 33.

40. John Baily, personal communication; Baily's source of information was Ghulam Sarwar, the leader of the Herat Nendarei orchestra.

41. Although I recorded a sampling of their language, I could not find a source which could give more information. I only made a connection between one phrase, *dag betabarein* (play an instrument) and the Iranian gypsy *taburdam*, meaning "to beat," collected by Sykes, "Anthropological Notes on Sourthern Persia," p. 347. The Persian equivalent would be *sāz bezanein*. Both use the verb "to hit" or "to beat."

42. John Baily, personal communication.

43. The cost of a *moqoladi* performance in 1971 was 7,000–10,000 *afghanis*, which was approximately equivalent to $100 at the time.

44. A radio transmitter was introduced to Afghanistan during the reign of Amanullah Khan (1919–29). In 1941 (A.H. 1320) the station of Radio Kabul was established at Pul-e Bagh Umumi, then in 1964 (A.H. 1343), the station was moved to Chaharah-ye Ansari (the present

site) and became known as Radio Afghanistan. This information was received from Parwin in private communication.

CHAPTER SIX: MUSICAL AND CONCEPTUAL RELATIONSHIPS

1. For more information on the realization of poetic meters in the Persian *āvāz,* see Tsuge, "Rhythmic Aspects of the *Âvâz* in Persian Music," pp. 205–27.

2. Browne, *A Literary History of Persia* 2:259–60.

3. See Blum, "Persian Folksong in Meshhed (Iran), 1969," pp. 86–114, for *chār baiti* as a melody type in the folk songs of Khorasan, Iran.

4. Zonis, *Classical Persian Music,* p. 75.

5. The sign ⸰ is known as *koron* and signifies a pitch slightly less flat than the sign ♭.

6. Zonis, *Classical Persian Music,* p. 75.

7. The "af" sound is often changed to the "au" sound in Afghanistan, as in the classical example "Aughan" for "Afghan."

8. Zonis, *Classical Persian Music,* p. 142.

9. Browne, *A Literary History of Persia* 2:41.

10. Chadwick and Zhirmunsky, *Oral Epics of Central Asia,* p. 300.

11. The text was transcribed into Persian by Enayatullah Shahrani. The English transcription was made with the help of M. Nazif Shahrani. The text was translated by M. Nazif Shahrani.

12. Sakata, "Music of the Hazarajat," p. 31.

13. Ibid., p. 47.

14. Ibid., p. 50.

15. Ibid., p. 78.

References

Afghanistan.
  1964 Constitution.
Afghanistan, Ministry of Planning, Department of Statistics
  1972 *Pocket-Book of Afghanistan 1350*. Kabul: Government Printing House.
Ali, Mohammed
  1954 *The Afghans*. Kabul: Prof. Mohammed Ali.
Arberry, A. J.
  1958 *Classical Persian Literature*. London: George Allen and Unwin.
  1967 *Aspects of Islamic Civilization*. Ann Arbor: Univ. of Michigan Press,
        Ann Arbor Paperbacks.
———— , ed.
  1969 *Religion in the Middle East*. Vol. 2, Islam. Cambridge: The University
        Press.

Babur, Zahiru'ddin Muhammad
  1970 *Babur-nama*. Trans. of original Turki text by Annette S. Beveridge. New
        Delhi: Oriental Books Reprint Corporation.
Bacon, Elizabeth E.
  1951a The Hazara Mongols of Afghanistan: A Study in Social Organization.
        Ph.D. diss. Univ. of California.
  1951b "The Inquiry into the History of the Hazara Mongols of Afghanistan."
        Southwestern Journal of Anthropology 7:230–247.
  1958 *Obok: A study of social structure in Eurasia*. Viking Fund Publications in
        Anthropology, No. 25. New York: Wenner-Gren.
Baghban, Hafizullah
  [n.d.] *An Overview of Herat Folk Literature*. Kabul: Peace Corps.
  1977 *The Context and Concept of Humor in Magadi Theater*. Ann Arbor:
        University Microfilms.
Baily, John
  1976 "Recent Changes in the Dutar of Herat." *Asian Music* 8 (1):29–64.
  1977 "Movement Patterns in Playing the Herati Dutar." In *The Anthropology
        of the Body*, ed. J. Blacking, New York: Academic Press.

1979 "Amateur Musicians in Afghanistan." *The World of Music* 21 (2):46–60.

1980 "A Description of the Naqqarakhana of Herat, Afghanistan." *Asian Music* 11 (2):1–10.

1981 "A System of Modes Used in the Urban Music of Afghanistan." *Ethnomusicology* 25 (1):1–39.

Barkechli, Mehdi

1963 *Les Systemes de la Musique Traditionnelle de l'Iran.* Tehran: Secretariat d'Etât aux Beauxarts.

Barth, Fredrik

1971 "The System of Social Stratification in Swat, North Pakistan." In *Aspects of Caste in South India, Ceylon and North-West Pakistan*, ed. E. R. Leach. Cambridge Papers in Social Anthropology No. 2: 113–46. Cambridge: The University Press.

1969 *Ethnic Groups and Boundaries.* Boston: Little, Brown.

Beattie, John

1964 *Other Cultures: Aims, Methods and Achievements in Social Anthropology.* New York: Free Press.

Beliaev, Victor M.

1975 *Central Asian Music: Essays in the History of the Music of the Peoples of the U.S.S.R.* Ed. and annotated by Mark Slobin; trans. from the Russian by Mark and Greta Slobin. Middletown: Wesleyan Univ. Press.

Bellow, H. W.

1880 *Races of Afghanistan.* Calcutta: Thacker, Spink and Co.

Blochmann, Henry

1970 *The Prosody of the Persians According to Saifi, Jami and Other Writers.* Reprint of Calcutta edition, 1872. Amsterdam: Philo Press.

Blum, Stephen

1972 "The Concept of the ᶜAsheq in Northern Khorasan." *Asian Music* 4 (1): 27–47.

1974 "Persian Folksong in Meshhed (Iran), 1969." *Yearbook of the International Folk Music Council* 6:86–114.

Bray, Denys.

1925 "The Jat of Baluchistan." *The Indian Antiquary* 54:30–33.

Browne, Edward G.

1920 *A Literary History of Persia.* Vol. 3, *Under Tartar Dominion (A.D. 1265–1502).* Cambridge: The University Press.

1925 *A Literary History of Persia.* Vol. 1, *From the Earliest Times.* Reprint, London: T. Fishcher Unwin.

1928 *A Literary History of Persia.* Vol. 2, *From Firdawsi to Saᶜdi.* Cambridge: The University Press.

1930 *A Literary History of Persia.* Vol. 4, *Modern Times (1500–1924).* Cambridge: The University Press.

Burling, Robbins

1970 *Man's Many Voices: Language in Its Cultural Context.* New York: Holt, Rinehart and Winston.

Burnes, Alexander

1843 *Cabool.* 2nd ed. London: John Murray.

Burton, Sir Richard
1898   *The Jew, the Gypsy and El Islam.* Chicago: Herbert S. Stone and Co.

Canfield, Robert Leroy
1973   *Faction and Conversion in a Plural Society: Religious Alignments in the Hindu Kush.* Museum of Anthropology, Univ. of Michigan, No. 50. Ann Arbor: Univ. of Michigan.

Caroe, Olaf
1965   *The Pathans, 550 B.C.–1957 A.D.* London: Macmillan and Co., Ltd.

Centlivres, Pierre
1972   *Un bazar d'Asie Centrale: Forme et organisation du bazar de Tashqurghan (Afghanistan).* Wiesbaden: Dr. Ludwig Reichert Verlag.

Chadwick, Nora K. and Zhirmunsky, Victor
1969   *Oral Epics of Central Asia.* Cambridge: The University Press.

Chodzko, Alexander
1971   *Specimens of the Popular Poetry of Persia.* Originally published, 1842. Reprint, New York: Burt Franklin.

Clébert, Jean-Paul
1963   *The Gypsies.* Trans. Charles Duff. Baltimore: Penguin.

Dumont, Jean-Paul
1978   *The Headman and I: Ambiguity and Ambivalence in the Fieldworking Experience.* Austin: Univ. of Texas Press.

Duprée, Louis
1970   "Aq Kupruk: A Town in North Afghanistan." In *Peoples and Cultures of the Middle East.* Vol. 2, *Life in the Cities, Towns and Countryside*, ed. L. E. Sweet. 344–86. Garden City: Natural History Press.
1978   *Afghanistan.* First Printing, 1973. Princeton: Princeton Univ. Press.

Duprée, Louis, and Linette Albert, eds.
1974   *Afghanistan in the 1970s.* New York: Praeger.

Duprée, Nancy H. [Nancy H. Wolfe]
1966   *Herat: A Pictorial Guide.* Kabul: The Afghan Tourist Organization.
1971   *An Historical Guide to Afghanistan.* Kabul: Afghan Tourist Organization.
1975   *Kabul City.* The Afghanistan Council of the Asia Society, Special Paper. New York: The Asia Society.

Elphinstone, Mountstuart
1819   *An Account of the Kingdom of Caubul.* 2 vols., 2d ed. London: John Murray.

English, Paul
1973   "The Traditional City of Herat, Afghanistan." In *From Madina to Metropolis: Heritage and Change in the Near Eastern City*, ed. L. Carl Brown. Princeton: The Darwin Press.

Farhadi, Rawan [Abdul Ghafur Farhadi]
1955   *Le Persan parlé en Afghanistan: Grammaire du Kâboli accompegneé d'un recueil de quatrains populaires de la région de Kâbol.* Paris: C. Klincksieck.

1970 "Languages," In *The Kabul Times Annual*, 121–24. Kabul: Kabul Times Publishing Agency.

Farmer, Henry G.
1967 *A History of Arabian Music to the XIIIth Century*. London: Luzac and Co.

Ferdinand, Klaus
1962 "Nomad Expansion and Commerce in Central Afghanistan." *Folk: Dansk Ethnografisk Tidsskrift* 4:123–59.

Ferrier, J. P.
1857 *Caravan Journeys and Wanderings in Persia, Afghanistan, Turkistan, and Beloochistan*. Trans. of original unpublished manuscript by Capt. William Jesse. 2d ed. London: John Murray.

Fraser-Tytler, W. K.
1962 *Afghanistan: A Study of Political Developments in Central and Southern Asia*. 2d ed. London: Oxford Univ. Press.

Grassmuck, G., L. W. Adamec, F. Irwin (eds.)
1969 *Afghanistan: Some New Approaches*. Ann Arbor: Center for Near Eastern and North African Studies.

Haim, S.
1962 *New Persian-English Dictionary*. Vol. 1: From ژ to ا . Vol. 2: From ى to ک . Tehran: Beroukhim.
1970 *Haim's One Volume English-Persian Dictionary*. Tehran: Y. Beroukhim and Sons.

Hall, Edward T.
1959 *The Silent Language*. Greenwich: Fawcett Publications, a Fawcett Premier Book.

Hanafi, M. Jamil
[n.d.] *The Central Asian City and its Role in Cultural Transformation*. Afghanistan Council of the Asia Society, Occasional Paper No. 6. New York: The Asia Society.

Hillmann, Michael
1976 *Unity in the Ghazals of Hafez*. Chicago: Bibliotheca Islamica.

Hitti, Philip K.
1970 *History of the Arabs from the Earliest Times to the Present*. 10th ed. New York: St. Martin's.

Hodgson, Marshall G. S.
1974 *The Venture of Islam*. 3 vol. Chicago: Univ. of Chicago Press.

Ivanov, W.
1914 "On the Language of the Gypsies of Qainat (in Eastern Persia)." Asiatic Society of Bengal, *Journal and Proceedings, New Series* 10 (11):439–55.

Jarring, Gunar
1939 *On the Distribution of Turk Tribes in Afghanistan*. Lund: C. W. K. Gleerup.

Karomatov, Faizullah
  1972 "On the Regional Styles of Uzbek Music." *Asian Music* 4 (1): 48–54.
Krader, Lawrence
  1971 *Peoples of Central Asia*. Indiana University Publications, Uralic and Al-
       taic Series, ed. J. R. Kruegar. Vol. 26. 3d ed. Bloomington: Indiana Univ.
       Press.
Kritzeck, James, ed.
  1966 *Anthology of Islamic Literature*. New York: New American Library, A
       Mentor Book.

Lane, William E.
  1973 *An Account of the Manners and Customs of the Modern Egyptians*. New
       York: Dover.
Leland, Charles G.
  1882 *The Gypsies*. Boston: Houghton, Mifflin.
  1962 *Gypsy Sorcery and Fortune Telling*. New York: University Books.
Levy, Reuben
  1923 *Persian Literature: An Introduction*. Language and Literature Series, ed.
       C. T. Onions. London: Oxford Univ. Press.
Lord, Albert B.
  1970 *The Singer of Tales*. [Originally published by Harvard Univ. Press as
       Harvard Studies in Comparative Literature, No. 24] New York:
       Atheneum.

Malleson, Col. George B.
  1880 *Herat: The Granary and Garden of Central Asia*. London: W. H. Allen &
       Co.
Mauss, Marcel
  1967 *The Gift: Forms and Functions of Exchange in Archaic Societies*. Trans.
       Ian Cunniso. New York: W. W. Norton.
Menges, Karl H.
  1968 *The Turkic Languages and Peoples: An Introduction to Turkic Studies*.
       Ed. O. Pritsak and W. Schlachter. Ural-Altaische Bibliothek, No. 15.
       Wiesbaden: Otto Harrassowitz.

Neuman, Daniel M.
  1980 *The Life of Music in North India: The Organization of an Artistic Tradi-
       tion*. Detroit: Wayne State Univ. Press.
Newell, Richard S. and Nancy Peabody Newell
  1981 *The Struggle for Afghanistan*. Ithaca: Cornell Univ. Press.
Nicholson, Reynold A.
  1969 *A Literary History of the Arabs*. 1st paperback ed. Cambridge: Univ.
       Press.
Nizami-ye Arudi-ye Samarqandi
  A.H.1340 "Chahar Maqala [Four Discourses]." In *Ganjina-ye Nasar Parsi* [A
  [1962]   Treasury of Persian Prose], ed. Hasan Sadr Haji Sayid Javadi, pp. 117–25.
           Tehran: Tabesh Press.

Nurjanov, Nizam
  1976 "Tajik Folk Theater and Puppetry." *Asian Music* 8 (1): 65–77.
Nutting, Anthony
  1964 *The Arabs: A Narrative History from Mohammed to the Present*. New York: New American Library, A Mentor Book.

Pickthall, Mohammed Marmaduke
  [n.d.] *The Meaning of the Glorious Koran*. New York: New American Library. A Mentor Book.
Popley, Herbert
  1921 *The Music of India*. London: Oxford Univ. Press.

Sakata, Hiromi Lorraine
  1968 "Music of the Hazarajat." M.A. thesis, Univ. of Washington.
  1976 "The Concept of Musician in Three Persian-speaking Areas of Afghanistan." *Asian Music* 8(1):1–28.
  1977 "Afghan Musical Instruments: The Rabab." *Afghanistan Journal* 4(4):144–46.
  1978a "Afghan Musical Instruments: The Dambura." *Afghanistan Journal* 5(2):70–73.
  1978b "Afghan Musical Instruments: The Dutar and Tanbur." *Afghanistan Journal* 5(4):150–53.
  1979a "Afghan Musical Instruments: Ghichak and Saroz." *Afghanistan Journal* 6(3):84–86.
  1979b "Afghan Musical Instruments: The Nai." *Afghanistan Journal* 6(4): 144–46.
  1980a "Afghan Musical Instruments: Drums." *Afghanistan Journal* 7(1):30–32.
  1980b "Afghan Musical Instruments: Sorna and Dohl." *Afghanistan Journal* 7(3):93–96.
  1980c "Afghan Musical Instruments: The Chang." *Afghanistan Journal* 7(4):144–45.
Sayf ibn Muhammad ibn Yaqub al Harawi
  1944 *Tarikhnama-i Herat* [History of Herat]. Ed. and introduction by M. Z. As-siddiqi. Calcutta: Imperial Library.
Schacht, Joseph
  1964 *An Introduction to Islamic Law*. Oxford: The Clarendon Press.
Schacht, Joseph and C. E. Bosworth, eds.
  1974 *The Legacy of Islam*. 2d ed. Oxford: The Clarendon Press.
Schurmann, H. F.
  1962 *The Mongols of Afghanistan*. Central Asian Studies, No. 4, ed. K. Jahn and J. R. Krueger. s'Gravenhage: Mouton.
Shahrani, Enayatullah
  1973 "The 'Falaks' of the Mountains." *Afghanistan* 26(1):68–75.
Shahrani, M. Nazif Mohib
  1979 *The Kirghiz and Wakhi of Afghanistan*. Seattle: Univ. of Washington Press.

Shiloah, A.
   1976   "The Dimension of Sound." In *Islam and the Arab World*, ed. Bernard
           Lewis. New York: Alfred A. Knopf.
Slobin, Mark
   1969a   *The Music of Afghanistan*. Vol. 1, *Music of the Uzbeks*. Anthology, AST
           4001.
   1969b   *Instrumental Music in Northern Afghanistan*. Ph.D. diss., Univ. of Mich-
           igan. Ann Arbor: University Microfilms.
   1970   "Persian Folksong Texts from Afghan Badakhshan." *Iranian Studies*
           3(2):91–103.
   1971   "Rhythmic Aspects of Tajik Maqam." *Ethnomusicology* 15(1):100–104.
   1972   "Review of Sakata, Music of the Hazarajat and Hoerburger, Volksmusik
           in Afghanistan, nebst einem Exkux über Qor'an-Rezitation und Thora-
           Kantillation in Kabul." *Asian Music* 4(1):69–74.
   1976   *Music in the Culture of Northern Afghanistan*. Viking Fund Publications
           in Anthropology No. 54, ed. Colin M. Turnbull. Tucson: Univ. of
           Arizona Press.
Sotoodeh, Manoochehr
A.H.1344 *Persian for English-speaking People*. Vol. 2. Univ. of Tehran Publica-
[1966]   tions No. 1025. Tehran: Univ. of Tehran.
Steingass, F.
   1970   *A Comprehensive Persian-English Dictionary*. Beirut: Librairie du
           Libnan.
Stewart, Desmond
   1967   *Early Islam*. Great Ages of Man: A History of the World Cultures, ed.
           M. A. Edey. New York: Time Inc.
Sweet, Louise E., ed.
   1970   *Peoples and Cultures of the Middle East*. 2 vols. Garden City: Natural
           History Press.
Sykes, P. M.
   1902   "Anthropological Notes on Southern Persia." *Anthropological Institute
           of Great Britain Journal* 32:339–49.

Tate, G. P.
   1977   *Seistan: A Memoir on the History, Topography, Ruins, and People of the
           Country*. First published 1910. Quetta: Gosha-e-Adab.
The Times Atlas of the World
   1967   Comprehensive edition. Boston: Houghton Mifflin.
Tsuge, Gen'ichi
   1970   "Rhythmic Aspects of the *Âvâz* in Persian Music." *Ethnomusicology*
           14(2):205–27.
Tyler, Stephen A., ed.
   1969   *Cognitive Anthropology*. New York: Holt, Rinehard and Winston.

Wensinck, A. J.
   1960   *A Handbook of Early Muhammadan Tradition: Alphabetically Orga-
           nized*. Reprint. Leiden: E. J. Brill.

Weryho, Jan W.
1962 "Sistani-Persian Folklore." *Indo-Iranian Journal* 5(4):276–307.
Wilber, Donald N.
1962 *Afghanistan: Its People, Its Society, Its Culture.* New Haven: HRAF Press.
Williams, John A., ed.
1961 *Islam.* Great Religions of Modern Man, ed. R. A. Gard. New York: Washington Square Press.
Wood, John
1872 *A Journey to the Source of the River Oxus.* London: John Murray.

Zonis, Ella
1973 *Classical Persian Music: An Introduction.* Cambridge: Harvard Univ. Press.

Index

Music Examples by Region
Featured in Music in the Mind and on Compact Disk

Example No., Artist, and Instrument	Title	Date and Place	Page Reference
Herat			
1. Mohammed Alishah Olfat Herawi, voice; Behzad Nendarei Orchestra	*Gul-e Zard*	December 16, 1971, Herat	108–109
2. Abdul Rahman Saljuqi, *chārtār*	*Gul-e Zard*	May 5, 1972, Kabul	111–112
3. Ghulam Dastegir Sarud, voice; Behzad Nendarei Orchestra	*Sarwe Gulpusham*	December 16, 1971, Herat	114–115
4. Mohammed Ibrahim Enayat, voice; Behzad Nendarei Orchestra	*Rafiq Karawan*	December 16, 1971, Herat	118–119
5. Mrs. Nafisa, voice; Herat Nendarei Orchestra	*Bela Ai Del*	January 11, 1972, Herat	120–121
6. Mohammed Farhat, voice; Herat Nendarei Orchestra	*Zaban-e Shekwa*	January 11, 1972, Herat	123–125
7. Ghulam Haidar, *dutār;* Mohammed Karim, *tabla*	*Sarhadi*	December 16, 1971, Herat	127–129
8. Zainab, voice and harmonium; Ghulam Haidar, *dutār;* Amir Mohammed, *zirbaghali*	*Sarhadi*	February 18, 1972, Herat	129–131
9. Ghulam Haidar, *dutār;* Amir Mohammed, *zirbaghali*	*Sarhadi Ghoriāni*	March 2, 1972, Herat	132–133
10. Abdul Rahman Saljuqi, *chārtār*	*Sarhadi*	May 5, 1972, Kabul	134
11. Saman Jan, voice	*Chār Baiti*	February 2, 1972, Herat	135

Example No., Artist, and Instrument	Title	Date and Place	Page Reference
12. Habibullah, voice	*Chār Baiti*	March 7, 1967, Neshin, Herat Province	136
13. Mohammed Omar, *sornā;* Khalifa Dohlchi Sarwar, *dhol*	*Aushāri*	December 27, 1971, Herat	137–138
14. Abdul Rashid, *tula;* Ghulam Mohammed, *zirbaghali;* Mohammed Qasem, *tāl*	*Aushāri*	January 11, 1972, Herat	138
15. Ghulam Haidar, *dutār;* Amir Mohammed, *zirbaghali*	*Aushāri*	March 5, 1972, Herat	139
16. Ghulam Mohiuddin, lead voice and *dutār;* Baidola, *zirbaghali,* voice and bird whistles	*Heinā Ba Kārā*	December 19, 1971, Herat	140–141
17. Khohar-e Sher Gul, voice and *daira*	*Heinā Ba Kārā*	February 5, 1972, Herat	142
18. Zainab, lead voice and harmonium; Shahpari and Nazgul, chorus; Ghulam Haidar, *dutār;* Amir Mohammed, *tabla*	*Mullā Mohammed Jān*	February 18, 1972, Herat	144
Badakhshan			
19-a. Aka Naim, voice and *rabāb;* Khan-e Baharaki, *daf*	*Ghazal*	May 30, 1972, Baharak	147–148
19-b. Aka Naim, voice and *rabāb;* Khan-e Baharaki, *daf*	*Ghazal*	May 30, 1972, Baharak	148–149
19-c. Aka Naim, voice and *rabāb;* Khan-e Baharaki, *daf*	*Ghazal*	May 30, 1972, Baharak	150
20. Khan-e Baharaki, voice and *rabāb;* Aka Naim, *daf*	*Ghazal*	May 30, 1972, Baharak	152
21. Faiz-e Mangal, voice and *dambura;* Dost Mohammed, *rabāb;* Mangal Zada, *sang* (stone clappers)	*Ghazal*	May 30, 1972, Jurm	152–153
22. Islam, voice and *ghichak;* Mohammed Yusuf, *tāl*	*Tarkib-band*	August 24, 1972, Faizabad	155
23. Mohammed Akbar, lead voice and *daf;* Maghul Beg, voice and *daf;* Adina, voice	*Wakhan Folk Song*	August 18, 1972, Ishmorgh, Wakhan	155–156
24. Jandar Shah, *nai*	*Nai Falak*	September 17, 1972, Bahshar, Sheghnan	156

Continued on next page

Example No., Artist, and Instrument	Title	Date and Place	Page Reference
25. Mohammed Akbar, voice and harmonium; Mardan, *rabāb,* Mahdi Asin, *zirbaghali;* Haji Latif, *tāl*	*Falak*	September 26, 1972, Faizabad	157
26. Ramazan, voice	*Chopāni*	August 19, 1972, Khandud, Wakhan	157–158
27. Islam, voice and *ghichak;* Khan-e Baharaki, *daf*	*Paron-e Falak*	May 30, 1972, Baharak	158
28. Awaz, voice and *dambura;* Nazar Mohammed, *ghichak*	*Falak*	September 15, 1972, Bahshar, Sheghnan	161
29. Nazar Mohammed, voice and *ghichak;* Gul Mohammed, voice and Pamir *rabāb*	*Falak*	September 16, 1972, Bahshar, Sheghnan	162
30. Ezrat Murad, voice and *daf;* Jandar Shah, *ghichak*	*Falak*	September 17, 1972, Bahshar, Sheghnan	162–163
31. Haj Begin, lead voice; Gulshan Begin, voice	*Wakhi Women's Song*	August 18, 1972, Ishmorgh, Wakhan	164
32. Gulshan Begin, voice	*Women's Song*	August 18, 1972, Ishmorgh, Wakhan	164
33. Palawan Asil, voice and *dambura*	*Gorgholi*	July 20, 1972, Faizabad	168–178
Hazarajat			
34. Mirza Husain, voice	*Musammat*	November 3, 1972, Khadir	179
35. Mohammed Asil, voice	*Hazara Folk Song*	June 1, 1967, Khag Bedak, Panjao	183
36. Ghulam Sauz, voice and *dambura*	*Hazara Song*	October 25, 1972, Khadir	184
37. Sakhidad, voice; Yusuf, voice; Anwar, voice; Bomand, *dambura;* Awaz, *pip* (tin can)	*Tamazāni*	October 27, 1972, Khadir	184–185
38. Mahtab, voice; Agha Gul, voice	*Hazara Song*	November 7, 1972, Khadir	185
39. Arbab Ghulam, voice and *dambura;* Awaz, *pip* (tin can)	*Kisawi*	October 25, 1972, Khadir	185–186
40. Baz Gul, voice	*Hazara Song*	October 25, 1972, Khadir	187

Author's Note: I am grateful to Laurel Sercombe, University of Washington Ethnomusicology Archives, for preparing the compact disk examples, and Gary Louie, University of Washington School of Music, for the digital mastering. The Ethnomusicology Archives holds the complete collection of recordings I made in Afghanistan from 1966 to 1973.